Computer S
Through
Applications

Steve Kennewell
Advisory teacher, City of
Birmingham

Peter Fox
Advisory teacher, City of
Birmingham

Chris Mitton
Lecturer in Education,
University of Birmingham

Ian Selwood
Advisory teacher, City of
Birmingham

Oxford University Press 1989

Section D

Section E

Oxford University Press, Walton Street, Oxford OX2 6DP

Oxford New York Toronto
Delhi Bombay Calcutta Madras Karachi
Petaling Jaya Singapore Hong Kong Tokyo
Nairobi Dar es Salaam Cape Town
Melbourne Auckland

and associated companies in
Berlin Ibadan

Oxford is a trade mark of Oxford University Press

ISBN 0 19 832744 7

Introduction

This is a new style of Computer Studies text, designed specifically to meet the needs of GCSE students. It can be used either as a class text or for independent study.

You will gradually acquire knowledge and understanding of Information Technology — the use of computers and electronic communications — as you work through the book. You will not immediately learn all about how a computer works. You will, however, meet a number of situations where information technology is used: in shops, offices, factories, homes, schools, and other public services. All the facts, techniques and issues are introduced as soon as they are relevant, and developed further in later chapters. The impact of the technology on people and society is considered throughout.

The book is divided into five sections:

Section A (Chapters 1 to 3) covers the use of microcomputer systems in small businesses, and introduces most of the ideas which are developed in later chapters;

Section B (Chapters 4 to 6) covers the use of special microelectronic devices and small computer systems to control processes in industry and the home;

Section C (Chapters 7 to 9) covers the use of mainframe computers in commercial and public administration;

Section D (Chapters 10 to 12) covers the use of various types of computer in other types of application — creative, leisure, community, personal, research, forecasting and military use;

Section E is a review and enrichment section: Chapter 13 provides reference material to be used in conjunction with the main chapters, with more detail on some of the topics introduced earlier, and summaries of various technical points for revision purposes; Chapter 14 shows the place of current information technology systems within a process of continual development, from earliest times through to visions of the future.

You should approach the work with a number of questions in mind. As well as 'How do computers work?', you will learn to answer questions concerning *how* computers are *used, who* uses them, and *why* they are used. It is important that you try the questions in the text.

You will not need to attempt *all* the questions, however, at least at first reading. They are classified into four types, for your guidance:

T which test your understanding of information in the text;

F which provide follow-up activity to practise or extend previous work;

D which require discussion — the answers can only be suggestions or opinions;

R which require some research — looking up information in other places, or seeking people's opinions.

Notes for teachers

A Teachers' Book is available separately, and this includes a large number of reproducible worksheets, covering all abilities, and notes on the text and questions.

Many of the questions do not have clear right and wrong answers, and the text cannot be expected to provide the answer to *every* question which may be found in a GCSE examination. The 'End-of-chapter Questions' follow a different format: they start with easy ones and gradually increase in difficulty. The last question in most chapters is structured differently however; it is a long question made up of a large number of parts, with the parts becoming progressively more difficult. The questions cover all the types and all the content likely to be found in GCSE papers at present. The Teachers' Book which is available separately provides some guidance on approaches to those questions for which the text does not provide direct answers, and also gives a list of those questions which introduce material not covered in the main text.

This book does not provide any detailed assistance concerning the production of coursework for assessment. This will depend very much on local resources. At the end of each section, however, there are three 'Project Briefs' which suggest work which could be carried out, relating to the work already covered. In addition, the Teachers' Book provides many more suggestions for practical work. The approach throughout the text gives guidance on good practice in systems development, and Chapter 13 contains a specific summary of steps to be taken.

Section A

Our study of the world of computers and information technology starts with the type of machine which you probably use already in some form: the microcomputer. We shall not concentrate on the detail of how the computer works, or even how to make it work. What we are most concerned with is *what* people use computers for, and *how* they use them. We shall also frequently consider *why* computers are used, and what the wider effects are.

We are starting with familiar types of computer user as well as familiar types of machine. Although we are using business applications as examples, the same sort of activity can be carried out by computers in other small organizations: schools, clubs, voluntary groups, and homes.

Your knowledge of how the technology works will build up gradually, and you will be able to use your own computers and other resources to solve problems similar to the ones shown in this book.

We shall look first at a small, simple business. Many such businesses do not use computers. They prefer instead to continue using paper for their information, as well as typewriters, calculators and electronic tills. We shall examine how even a small business can benefit from using a computer, and what the effects are on the business and on the people involved. We shall study a particular firm, which started without a computer, but introduced one at an early stage. This will provide an introduction to many of the ideas and techniques to be developed further in later chapters.

Business information

Many people have video recorders in their homes. Pre-recorded cassette tapes of feature films, sports events and concerts are expensive to buy, and there is a great variety to choose from. Every town has shops that will hire video tapes, and *VIP Video* is one of these. VIP Video is owned by three people: Vicki, Ian, and Parvesh. Ian acts as the shop manager, Vicki looks after the money and the films that are hired, and Parvesh works with computers. The shop has a very wide selection of video tapes, and the owners employ an assistant, Sharon, to help serve customers in the shop.

To hire a tape you need to be a member, and VIP has around 6000 members. A video cassette player will probably be either a VHS type or a Beta type, and will only play tapes of the right type. VIP have almost 10 000 tapes, in both VHS and Beta formats, for their members to choose from. Any member can have up to three tapes at any one time. The tapes are displayed on shelves, divided into categories such as horror, comedy, war, sport, etc. Some of the most popular films are very expensive to

buy, and there is a high demand to rent them from the shop.

What is important about information?

Ian and Vicki have realized that the success of their business depends on their keeping a close check on their tapes and on the members. As you may imagine, this is not an easy job.

The actual cassettes are stored in serial number order in a stock room at the rear of the shop, and only the covers are displayed on the shelves. Each cassette cover has a picture on the front advertising the film. There are also two small paper stickers attached to the cassette. One of these is coloured, and on the wall of the shop there is a chart showing the hire charges and the colour corresponding to each charge. The other sticker has a serial number, such as 2612V, which is different for each film.

The numbers and letters on these stickers are called *data*. The numbers and letters do not mean anything in themselves, but when Sharon or Ian look at a sticker, it tells them something. The colour of the sticker tells them the hire charge: for example, a red sticker means £1.50 per day; the serial number tells them the name of the film. They use the data to get the *information* they need. When Sharon looks at the sticker, and sees it is red, she automatically works out the meaning, £1.50. This is called *processing* the data to obtain information. In this case the process is simple, but some of the processes that are carried out on data can be very complex, as we will see later in this book. The red colour is a form of *code*. Coded data is often used to make information shorter, easier to remember, or secret.

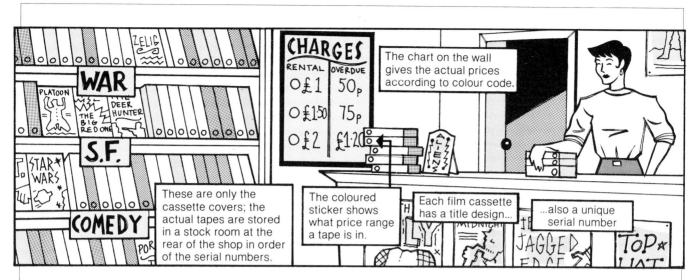

Fig. 1.1   VIP Video.

1.1

VIP use a coloured sticker on the tape to indicate the rental charge.

a   Why are there different charges?

b   Why do VIP not use a sticker showing the actual price?   (*T*)

1.2

Here are the serial numbers on four of VIP's tapes: 918V   342V   454B   1234V

a   Why do you think some tapes have a V and some a B following the number?

b   Why is this information coded, rather than written in full?

c   Does this coding help the customer?

d   Do the numbers help the customers? (*T*)

1.3

What do these words mean, as used above?

a   data

b   information

c   code   (*T*)

1.4

When a tape is hired, VIP insist that certain pieces of information are written down.

a   What pieces of information do you think Vicki needs so that she knows where all the tapes are at any time?

b   Why do you think that VIP insist that only members may hire a tape?   (*D*)

It takes a lot of care to collect and record all the data, and to obtain the information that VIP require. An ***information system*** organizes this data.

What is VIP's information system?

New members have to fill in a form, showing their name and address. They are given a membership card with a unique number written on it. The number and personal details are also typed on a record card which VIP stores in a box.

Fig. 1.2   Completing the Membership form.

When a customer hires a tape, Sharon fills in some data on a *rental sheet*. She writes down the customer's membership number (from their card), the tape number (from the label on the tape case), and the number of days paid for. Whenever data is collected in this way, the process is referred to as ***data capture***.

1.5

The information used by VIP is based on unique membership numbers and unique film codes.

a   What does *unique* mean?

b   Why is it important that each membership number is unique?

Fig. 1.3 Booking out a video (manual system).

c Explain why it is important that each film has a unique serial number.

d Why are tapes stored in serial number order in the stock room, instead of the way that they are stored in the shop? (*D*)

1.6

VIP often buys several copies of the same film.

a Why do you think they do this?

b Should all the copies of a particular film have the same serial number?

c Suggest a system of codes which could be used to distinguish between different copies of the same film.

d How could Vicki predict how many extra copies of a tape she should buy? She must have enough copies to satisfy the demands of the members, but she doesn't want to waste money on too many copies. (*D*)

When someone returns a tape, Sharon has to look through the rental sheets until she finds that tape, and then she crosses out the record of the rental. If a customer owes some extra money because the tape is overdue, then the customer may pay it immediately. If they do not pay, then the amount owing is

recorded on the member's record card, ready for the next time they come in.

There are several customers who do not return tapes promptly. To find out who has overdue tapes, Vicki can look through the rental sheets, noting the membership numbers for all the people who haven't returned their tapes. She must then look through the members' record cards to find their names and addresses, so that she can write to them.

1.7

When a tape is returned, sometimes it is overdue.

a Explain what is meant by *overdue*.

b How can Sharon tell how long a tape is overdue when it is returned? (*T*)

1.8

Some video shops record their rentals by having a card for each tape, and recording the hirer's membership numbers on these. Describe the procedures the shop owner might carry out in this case:

a when hiring tapes out

b collecting tapes in

c recovering money for overdue tapes. (*R*)

1.9

The rental sheet used by VIP is shown in Fig. 1.4. A rental sheet should be easy to fill in and easy to look through to find the record when the tape is returned. Either:

a design a better rental sheet for VIP, or,

b design a tape rental card for the system suggested in question 1.8. (*F*)

For the system we have described VIP need only pens, paper, typewriters and calculators to handle the data: this is called a **manual system**. If Sharon knows the number of a tape and wants to find out the title, then with a manual system she would have to look on the shelves to find the tape. This is clearly not very satisfactory for a company with 6000 members and 10 000 tapes.

Many processes are difficult and time consuming using a manual system. In the case of VIP's system, there are important questions which are hard to answer, such as:

● Which tapes are being hired regularly?

● Which customers are slow in returning tapes?

● How much money is being made from the business?

1.10

Suppose that a member comes into the shop to tell Sharon that his house has been burgled and that three tapes were taken along with the video equipment. The police want a full description of the missing goods, but the customer cannot remember the names of the tapes.

a   In VIP's manual system, how could Sharon find the serial numbers of the missing tapes?

b   Could she find out the names of the tapes?

c   In what other situations would such information be needed?

d   Suggest what VIP could add to their manual system to help deal with these problems.   (*D*)

What will be needed for a computer system?

A computer could handle the processes by which VIP keep a record of all their customers and tapes. As well as the main part of the computer which does the processing, they will need to attach other devices, called *peripherals*.

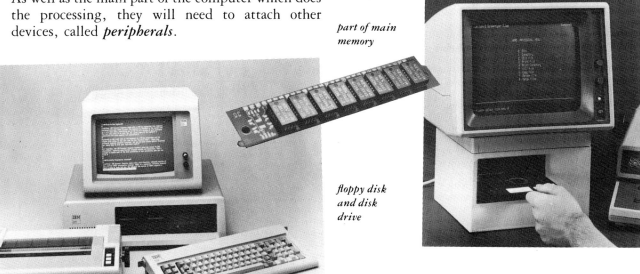

Fig. 1.5   A computer system including peripherals.

1.11

On the rental sheet, it was easy to see which tape was hired out to a particular member.

a   How do you think you would see this information if you were using a computer?

b   Suggest another way of displaying this information.

c   Explain why there should be two different methods.   (*T*)

1.12

Keyboards were designed to be like typewriters, because until recently, most keyboard operators first trained as typists.

a   Do you think that most people who use keyboards now learn to type first?

b   What changes would you make to the normal keyboard to make it easier to type data quickly and accurately?

c   What other input devices have you seen that could be used instead of a keyboard?   (*D*)

All computers have a built-in memory where data can be stored and retrieved again rapidly.

To keep the data over a period of time, and to be able to find it or change it later on, the computer stores the data in magnetic form, similar to music recorded on an audio tape or films on a video tape.

part of main memory

floppy disk and disk drive

cassette tape and cassette unit

Fig. 1.6

This long-term memory is called **backing storage**, and the storage *medium* (plural *media*) is usually a **disk**, though it can be a **tape** (not a video tape!). The storage *device* is a peripheral, either a **disk drive** or a **tape unit**. A computer can search through data stored on a disk or tape in the same way as a person looks through a card box.

1.13

Various devices are used as part of computer systems, and most of them record data on particular media.

For each of the devices listed below, state what medium would be used by each:

a tape unit

b printer

c disk drive   *(T)*

1.14

The membership record cards were stored in a card box and the rental details were stored on a form.

a How would the rental details and membership numbers be entered into the computer system?

b Where would all the data be stored in the system?

c Which part of the system would organize the storage?   *(D)*

1.15

Does the computer system which you use have disk or tape for backing storage? Describe the advantages of the kind of backing storage available to you.

A collection of connected data, such as the card box or a folder containing the week's rental sheets, is often called a **file**. Computers also store data in files. Each card in the box is the record of a member; each line on the rental sheet is the record of a tape rental. Computer files are also made up of **records**.

The data is stored on the backing store in an ordered way. The card index was limited in the quantity of data that could be stored conveniently: the computer system can easily handle a lot more data. The records on the membership file are stored as a sequence of symbols.

Each item in the record, such as a number or name, is called a **field**. Parvesh chose which fields to use

when he designed the system. The way that the data is divided into fields is called the **structure** of the record or file. Files for different purposes may need just one or two fields, or they may need hundreds. A field may need to store just a single letter or it may be pages of text. These points are important when designing a computer system, and we shall look at file structure in more detail in Chapter 2.

1.16

Using examples and diagrams to help, explain the meaning of the following words:

a file

b record

c peripheral   *(T)*

1.17

a Copy the record (Fig. 1.7) on this page.

b Mark where each field starts and finishes.

c For each field, write down a short name which describes the information which is stored in it.   *(F)*

1.18

Here is one way of organizing a file. It contains a record for every tape that VIP owns:

Tape code	Tape title	Number of member hiring tape
101V	Airplane	2986
102V	Death Valley	
103V	Rocky 19	4006
104V	Gandhi	1489
105V	Star Wars	
106V		

Fig. 1.8

a Why do you think records 2 and 5 have the last column blank?

b Suggest one extra field that might be added to this record. Explain what data it should contain, and how it could be useful.

c Draw a similar diagram for the file which contains records of members.

d What other files might VIP use to store data? For one of these, draw a diagram showing what type of data is stored in each record.   *(D)*

| 2 | 1 | 7 | 6 | | R | | J | O | N | E | S | | | | | 4 | | M | A | R | K | E | T | | S | T | R | E | E | T | | E | L | L | I | N | G | T | O | N | | ⋯ |

| ⋯ | | 2 | 0 | 4 | 2 | V | 0 | 4 | 0 | 7 | 8 | 6 | | 1 | 6 | 7 | 9 | V | 0 | 8 | 0 | 7 | 8 | 6 | | | | | | | | | | | | | 1 | . | 5 | 0 |

Fig. 1.7   A record from the membership file.

A computer system for VIP

We have looked at the information that VIP need to handle, and at some of the equipment that they could use. We shall now consider some more detail concerning the computer system, the programs it needs, and the way it is used to process and store data.

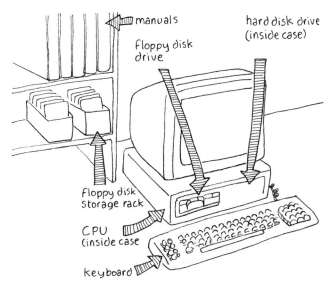

Fig. 1.9

At the heart of the system is the *central processing unit* (**CPU**). This is the main part of the computer system, and the peripherals cannot work without it. The central processing system

- remembers data and instructions,

- calculates and makes decisions,

- controls the order of instructions,

- controls the memory and peripherals.

In a small computer system, this device is made up from tiny electronic components, put together on a piece of silicon to form a **microprocessor**. We shall examine *microchips* like these in later chapters. The memory inside the CPU is called the **immediate access store**. This memory will need several more microchips, each connected to the microprocessor by thin copper wires attached to the chip's 'legs'.

A computer system is made up from some or all of these devices. Before a company buys a computer to replace their manual system, a lot of careful thought and planning is needed. Ian and Vicki would have to be sure that they would gain some benefit from buying a computer system. Vicki and Ian thought

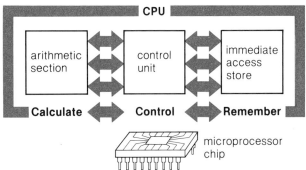

Fig. 1.10 *The central processing unit.*

they might save money by being more efficient, or be able to do extra jobs that would increase their volume of business. They asked Parvesh to work with them to find out how best to use a computer system, to produce computer programs, and to sell the programs to similar firms. We shall see later what this involves.

1.19

Which *one* of the following devices cannot be missed out of a computer system?

a monitor

b keyboard

c disk drive

d CPU

e printer

Give a reason for your choice.

1.20

Vicki and Ian must decide if they want to spend money on a computer system, rather than continue with their existing manual system.

a What are the main items on which VIP spend money?

b What are the main ways in which VIP gain income?

c What benefits did they think they would gain by using a computer system?

d What other benefits do you think they would discover if they were to change? (D)

How does the system work?

In the end, Ian and Vicki decided to buy a computer system. The system is used whenever a customer comes in to hire or return a tape. It is also used to give information at the end of the day about various aspects of the day's business.

The set of instructions which the computer uses to calculate, store data, select data, display results and give messages, is called a *program*. Parvesh wrote several different programs and these were collected together into an *application package*. In this case, the package Parvesh produced was mainly for use by video rental companies. Other businesses would need different collections of programs; some may be the same as the ones in VIP's package, others would be special ones.

When Parvesh had finished writing the programs, he wrote detailed instructions for the people who were going to use the package on how to operate the programs. This is called *documentation*. He also wrote down notes explaining how the programming instructions made the computer perform the right processes, so that if VIP wanted to change the *processes*, another programmer could change the *instructions*.

Fig. 1.11 Software packages.

Writing programs is an expensive way of obtaining a package, because Parvesh needed many hours designing and writing, and many more hours to test that the programs worked correctly. However, other shops have bought the VIP package, and so the cost to VIP of producing the package has been greatly reduced. The sale of the package is now another way that the company makes its profits.

The programs and data are called *software*, in contrast to the equipment, which is called *hardware*. A computer system has to have both hardware and software to be of any use.

1.21

Under the headings *software* and *hardware*, list the items that you use in your classroom or computer room.   (*T*)

How do VIP use the computer?

First, think about a customer hiring a tape.

To make it as quick as possible for Sharon to type in the details without making mistakes, some of the values appear on the screen automatically. These are called *default values*, and the computer will use these unless Sharon types in something else.

Default values are written into the program. The *date* is another piece of information which is very important, and Sharon has to type this in every morning before the shop opens. The computer remembers the date for as long as the computer is switched on, so Sharon does not have to type it in each time a tape is hired or returned.

1.22

The programs used and data in VIP's computer system are stored in various parts of the computer system. For each of the following, say whether they will be stored in the immediate access store or backing store while Sharon is using the system. Give reasons for your answers.

a The program which records rentals and returns.

b The program which lists members with overdue tapes.

c The date.

d The membership file.

e The record of a member who is just paying the rental on a tape.   (*D*)

When a customer has finished with a tape, it has to be returned to the shop before it becomes overdue. To keep the information about this film up to date, Sharon chooses the *return* option and records the return of the tape by keying in its number.

It is very common for some people to keep tapes for extra days which they have not paid for. The overdue charge is half the daily rate. With the manual system, the only place to record the customer's debt was on the member's record card. This was a lengthy process and when the customer came in again, their card might not be checked anyway, so the fees were very often not collected. With a computer system, the amount is automatically calculated and stored on disk. So when a customer comes in again to hire a tape, and their record is accessed by the computer system, a flashing figure is displayed on the screen to show how much they owe.

the customer brings the tape he wants to hire from the shelf to the desk

1 RENTAL OF TAPE
2 RETURN OF TAPE
3 SEARCH
4 SEARCH
5 END

Sharon chooses from the menu by pressing number 1

MEMBERSHIP NUMBER 2176
TAPE NO. 2042V
DAYS RENTAL 1
AMOUNT DUE £1.50

R Jones
4 Market Street

Sharon types these in

default value — can be changed

computer displays these automatically

Sharon keys in the membership number which she finds on the card. The computer searches for the member's record on the disk and displays the data on the monitor

Fig. 1.12   Booking out a video (computerized system).

1.23

When a tape is returned:

a   How will Sharon know if the tape is overdue?

b   If the tape is returned during the night, how might the money overdue be collected?

c   What would be the effect on the shop if this overdue money were not collected? (*T*)

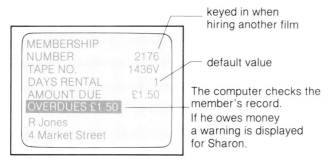

MEMBERSHIP NUMBER 2176
TAPE NO. 1436V
DAYS RENTAL 1
AMOUNT DUE £1.50
OVERDUES £1.50
R Jones
4 Market Street

keyed in when hiring another film

default value

The computer checks the member's record. If he owes money a warning is displayed for Sharon.

Fig. 1.13

1.24

a   What would be due for a tape that was overdue by three days if the daily hire charge was £1.50?

b   What part of the computer system will work out this extra charge?

c   What data does it need to do this?

d   What calculations must you tell it to do?

e   Which data is typed in, and which is already stored on the disk?   (*F*)

1.25

When Sharon asks the computer for information about a member, several peripherals are used.

a   List the peripherals attached to the computer.

b   Which peripherals are used when Sharon asks for membership information?   (*T*)

1.26

Using the manual system, Sharon recorded overdue amounts on the member's record card.

a   Where does the computer record overdue amounts?

b   Write down some advantages that the computer system gives in recording these amounts.   (*D*)

Ian often wants a permanent record of all tapes hired out, or especially a list of those which are overdue. The screen only gives a temporary output, and to get a permanent copy he uses a printer. The output from the printer is called **hard copy**. The CPU accesses all the members' records and selects those members who have overdue tapes. Their names and addresses are printed out.

How are the records kept up to date?

The stored records of members and tapes are very valuable to VIP. Vicki must be sure that all the names, addresses and serial numbers are correct. She could easily lose video tapes if the computer had stored incorrect addresses of the members.

Ian was concerned about what would happen if the computer broke down during the day, and Sharon could not find members' name or keep track of rentals and returned films. The loss of business would be serious, and if the files were completely wiped out (*erased*), or mixed up with wrong data (*corrupted*), then this could be the end of VIP.

Parvesh was asked to design a system to prevent this happening. He had to make the files *secure*. His security system involved some extra work for Ian and the use of floppy disks as well as the hard disk.

This process is called a **dump**.

The **backup** copies are placed in a safe in the office.

hard disk

Every evening after the shop closes Ian copies the main **master** files onto a floppy disk.

Fig. 1.14

The master files are stored on the hard disk fixed inside the computer. Ian can type instructions on the keyboard, telling the CPU to copy a file from the hard disk to any floppy disk which he places in one of the floppy disk drives. This is called a *backup* copy of the file, and it can be locked away.

If the computer breaks down, and the master files are lost, then the backup disks can be retrieved from the safe. Although they are out of date, the backup master files can be *updated* by typing in again details of all the day's business. Parvesh decided that while the computer was working, it could record details of all the tapes hired out and returned on a separate floppy disk, as well as updating the master file there and then.

This record of all the day's business is called a *transaction file*. Parvesh wrote a special program to read in the transaction file and update the old master file again should the new master file be corrupted.

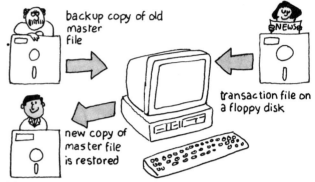

backup copy of old master file

transaction file on a floppy disk

new copy of master file is restored

Fig. 1.15

The details written on the forms can then be keyed into the computer when it is running again.

1.27

Explain the following terms:

a   security of files

b   backup

c   updating   (*T*)

1.28

While the computer is out of action, the old manual system of rental sheets must be used.

a   Explain why VIP need written records of tapes hired and returned when the computer is not working.

b   Suggest which items of data should be written down when the computer is not working.   (*D*)

1.29

Floppy disks cost money, and VIP does not want to keep buying new ones just to store more and more transaction files. They decide that they can record over the top of old transaction files after a certain amount of time.

a   Why did Parvesh design the system so that the transaction file is recorded on a floppy disk rather than on the hard disk?

b   How long do you think that a particular day's transaction file should be kept before the disk is used for something else? Give reasons.   (*D*)

Ian was concerned that some of the data stored on the computer system could be useful to other people. It is easy to make a copy of computer files, and no one would know it had been done, whereas if the box file was taken it would be immediately obvious.

Criminals could use the list of names and addresses to choose houses to break into, knowing that these people had a video recorder that they could steal. Information about people stored on a computer system must only be seen by those entitled to do so. This control is called *privacy* of information. We shall look at this problem in more detail in Chapter 8.

1.30

a Suggest ways that could be used to stop the wrong people using the computer system.

b Sharon is only allowed to choose *some* of the options on the menus which appear on the screen, but Ian can use the others as well. Explain why they do not allow Sharon to operate all of the tasks that the computer can perform.

c Suggest a way Parvesh could allow only Ian and Vicki to use a particular section of the computer system. (*D*)

Did VIP find the computer helpful?

Ian and Vicki were delighted with their computer system. They found that the cost of buying it was recovered in the first six months of its use, due to the efficient collection of the overdue amounts. They did not leave the system as it was, however, because they used it for many other processess. Vicki found that she could do all the business accounts directly on the system, and with the help of Parvesh she continually used the computer to improve and increase VIP's business.

Parvesh was also very pleased with the computer system and the application package he had produced. This was sold to many other shops and proved a great success. He was able to join the company full time to produce more software and to keep the programs up to date.

Sharon was very worried when the computer was first installed as she thought she might lose her job. In fact she found it very useful, and it saved her a lot of boring and repetitive paper work. She could spend more time in the shop helping customers choose tapes.

The customers appreciated the rapid service offered. The queues to hire films had gone, and they appreciated the time that Sharon and Ian had to talk and offer advice and help in choosing films.

1.31

Explain how the computerized system benefited:

a Ian, the shop manager

b Vicki, who looked after the money and accounts

c Sharon, who dealt with the members

d the members (*T*)

End-of-chapter Questions

1.32

Explain what is meant by a default option or default value.

1.33

Explain the difference between:

a storage and processing

b immediate access store and backing store

c software and hardware

d temporary and permanent output

e file, record and field

f program and application package

g erased and corrupted files

h master and transaction files

1.34

Imagine that VIP's computer system breaks down.

a How will Ian and Vicki continue to operate the business?

b What precautions could they take to enable them to continue when the system is repaired?

1.35

a When a tape is hired by a customer, what type of data is stored on the member's file?

b What is this data used for later?

1.36

a Using the manual system, how would the manager find the names and addresses of the people who had overdue tapes?

b How would the computer system find this information?

1.37

The data collected by VIP's manual system had to be organized in a particular way if information was to be gained from it.

a In what order would you store the members' record cards in the card box?

b How would you organize the information about the video tapes?

c　Would the membership records be in the same order in the computer file? Explain your answer.

1.38

a　What is the difference between *privacy* and *security* of computer files?

b　Describe how VIP could keep their data secure.

c　Describe how VIP could ensure the privacy of their files.

1.39

For some processes that the computer carries out it is useful to have hard copy output.

a　Describe one such process.

b　Explain why the printout is preferred to a temporary display.

1.40

a　Describe the ways in which a customer might return a tape.

b　Write down instructions which Ian would give Sharon, if she had to carry out manually the procedure for recording overdue amounts.

c　What would be different about the instructions which the computer needs to do this?

1.41

Describe three different types of code used to represent information in everyday life, and explain why you think a code is used in each case.

1.42

a　The programs in the package perform a variety of different processes. List as many as you can of the processes which have been mentioned.

b　What other processes might have to be carried out on the files in order to keep them up to date?

1.43

Describe any other procedures that VIP might occasionally use the computer for to help them in running the business, such as predicting the number of copies of a new tape to buy.

1.44

There are advantages gained from use of the computer system by the owners of VIP, the employees, and the members.

Explain whether you think there are any *disadvantages*

a　for any of the groups listed above,

b　for any other people that we have not mentioned.

1.45

a　What information does the VIP computer store about each member who has hired tapes?

b　What does the manager do with this information once the tapes have been returned?

c　Would anyone else be interested in this information? If so, what might they do with it?

1.46

If VIP decide to modernize their computer system, what other peripherals do you think they might use, either instead of, or as well as, the equipment they have at present?

1.47

Imagine that some friends have decided to open a shop where people can hire compact discs for hi-fi systems. They have decided to charge per week, but not to have a membership system. Instead, customers will simply pay a deposit on each disc they borrow, which they will get back when they return the disc. The charges will vary, as some albums contain two discs.

They think that a computer system would be helpful in running their business effectively.

a　Explain the purpose of a deposit, and suggest how much they should charge for each disc.

b　Describe the procedure they would use when a customer borrows and returns a disk, explaining what steps must be carried out manually and which could be carried out by the computer.

c　What information would they need to record about each disc?

d　Will they need to record information about customers? Give reasons for your answer.

e　Describe briefly two types of files that they will need to use.

f　For each of the files you describe in (e), list the names you would suggest for the fields, and draw a typical record.

g　Describe briefly the hardware you would choose for their system, explaining what the purpose of each part will be.

h　Give two ways in which they could obtain software to run the system, explaining the advantages of each one.

a most desirable residence

The owners of the video shop used a small computer system for certain special purposes, because they needed to keep accurate records of a large number of items and find information quickly. We shall now look at another business that uses a similar computer system for a wide range of tasks concerned with large amounts of information. We shall also see how one computer can be linked to others, so that the data stored on disk can be accessed by several computers in different places.

Houses, vendors and purchasers

A house is the costliest item that most of us will buy in our whole lives. We may quite often move from one house to another, perhaps because we have obtained a job in another part of the country, or we may just want a bigger or better house. Selling one house and buying another involves large amounts of money, adding up to several years' wages. The information needed by people moving house is complex and it must be correct and complete.

What information does a house-buyer want to know?

When it comes to buying a house the first problem is finding the right house, in the right place, and at the right price. A number of questions must be considered carefully, such as:

Does it cost too much?

Has it got enough of each type of room?

Are the rooms large enough?

Is there a garden?

What is the surrounding area like?

How far away are the shops and schools?

Is public transport nearby?

Are there legal restrictions concerning the house?

2.1

a What information in addition to the list above would *you* need to decide whether you wanted to buy a particular house?

b For each point you suggest, explain how you would find the information.   (*D*)

2.2

A lot of the information in the newspaper advertisement shown here is coded by means of abbreviations.

> **Newport**, Barton Road. Attractive freehold modern det. house. Full gas c/h. 2 rec, kit, 3 beds, bath, sep w/c. Gdn, grge. £35,000. Tel 345 5111.

Fig. 2.1   A typical newspaper advertisement for a house.

a Why is this often done?

b Write out the advertisement in full.   (*F*)

Selling a house is not an easy job. House prices may change rapidly, and it is hard to estimate what people will pay for your house. There may be other problems:

Does the buyer have the money?

Does he need to sell his house first?

Can he get a mortgage from the building society?

You can put up a *For Sale* sign, and advertise in the local paper. But there are many possible problems in dealing with the amount of information and large sums of money concerned with buying and selling houses, and most people use the services of an *estate agent*.

What does the estate agent do to help sell a house?

Mr Adams, the estate agent, will start by visiting the house he has been asked to sell. He will examine

the house and record details of it. When he has finished this, he will be able to produce advertising handouts, advise on the price to expect, and suggest any repairs that are needed.

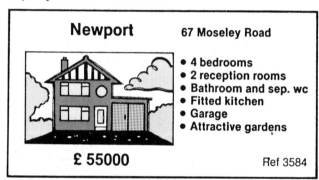

Fig. 2.2   Card from an estate agent's window.

The agent's bill is normally based on a percentage of the final selling price of the house, but often includes extras such as advertising, the notice board, the photographs and the printing of house details.

2.3

Write an estate agent's handout for one of these:

a   The place where you live. Be careful to highlight its good points!

b   A house which is near a pig farm, two miles from the nearest road, has no bathroom, has not been painted for 20 years and has holes in the roof. Use plenty of imagination!   (*F*)

After Mr Adams has visited a house which he is going to sell, he asks his secretary Jean to type and duplicate a set of details. Brief information is placed in the shop window and the house may be advertised in the local paper. Jean will check through a list of people looking for a house to buy, and send full details to anyone on the list whom the house might suit. She must take care with this, because buyers will not want to receive details of houses which are too expensive, or in the wrong area. It is a time-consuming task.

Fig. 2.3   Manual storage: filing cabinets.

The remaining copies of the details will be stored in a filing cabinet to give to customers calling at the office. A separate record will be kept of the person selling (called the vendor), and of his house. This record will contain a variety of information:

Name of vendor
Address of vendor
Details of property for sale
Name and address of solicitor
Date when first advertised
Details of advertising carried out
Copies of letters sent
Costs incurred

All this will be handwritten or typed and stored in a filing cabinet.

2.4

The vendor's record is just for Mr Adams and his secretary to refer to when necessary.

a   What do you think the *details of property for sale* would be?

b   Would you use codes for any of this information? If so, explain why and suggest suitable codes.   (*D*)

2.5

a   In what order do you think the records of vendors would be stored?

b   Explain how the data in the records might be used in preparing a vendor's bill.   (*R*)

How does an estate agent help a buyer?

Most of an agent's services to the buyer are free. People looking for a house to buy can just look through the property advertisements in local newspapers but, if they visit an agent, they will find full details of a large number of properties in that area. The agent may have links with other agents in neighbouring towns or areas.

Prospective buyers can examine the display boards that are a feature of most agencies. These have cards mounted on them containing a photograph and brief details. If the customer decides to go in, Jean will ask for details of their requirements, such as:

Price range

Area

Number of bedrooms

This information will allow Jean or Mr Adams to search the files efficiently. But it would take a long time to look at *all* the details of *every* house, and unless Mr Adams' memory is very good, the customer may not receive details of all the properties that might suit her.

2.6

Jean's task of searching the records for suitable houses will be much easier if the house details are stored in a particular order.

Which of the following do you think would be the two most important factors to help sort the records into order?

The area of town

The number of bedrooms

The number of the house in the street

The price

The colour of the front door   (D)

2.7

Design a form that prospective buyers might be asked to fill in to specify what type of property they are looking for.   (F)

2.8

Make a list of all the machines that you are likely to find in a traditional estate agent's office.   (R)

2.9

Many of the tasks described in Mr Adams' office could be carried out using a computer system. For each one:

a   Explain why a computer could be used.

b   Describe any benefits to the vendor.

c   Describe any benefits to the purchaser.

d   Describe any benefits to the agent.

(*Advice:* consider savings of time and money)   (R)

How can a word processor help in the office?

One of the first steps to automating or computerising Mr Adams' office would be the introduction of word processing facilities.

A ***word processor*** is a computer system which can help people to produce letters and documents. The system which Jean will have allows her to store the text that she has typed, and change it easily if Mr Adams changes his mind. She can include the same piece of text, such as the description of a particular area, in many different documents.

In general, a word processor consists of:

● A standard keyboard, like an ordinary typewriter, but usually with extra keys that tell the computer to perform particular tasks, such as deleting a word. The effect of each of these ***function keys*** can often be changed.

Fig. 2.4   Keyboard with function keys and mouse.

● A screen to display the text which is being typed in or altered (*edited*).

● A processing unit to carry out the instructions in the word processing program.

● Some form of backing store to store the text.

● A printer which produces 'letter-quality' print (as least as good as the print that a typewriter produces), such as a ***daisy-wheel***, ***ink-jet***, or ***laser*** printer. These are more expensive than VIP's printer (see Chapter 1), which was a ***dot-matrix*** type. There are diagrams of these other types of printer in Chapter 13.

```
A  quick,  informal  evaluation  of  all  our  word
processing  output  showed  that  our  documents  can  be
divided  into  three  major  types.
```
laser

```
A quick, informal evaluation of all our word processing
output showed that our documents can be divided into three
major types.
```
daisy wheel

```
A quick, informal evaluation of all our word processing
output showed that our documents can be divided into three
major types.
```
ink-jet

```
A quick, informal evaluation of all our word processing
output showed that our documents can be divided into three
major types.
```

```
A quick, informal evaluation of all our word processing
output showed that our documents can be divided into three
major types.
```
dot matrix (two styles)

Fig. 2.5 Different types of printer output.

The word processor may be a ***dedicated*** machine, designed and used for just one application, or a general-purpose computer that can run a word processing program. Its main advantage over a typewriter is that a good document can be produced in a short time, even by someone who is not an expert typist.

Fig. 2.6 A word processing system.

These are some of the ways in which a word processor helps to produce a good document:

- Simple mistakes can be corrected before printing.'

- Extra text can be added later, or sections can be removed.

- Blocks of text (words, sentences, paragraphs, pages) can be moved from one place to another or from one document to another.

- The text starts a new line when necessary, without splitting words (***automatic carriage return***).

- A straight right margin can be produced (called ***right justification***), or text can be placed automatically in the centre of the page (called ***centring***).

2.10

There are word processing programs available for most computers.

a Choose a word processing program and describe how to use the facilities for typing in, editing, moving blocks of text and printing.

b Can your program print several copies of a letter with different names and addresses in each copy? Explain the advantage of this facility.

c Briefly describe one other advantage of a word processing system compared with a mechanical typewriter.

2.11

How do you think the use of word processors has affected the training of typists and the number of typists employed?   (*D*)

The word processing system that Jean is going to use includes a device called a ***mouse***. This is a small input device that Jean moves around on a flat surface. As the mouse moves so will the ***cursor***, the mark on the screen that shows where Jean is typing. This speeds editing considerably. Jean first uses the mouse to place the cursor over a symbol which indicates what she wants to do, such as storing the text on disk. She then presses a button on the mouse, and the task is carried out.

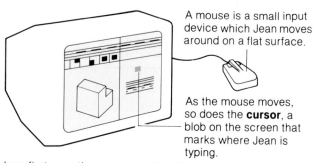

A mouse is a small input device which Jean moves around on a flat surface.

As the mouse moves, so does the **cursor**, a blob on the screen that marks where Jean is typing.

Jean first uses the mouse to place the cursor (or pointer) over a symbol which indicates what she wants to do, such as storing the text on the disk. She presses a button on the mouse, and the task is immediately carried out.

Fig. 2.7 Using a mouse.

2.12

Explain, with examples, what is meant by:

a Automatic carriage return

b Right justification

c Centring   (*T*)

2.13

a What input and output devices are normally used with a word processing system?

b What other peripherals could be used?   (*R*)

Enter text into CPU using keyboard, with display on screen.
Store text on disk.
Repeat the following until the document is perfect:

Correct errors seen on screen, using keyboard and mouse
Store text on disk
Arrange layout of text using mouse or keyboard
Store text/layout on disk
Print document out
Check for errors

Fig. 2.8 Producing a document with a word processor.

You may have seen, or perhaps received, letters addressed to you which are identical to letters sent to thousands of other people. Circular letters like these can be made more personal using a method called *mail-merge*: Jean can write a letter with blanks left for personal details, called a *form letter*. If personal details about everyone who is to receive the letter are stored on disk, then the word processing program can access these one by one and place the details in the blank spaces left in the form letter.

Mr John Smith
15 New Road
Anytown

Dear **Mr Smith**

There is a large demand from prospective buyers of houses in **Anytown** for properties in the **New Road** area.

Have you considered putting number **15** on the market? If you do we should be happy to handle the sale for you, and we have an attractive range of larger houses available for purchase.

Yours sincerely

John R Adams

Fig. 2.9 A personalized circular letter.

2.14

What is special about the parts of this letter which are in bold print?   (*T*)

2.15

Which of Jean's tasks will be easier when she has a word processor?   (*D*)

2.16

Most offices will eventually have word processors. Do you think that:

a There will still be as many jobs for typists?

b More or less paper will be used in offices?

c There will be more or less personal contact between people?
Give reasons for you answers.   (*D*)

2.17

It is possible for several word processors to share one backing store and one printer. Why is this sensible? (*R*)

2.18

In Chapter 1, VIP Video only had a cheap dot-matrix printer.

a What advantages do you think a more expensive one would give them?

b Would you advise VIP to purchase a more expensive type of printer?   (*R*)

One of the major and most time consuming tasks in an estate agent's office is the recording, storing and retrieval of information. In the manual system details of houses must be recorded (typed), stored (on paper in a filing cabinet) and found (taken out) when required. The computer can help in two ways.

As well as producing letters a word processor can be used to produce typed details of houses. Indeed, the agent would probably use it very effectively by storing standard paragraphs and using these in several house details with only slight changes. This is called *boiler-plating*.

This <u>most</u> desirable residence, situated in one of the most sought-after areas of the town, offers deceptively **spacious accommodation** at a *very* affordable price. An early inspection is recommended.

Fig. 2.10 A standard paragraph suitable for boiler-plating.

2.19

Which parts of the text in Fig. 2.10 are:

a Underscored?

b In bold print?

c Italic?

d Justified?   (*T*)

Matching houses and purchasers

We have seen how Mr Adams collects information and how Jean uses a word processor to store the information on a computer system for various purposes. We shall now look at how some of the information is stored so that the computer can search through it easily and print out lists.

We have seen that the problem of matching prospective buyers with the type of house they require is considerable and can be very haphazard when done manually. Using a computerised *information retrieval* system may well solve this problem.

Stored data is only valuable if it can be found and turned into useful information when required. So data must be organised into records and files.

As we have seen in Chapter 1, a *file* is a collection of related items of data, usually made up of smaller sections called *records*. In the case of the estate agent, the file may contain all the details of all the houses he is currently trying to sell, or it may just be a particular part of this information, such as all the properties in a certain area.

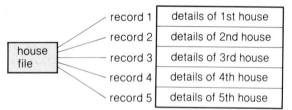

Fig. 2.11   File structure.

A *record* is a collection of data with some factor in common. In the case of the estate agent, one record may consist of the details of one house.

A record is a collection of data with some factor in a specific part of a record which normally stores the same type of data item. In the case of the House File, each field refers to some aspect of the house. There are fields for price, address, number of bedrooms, etc; each one is always in the same position in each record.

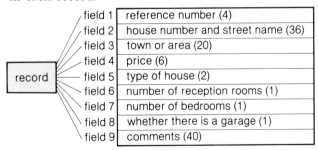

Fig. 2.12   Record structure.

Each item of data is made up of a number of *characters*: letters, digits, punctuation marks and spaces. The *length* of a field is the number of characters which are needed to store the data. You will find that some items of data can vary in length, whilst others will always be the same length. For example, the street name may be up to 30 or 40 characters, whereas the number of bedrooms will only need to be a single digit.

A *record structure* describes the way a record is divided into fields of particular lengths.

2.20

If there is only one character allowed for the number of bedrooms, what do you think Mr Adams should do if he is asked to sell a mansion with 16 bedrooms?   (D)

2.21

Draw a list to show what you think the record structure should be for the file which stores details of purchasers, the people who wish to *buy* houses. (F)

2.22

Mr Adams uses a two-character code for each type of house.

a   Decide what types of house he should include, and suggest a code for each one.

b   What are the advantages of using a short code instead of a full description?

c   Are there any disadvantages?   (F)

The designer of a record structure must decide if he is going to use a *fixed length* field format or *variable length* field format. With a fixed length field, any data must fit within a given number of characters, and extra spaces are added to the end of short items of data. This makes it possible for the computer system to calculate exactly where any item of data is to be found on the disk, and to read it directly without searching through the whole file. Fixed length fields clearly waste disk space, but are easier to handle.

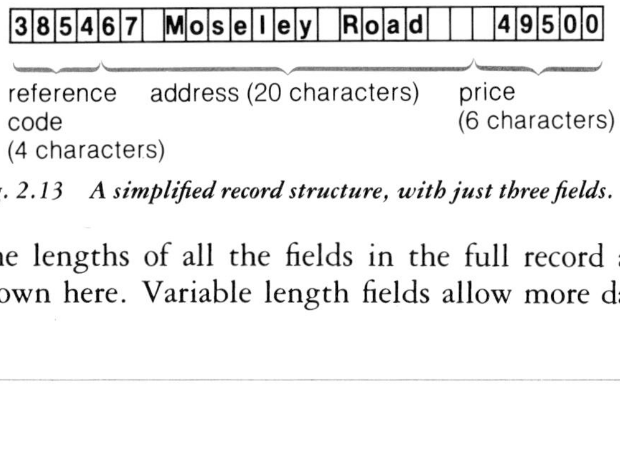

| 3 | 8 | 5 | 4 | 6 | 7 | | M | o | s | e | l | e | y | | R | o | a | d | | | | 4 | 9 | 5 | 0 | 0 |

reference code (4 characters)   address (20 characters)   price (6 characters)

Fig. 2.13   A simplified record structure, with just three fields.

The lengths of all the fields in the full record are shown here. Variable length fields allow more data to be packed onto a disk, since there is no 'padding', but there does need to be some way of marking the end of one field and start of the next. A special symbol can be used which will not appear as part of any item of data.

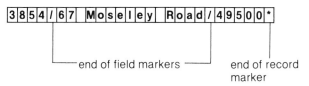

Fig. 2.14 *Alternative structure for a simplified house record.*

How is information put into the system?

There are two sets of data to be collected: the details of the house and the requirements of the customer. Only the bare details will be stored in the file; full details will be kept as text on a disk that the word processor can access. A special form may be used by the estate agent to collect the information for typing into the computer.

2.23
The houses file stores only brief details of each house. The full details collected by Mr Adams are also stored on disk, however, and Jean can access them using the word processor. Describe two situations in which the full details will need to be accessed. (*T*)

2.24
Design a form for collecting details of a house to be sold. (*F*)

2.25
Using the same record structure as for the house in Moseley Road, suppose that you have to find the price of the 11th house on the file, by looking at each character one at a time in sequence. Calculate how many characters there would be before this item of data. (*T*)

The next stage is ***data entry***. Part of the information retrieval package allows Jean to type in the details of the house which she copies from the form used for collecting information. A series of questions (called ***prompts***) lead her through the input of data.

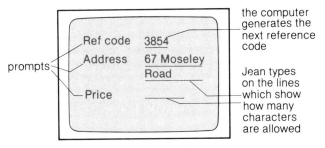

Fig. 2.15 *Entering details of a new house.*

Once Jean has entered all the information requested by the computer, the program asks her whether all the details are correct. If she responds 'Yes', then data is stored on disk in the House File. This checking of input data by comparing the data on the form with the data on the screen is called ***verification***. For really important information, some systems expect all the data to be typed in *again* by a different operator so that the computer can check for any errors. It would do this by comparing the two sets of data and highlighting any differences.

When a prospective buyer visits the office, Jean will first ask her to fill in an enquiry form. Jean then enters these details into the computer, watched by the buyer. This data forms a record on the Purchaser File.

Property Enquiry Form

Name...
Address...
....
....
Tel no. (home)...............................
    (work)...............................
Mailing list:
yes.......... no..........

Free mortgage consultation:
yes.......... no..........

Property to sell:
yes.......... no..........

Price...
Location required:
   1...
   2...
   3...
Type of property sought:
House .... Bungalow...............
Det............S/Det............Terr...........
New .... Mod .... Old ....
Beds required...............................
Rec. rooms required.........................
Garage required?.............................
Garden required?.............................
Other ....

Fig. 2.16 *A property enquiry form.*

At the data input stage, it is useful if the computer is programmed to make checks on the data; this is called **validation**. For instance, Jean should only be allowed to type *numbers* into the *Price* field. If she types a *letter* instead, the computer will not accept it, and perhaps will make a noise to draw her attention to the mistake. Furthermore, some numbers may have to be within a certain range, such as a person's age, or a code may have certain characters in certain positions, for example VIP's film code in Chapter 1 (three digits followed by V or B). Other fields are allowed to have any set of characters (often called a **string** of characters), but there may be a check on the length.

2.26

What validation checks could be made on the fields in the House File?
(*Advice:* consider the type of character, range of number and length of string.)   (*F*)

2.27

Absolute accuracy is more important in some fields than others. Which fields do you think are the most important in:

a   The House File?

b   The Purchaser File?

c   VIP's Membership File (see Chapter 1)?

d   VIP's Film File?   (*D*)

2.28

List the fields that make up one record of the Purchaser File. What should be the maximum length of each field?   (*F*)

2.29

a   Design the screen layout for entry of data from the property enquiry form.

b   Default values can be used for suitable fields to reduce typing; show what you think would be the best default values.   (*F*)

2.30

Can you suggest ways in which the *computer* can check whether the data has been typed in accurately?   (*D*)

How is information retrieved from the system?

Consider now the lady wishing to buy a house who visits Mr Adams' office. She has looked in the window and seen two houses that are of interest to her. She enters the office and asks for further details. If Jean is going to use the computer system to look up information on a particular house quickly, she

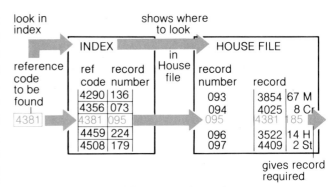

Fig. 2.17   A section of the index of the Master House File.

will need to know its reference code. This is no problem, because she previously typed the reference code onto the card before it went into the window.

The computer filing system will have an **index** which enables it to access the record directly when Jean types in the reference code. The reference code is called a **key** field, and identifies a record uniquely.

There may be other houses that will interest the customer, however, and she can fill in the Property Enquiry Form. Jean enters the details from this form into the computer and starts up the program that searches through for properties that match the requirements. This is called **interrogating** the file.

The computer will not be able to have **direct** access to these records this time (as she did when using the reference code), as there is no way of working out where on the disk they are stored. So **serial access** will be used: each record will be accessed in turn, in the order that they appear on the file.

```
Name        _____
Address     _____
Tel. (home) _____   Tel. (work) _____
Mailing list           Price _____
Location 1 _____ 2 _____ 3 _____
House    Yes     Bungalow  Yes    Terr    Yes
Det      Yes     Semi      Yes    Old     Yes
New      Yes     Modern    Yes    Garden  Yes
Beds     ___     Recep     ___
Garage   Yes     Other
```

Fig. 2.18   Data entry screen for input to purchaser file showing default values and prompts.

Ref. no.	3854	Bedrooms	4
Location	Newport	Reception	2
Address	67 Moseley Road	Garage	Yes
Price	49500	Garden	Yes
Type	Detached house	Other	Fitted kitchen
Age	Modern		

Fig. 2.19   A set of house details.

The computer will display several sets of house details for the customer to examine. Remember that these are only brief, however, and if the customer wants the full sheets, which include a picture, Jean will use the reference code to retrieve them from the filing cabinets. If the purchaser answered 'yes' to inclusion on the mailing list, her details will be stored on disk in a temporary file.

Search: price less than 50000				—description of houses required
and beds more than 3				
Display: reference, location, beds, price				—list of fields to be shown
23 records found				
reference	location	beds	price	—list of houses satisfying conditions specified, showing fields requested
3854	Newport	4	49500	
2908	Melton	5	45000	
3775	Newport	4	38500	
more . . .				

Fig. 2.20   Screen layout for typical information retrieval package.

The software package that Mr Adams bought to help find suitable houses from his file is one specially designed for estate agents. But similar programs are used by very many organisations to make it easy for them to store and retrieve selected data. These are the typical features of a general information retrieval package:

- It allows users to specify fields and type in data.

- If displays particular records and allows users to edit the data.

- It searches for records which match a particular requirement for the contents of a field.

- It can carry out a keyword search, matching specified words wherever they occur in fields, for instance finding houses where *fitted kitchen* is listed in the field Other.

- It can print particular fields for selected records.

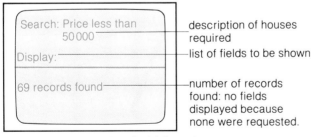

Fig. 2.21   Screen display of initial search.

2.31

It is unlikely that there will be an exact match between the purchaser's requirements and any one house on the file.

a   Why do you think this is the case?

b   Is it a good idea for the computer to tell most customers that there are no houses that are exactly right for them?

c   Which of the purchaser's requirements are the most important to match?

d   Suggest a procedure for the computer so that it always finds about six possible properties during a search.   (D)

2.32

For an information retrieval package that runs on your own computer, describe briefly:

a   How to specify the fields.

b   How to type data into new records.

c   How to show a particular record on the screen.

d   How to list particular fields for records selected by a condition.

e   Can your package do keyword searches? If so, explain how.   (R)

How are the files kept up to date?

We have seen that a temporary file of purchasers' requirements is built up during the day. Mr Adams will also be visiting houses that he has been asked to sell, and Jean will use the data entry program to type in the data required for the House File. The computer will issue the unique reference number and store the record on another temporary file. She then types in the full details that Mr Adams has noted about each house, including the measurements of every room, using the word processor. These will be stored on disk, and one copy printed out. She notifies a photographer, who will send pictures of the house a few days later. Jean attaches a photo to the printed details, makes a number of photocopies, and stores them in the filing cabinet, using a folder labelled with the reference number. This procedure may be carried out several times a day.

At the end of the day, a program is run which tries to match houses on this temporary House File with the requirements of prospective buyers. When a close match is found, the computer prints out the reference code of the house and an address label for the purchaser. Jean can then pull out printed details from the filing cabinet, and post them off to the customer. The process is shown in Fig. 2.22 at the top of the next page; this type of diagram is studied further in Chapter 3.

Fig. 2.22 *Search procedure: matching purchasers with houses.*

Fig. 2.23 *Updating the Master House File.*

The House File and the Purchasers File must be *updated* each day. This means that the information on the transaction files is added to the master files, and also any houses which have definitely been sold are removed from the House File, and any errors which have been made are corrected.

Updating consists of *inserting* new records, *deleting* records no longer required, and *amending* incorrect or incomplete records. The transaction file will just store the information needed to do this. Fig. 2.23 shows the flow of information involved in updating a master file.

2.33

Draw a system diagram, similar to Fig. 2.23, for the process which matches enquiries from new purchasers to properties on the master House File. (*T*)

2.34

There is usually a long time between a buyer making an offer for a house and the sale being completed. During this time, Mr Adams doesn't want the house details to be seen by other buyers, but he doesn't want to erase the record completely in case the deal falls through.

Suggest a possible solution to this problem. (*D*)

2.35

At what stage would Mr Adams decide to delete a record from the Purchasers File? (*D*)

What hardware will be needed for the information retrieval system?

A small estate agent's business could carry out word processing and information retrieval with the same sort of hardware system as we found at VIP

in Chapter 1, with a processing unit, screen, keyboard, disk storage, and printer. A single computer system, with peripherals directly attached, is called a *stand-alone* system. If Mr Adams wishes to expand, he may need more than one computer system. There are two main ways of doing this.

The first method would be to duplicate completely the hardware configuration (buy a second identical set of equipment), and make a second working copy of the files every time they are updated. The second, more sensible method, would be to have a *network* of computers. Each *terminal* (or *workstation*) on this network could share resources, such as disk storage and printers, and extra terminals could be added for less cost than another complete stand-alone system.

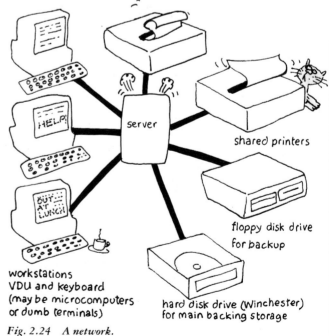

Fig. 2.24 *A network.*

Each terminal can be a complete computer system, or it may just be a screen and keyboard. The *server* is a processing unit dedicated to handling communication between the terminals, and the backing storage and output devices. One backing storage device could be a **hard disk drive** with large capacity, and the other could be a **floppy disk drive**. Further details on these devices can be found in Chapter 13.

2.36

Give one reason why the system would need a floppy disk drive in addition to the hard disk drive. (*Advice:* look back to VIP Video's procedures.)   (*T*)

2.37

If an office is to have more than about six workstations, it is probably cheaper to purchase a networked system rather than several stand-alone systems.

a   Explain why a network is cheaper in this case.

b   What other advantages might a network system offer?

c   Are there any disadvantages?   (*D*)

2.38

Mr Adams decides to invest in some computer equipment. He thinks he will be able to attract more customers and give a better service without taking on more staff.

Do you think the computer system will help him to do this? Explain your answer in detail.   (*D*)

A network can also link computers in different offices — within a building, across a city, or in different parts of the country. Mr Adams could open several branches, and give customers in each one access to information about all the houses he has for sale. Alternatively, he could link with other estate agents serving different areas and attach the computer to a telephone line to share information about the properties they each have available.

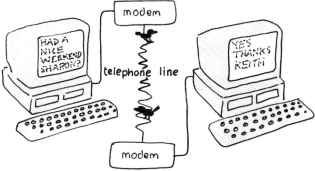

Fig. 2.25   Computers 'talking' over the telephone.

End-of-chapter Questions

2.39

For each of the following descriptions of sets of data, write down which would be a file, which would be a record, and which would be a field:

a   Details of all houses in a certain street.

b   The number of bedrooms in a house.

c   Details about a particular vendor.

d   The postcode of a house.

e   A list of people interested in buying a certain house.

2.40

Explain briefly the difference between:

a   Serial and direct access to information on disk, giving examples of when each method would be used.

b   A form letter and a boiler-plated document.

c   A networked and a stand-alone workstation.

2.41

Draw the layout of a *full* house record,

a   Using the structure in Fig. 2.13,

b   Using the structure in Fig. 2.14.

2.42

Mr Adams bought a word processing package and an estate agent's information retrieval program from a dealer. These could be described as **off-the-shelf** packages.

a   Describe what the package would contain, in addition to disks of software.

b   Why did VIP design and write their software themselves, rather than buy off-the-shelf packages?

c   Explain the advantages to Mr Adams of buying packages from a dealer.

d   What disadvantages might he find?

2.43

Jean uses a separate word processing program and information retrieval program. It is possible to buy an **integrated package** which allows the user to carry out word processing and information retrieval tasks on the same data.

a   What advantages would this have?

b   Can you think of any disadvantages that there might be?

2.44

Many people buy a spelling-checker as part of a word processing package. This program uses a file, called a *dictionary*, in which each record has just a single field containing one word. It prints out any of the words in a document which are not in the dictionary file.

a Describe the difference between the structure of the dictionary file and the structure of records in a normal printed dictionary.

b Which types of words which might appear in documents would not appear in the dictionary file?

c Explain how people can use this program to help correct spelling mistakes in their documents.

2.45

Mr Adams would like to get rid of his filing cabinets altogether.

What extra hardware and software do you think would be required to enable him to computerise *all* the files?

2.46

When Mr Adams is out visiting a house, Jean sometimes has to leave the office unattended for a few minutes. She locks the filing cabinets, but leaves the computer running.

a In what ways could this be harmful to the business?

b Is it more important to protect the computer files or the printed files?

c What precautions could be taken to protect the computer files?

2.47

There are a number of benefits and possible disadvantages associated with introducing information technology into the estate agent's office. There will be changes in:

speed,   quantity of information,
cost,   working conditions,
accuracy of information,   quality of service.

Suggest what the effects of these changes would be, for:

a Mr Adams.   *c* The vendors.
b Jean.   *d* The purchasers.

2.48

An estate agent might provide certain other services in order to help sell a house, such as arranging a loan (mortgage), showing people round, and advertising in local newspapers.

Describe how a computer system could help with *one* of these.

2.49

a What other organisations will a person buying or selling a house need to consult? Two have been mentioned in this chapter.

b For one of these, describe the ways in which they might use computers.

2.50

A dentist uses a small computer system to store information about his patients. His equipment includes a keyboard for input, screen for output and two floppy disk drives. His main Patients File contains a record for each patient, giving surname, forenames, date of birth, sex, address. This patient record also contains, for each visit, the date and type of treatment. There are 12 different types of treatment, each represented by a one-letter code such as C for check-up, F for filling. His secretary keeps the records up-to-date from his scribbled notes, using an application package designed specifically for dentists.

a What general name is given to the input, output and backing storage devices?

b What other output device would he need?

c What other hardware will be a necessary part of his system?

d What term is used to refer to the section of each record which stores a particular item of data?

e Why is each type of treatment given a code, rather than being written in full?

f What events would produce a need to update the file?

g The dentist usually wants to know the *age* of a patient rather than the date of birth. Why do you think the date of birth is stored and not the age?

h Choose two of the items of data and describe what validation checks could be carried out.

i What is meant by an *application package*?

j What advantages and disadvantages are there for a specific application package compared with a general information retrieval package?

k What changes to the system would you advise if the system was to serve a group of four dentists, with two secretaries?

l The dentist wishes to send out reminders to patients eight months after their last visit. Explain how the computer can help with this task.

m Describe briefly three other purposes for which the dentist could use a computer to improve efficiency.

fashion with a message

We have looked at two real businesses. In both cases, they were trading successfully before they started to use computers. Information technology has enabled them to expand their services and operate more efficiently. They will no doubt continue to develop their systems and take advantage of new devices. As you learn more techniques, you may be able to see for yourself what they could do to expand their use of computers and communications.

We shall now consider the start of a new company. This company is completely imaginary, though the activities described can all be found in real businesses. The business is being set up by four students of Design: Elaine, Alan, Mark and Tina, who decide to form a cooperative when they obtain their qualifi-

Fig. 3.1

Starting a new business

Many schools, colleges, clubs, teams and companies sell clothes with their names printed on. People also wear T-shirts with slogans printed on — perhaps to be different from everyone else.

Mark, Elaine, Alan and Tina have formed a company called TEAMSHIRTS. They chose the name for three reasons:

— they want to produce shirts which might be worn by teams;

— the initial letters of their names make up the word TEAM;

— they intend to work as a team.

They don't want a boss, but they *do* think that they ought to have a computer. They expect that the computer will do a lot of the boring paperwork for the business, leaving them to get on with having ideas, making decisions, giving a high standard of service and, of course, printing shirts!

3.1

The team want the computer to handle 'boring paperwork'.

a List some of the information you think they might need to record, such as the number of shirts they have of each colour and size.

b What processing tasks would they need to carry out on the data?

c Which tasks will a computer be able to assist with?

d Do you think the computer will be able to do the tasks better than people?

e Will the team be able to do without paper for their record keeping if they use a computer?   *(D)*

The team decides to sell by mail order, and advertise two types of shirt:

1 A light coloured T-shirt with large black writing across the front at £5.95.

2 A dark coloured sweatshirt with small white writing at £11.95.

Fig. 3.2

People who want to buy will be asked to state the number, type, size (Small, Medium or Large), and colour (White, Yellow or Pink for T-shirts; Green, Blue or Red sweatshirts) as well as the message that they want to appear. Private customers will also have to enclose a cheque or postal order.

Fig. 3.3   *They all agree to swap jobs after six months.*

3.2

Design an order form that TEAMSHIRTS could include in their advertisement.

(*Advice:* look at magazines and newspapers.)   (*F*)

3.3

a   Explain what is meant by mail order.

b   Find three advertisements for goods which are sold in this way.

c   Why do you think that some firms use this method instead of selling through shops?

d   How do customers know what they are buying?

e   What different ways are there for customers to tell the company exactly what they want to buy?

f   What different ways are there of paying for the goods?

g   Do you think all the firms use computers?   (*R*)

3.4

Mark and Elaine will both need to keep files of data.

a   List the items of data that you think Mark will need to record.

b   List the items of data that you think Elaine will need to record.

c   How many different master files will they need? (Note that VIP had two: a *tapes* file and a *members* file; Mr Adams also had two: a *houses* file and a *purchasers* file.)

d   Should Mark and Elaine both have access to the files?   (*D*)

The team expect a lot of orders to come from other businesses. Companies do not usually send cash with their orders; instead, they will expect an ***invoice*** to be sent with the goods. This gives a description of the goods and states how much is to be paid. There are rules which specify what information must appear on an invoice, and TEAMSHIRTS decide that they may as well use the same document for all their sales.

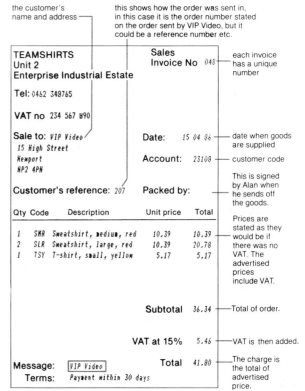

Fig. 3.4   *A typical invoice.*

How does the team decide what to buy?

The team wisely decide that they do not know enough about the use of computers to decide what hardware and software they need to buy. Before they start to do anything at all, they decide to seek pro-

`2 3 1 0 8 V I P V i d e o                15 H i gh S t r e e t          N e w p o r t        NP 2 4 PH V I PV\      4 1 . 8 0`

Fig. 3.5   *A typical record.*

fessional advice. They cannot afford to pay a firm of computer consultants, but they know that a friend from college studied *systems analysis*, and decide to ask her for advice. As well as suggesting equipment that they should buy, she will be able to tell them what steps they should take to make the system do what they want.

The first step that Dawn (the systems analyst) takes is to carry out a *feasibility study*, to find out whether a computer is going to be worthwhile for TEAMSHIRTS. It may be that the *benefits* of using a computer do not justify its *cost* and first Dawn will discuss with the others exactly what they expect the computer system to do. She will then report on what they will need to buy, how well this will do what they want, and whether the computer system will save money compared with a manual system.

Dawn identifies a number of tasks that the computer should take over. The system will keep a full record of orders and details of people who owe money, as well as keeping count of the blank shirts that TEAMSHIRTS need to buy, making sure that they know when they are running short of anything. These tasks are common ones in business, and there are many microcomputer systems and standard applications packages designed for the purpose. They could buy these 'off-the-shelf' and they would do the job quite well. But Dawn advises them that to do *exactly* what they want, the team should buy general-purpose equipment and software, and pay a programmer for software tailored to their needs.

How is the computer system developed?

Dawn will move on to a detailed *investigation* of the way that the business handles information, so that she can *design* the computerised system. She will then talk to each of the others about their jobs, and work out exactly what information they produce, how they produce it, and what information they need from others. She can then produce diagrams and notes which *specify* the system:

Record structure of files   Input documents

Output documents   Processes involved

Input documents are referred to as *source documents* if they contain information that is not already stored. For example, the order (Fig. 3.7) is a source document.

An example of an output document is the customer invoice shown on page 30 (Fig. 3.4).

3.5

a Suggest improvements to the structure for the customer file, shown in Fig. 3.6, explaining how the changes will improve the system.

```
customer number (5 digits)
customer name (20 characters)
customer address line 1 (20 characters)
customer address line 2 (12 characters)
postcode (8 characters)
message to be printed (20 characters)
amount owing (5 digits including 2 decimal places)
```

Fig. 3.6   Example record structure: file of customer information.

Name _____

Address _____

_____

Customer ref. _____

T-shirts

Number	Size (S, M, L)	Colour (W, Y, P)	Unit cost	Total cost
			£5.95	
			£5.95	
			£5.95	

Sweatshirts

Number	Size (S, M, L)	Colour (B, G, R)	Unit cost	Total cost
			£11.95	
			£11.95	
			£11.95	
		Total of order		

Fig. 3.7   Example input document: customer order from magazine advert or circular.

b Design the structure for a file which would store details contained on orders such as the one in Fig. 3.7. Set it out like the typical record shown (Fig. 3.5)   (*F*).

3.6

What information from orders will Mark and Tina in the production department need?   (*T*)

3.7

a Which of the items of data on the invoice will have to be typed in, and which will the computer be able to put on automatically?

b TEAMSHIRTS could buy forms with information already printed on them; this is referred to as *pre-printed stationery*. What are the advantages and disadvantages of using pre-printed stationery?   (*D*)

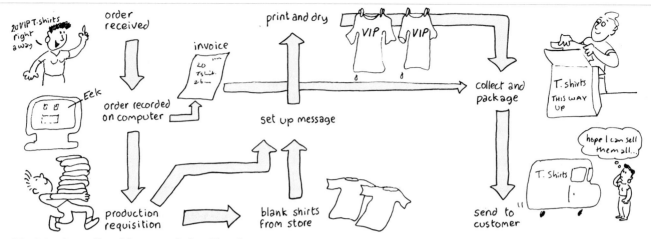

Fig. 3.8 An outline of the system for handling the production and the information processing. The arrows show the flow of information and goods.

3.8

What would you suggest the system should do if a customer sends too little money:

supply the whole order, and send the customer a bill for the extra needed?

supply as many shirts as the money will pay for?

supply nothing at all until the full amount is paid?

Give reasons for your answer.   (D)

3.9

What data will the team want to store permanently? Give a reason for each item you include.   (D)

When an order is received, Elaine will first record the details of the order and give the customer a reference code if they do not already have one (this is the account number in the invoice). She will pass on to Mark and Tina the information they need to draw stock and produce the shirts, written on a form called a *requisition*.

Requisition	Order no: 048
	Customer ref: 23108
	Date: 25/06/86

| Message | VIP Video |

Product	Quantity
SMR	1
SLR	2
TSY	1

There will be two copies: one for Mark, one for Tina.
Fig. 3.9 A requisition.

She will also give Alan a copy of the invoice. When the printed shirts are ready, Tina will pass them on to Alan, with the requisition. Alan checks the shirts, the requisition and the invoice are all correct, and then sends off the shirts and the invoice. He ticks off the items on the requisition and files it away.

3.10

Why is each customer given a reference code?   (T)

3.11

What problems may arise with this system? (*Advice:* consider what might be wrong with an order, or with stocks, and what mistakes the staff might make.)   (D)

3.12

What validation checks would you suggest they carry out to help reduce mistakes in recording data?   (D)

3.13

a   List the items of hardware that you think TEAMSHIRTS will need for the tasks that Dawn has planned.

b   Which standard software packages do you think they should buy, in addition to the special programs which are being written?   (D)

What files will they need?

The main files which Dawn decided they should use (master files) are:

● The *stock file*, which will have a record for each type of blank shirt, containing:

Reference code (3 letters)
Number in stock (3 digits)
Reorder level (3 digits): when the stock goes down to this number, more supplies must be ordered
Supplier code (2 digits): the reference number on the suppliers file of the firm which the stocks are ordered from

Here is the complete stock file:

Ref code	number in stock	reorder level	supplier code
TSW	242	250	19
TSY	160	200	19
TSP	250	150	19
TMW	329	300	19
TMY	258	300	19
TMP	357	250	19
TLW	212	250	19
TLY	290	200	19
TLP	167	150	19
SSB	109	100	27
SSG	156	100	27
SSR	98	100	27
SMB	203	150	27
SMG	187	150	27
SMR	148	150	27
SLB	123	100	27
SLG	109	100	27
SLR	73	100	27

- The *sales ledger file*, which will have a record for each order, containing:

  Invoice number

  Customer number

  Date

  for each item on the order

  — Reference code

  — Quantity

  — Unit price

  — Total price for item

  Total price for order

  VAT

  Amount charged

  Amount received

- The *customer file*, with the record structure shown in Fig. 3.6

- The *purchase ledger* file will be similar in structure to the sales ledger file, keeping records of what supplies have been ordered, who from, and whether they have been received and paid for.

- The *supplier file* will just contain details of companies that TEAMSHIRTS order from.

3.14

Which of the files listed above contain each of the items listed at the top of the next column?

a The cost of a blank T-shirt

b The name of the company which makes blank T-shirts

c The number of small, white T-shirts in stock

d The price for an order from VIP Video

e The address of VIP Video

f The customer number for VIP Video   (*T*)

3.15

The stock file on the left does not contain a full description of each item in stock. Instead, codes are used which represent the types of blank shirt.

a What do you think TSW and SLB stand for?

b Why is the information stored in coded form? (*T*)

What documents are to be used?

The input documents for the system that we are considering are:

  Customers' orders

  Customers' payments

  Requisitions

  Invoices from suppliers

The output documents are:

  Invoices

  Requisitions

  Orders to suppliers

  Other items, such as reminders to customers who have not paid, lists of stock for checking, sales figures for discussion

Note that a requisition is both an input and an output document. It is output from the order entry process, and input to the stock control process.

3.16

Draw out, as in Fig. 3.6, a typical record for

a the sales ledger file (use the details in the customer invoice on page 30 (Fig. 3.4).

b the purchase ledger file. (Invent suitable data.) (*F*)

3.17

a Explain what is meant by VAT, and how it is calculated.

b Why will stocks still need to be checked manually from time to time?   (*R*)

3.18

It would be possible to have just *one* file for sales, by including the data about the customer along with the order data in the sales ledger file.

a   Design the structure for such a file.

b   Why do you think that instead there are two separate files? (*Advice:* consider the situation where there are several orders from one customer.)   (*F*)

How does Dawn show how the whole system works?

Dawn uses a method called a **system flowchart** to show the flow of data through the system. This is a diagram showing an outline of the processes used to produce the output documents from the input documents and the files. Certain special symbols are used, and connected by arrows to show the flow of data through the system.

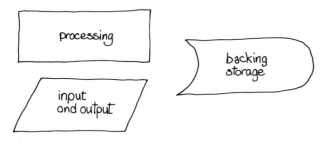

Fig. 3.10   System flowchart symbols.

The computerised system

Plans have been made for the work of the team and also for the documents they will need to keep records of their business information. We shall now look at how the computer system will be organised, and how they will try to prevent mistakes.

How will the system operate?

Dawn decides that the parts of the system dealing with sales and purchases will be **on-line**. This means that information entered at the keyboard is stored straight away on the master files, so that the files are always up-to-date. Operation of the computer will be **interactive** (or *conversational*); this means that the computer will respond as soon as the operator types something in, and the operator will then type in the next set of data or instructions.

This causes a problem concerning security, of course. If something goes wrong, all the data typed in could be lost. Dawn has considered what would happen if there were a breakdown of part of the computer system that as a result corrupted the master file.

3.19

a   What is meant by *corruption*?

b   What precautions would you suggest to reduce the problems that this would cause?
(*Advice:* refer to Chapter 1.)

c   What faults might cause such a breakdown? Consider software as well as hardware.   (*R*)

One solution to the security problems is to make regularly a complete backup copy of each master file. This could be once a day, or more often if there are a lot of transactions. This is called a *dump* of the file, and the copy will be put onto a separate tape or disk and stored safely. The source documents for

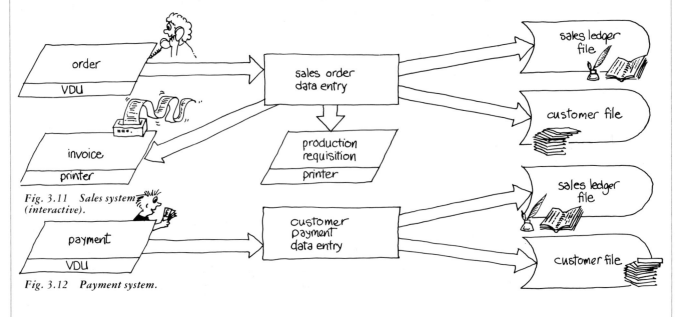

Fig. 3.11   Sales system (interactive).

Fig. 3.12   Payment system.

the data typed in since the last dump will be kept together, so that they can be entered again if necessary.

Dawn also decides that the system for keeping track of supplies in stock and ordering more when necessary will be handled by a **batch processing** system. This means that all data concerned with changes to stock will be collected together over a period of time and processed in a batch, rather than being entered and processed on-line as it comes in. The difference between batch and interactive processing is much more important in larger systems, and will be shown in detail in Chapters 7 and 8.

Fig. 3.13

The input documents for the stock control system are the production requisitions, which tell Mark that stock is to be taken from store to the production area, and suppliers' delivery notes, which tell Mark that new stock has been delivered.

3.20

VIP and Mr Adams (Chapter 1 and Chapter 2) both used on-line computer systems in their businesses.

a Explain what is meant by on-line processing.

b For either VIP or Mr Adams, explain why they used on-line systems rather than batch processing. (*T*)

3.21

What do you think are the advantages and disadvantages of using batch processing for the stock control system? (*D*)

How does the system allow for difficulties?

Of course, things can go wrong, and the staff must carry out checks so that mistakes and other problems can be prevented, or at least discovered as soon as possible.

One possible problem is that there may be things on the invoice that have not been delivered. Mark must check this and make sure that Elaine does not type in the data and send off payment until the rest of the goods are delivered.

Elaine herself may make mistakes when she types the data in, and so the system has another type of validation check included. Before Mark takes a batch of documents to Elaine, he adds together all the important figures on each document, such as the invoice number, the number of each item on the invoice, and even the date.

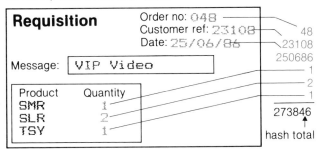

Fig. 3.14   Producing a hash total.

This is called a **hash total**, and the actual value calculated is of no interest at all. Its only purpose is to be checked by the computer. When Elaine types in the information from the documents, she also types Mark's hash total. The computer is programmed to add together the same figures and compare them with Mark's figure. If they are not the same, Elaine will check all the figures to find the mistake before the data gets into the files. Another method of validation is to just produce a single total of a particular value (such as the amount charged on an invoice) for the whole batch. This is called, not surprisingly, a **batch total**.

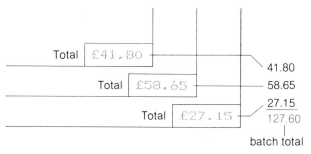

Fig. 3.15   Producing a batch total.

These methods check the **integrity** of the data, ensuring that it has not become corrupted as it passes through the system.

3.22

Write out the figures and form a hash total for the invoice on page 30 (Fig. 3.4). (*F*)

3.23

What other validation checks could be carried out in the TEAMSHIRTS system, using the methods described in Chapter 2? (*F*)

When typing the data from a supplier's invoice into the computer, Elaine does not have to type in the supplier's name and address. This will already be stored in the supplier file, and can be accessed by the program as long as the supplier *number* is typed in. It is also possible that a mistake may be made in entering this number, and so it must be validated.

One way of validating an important number like this is for it to include a ***check digit***. This is an extra digit placed on the end of a number the very first time that it is entered into the system, and it is treated as part of the number from that moment on. It is usually calculated by a method similar to this one, using supplier number 2394 as an example:

To calculate the check digit for a reference code such as 2394, multiply the units digit by 2, the tens by 3, the hundreds by 4, etc.

$$\begin{array}{cccc} 2 & 3 & 9 & 4 \\ \times\ 5 & \times\ 4 & \times\ 3 & \times\ 2 \\ \hline 10\ + & 12\ + & 27\ + & 8 \end{array} = 57 \text{ add up the}$$

answers, divide by 11, and note the remainder

$57 \div 11$ gives remainder 2

Subtract this from 11 to give the check digit:

$11 - 2 = 9$

Place this to the right of the units digit to give the complete reference number: 23949.

When this is typed into the computer, the program does this:

$$\begin{array}{ccccc} 2 & 3 & 9 & 4 & 9 \\ \times\ 5 & \times\ 4 & \times\ 3 & \times\ 2 & \times\ 1 \\ \hline 10\ + & 12\ + & 27\ + & 8\ + & 9 \end{array} = 66$$

The result should divide *exactly* by 11; this provides the required check.

Fig. 3.16

3.24

The most common types of error are to write 23949 as:

— 23999 (*transcription* error)

— 29349 (*transposition* error)

— 2399 (*omission* error).

For each of these, carry out the computer's check to see if it finds the error. (*F*)

3.25

a Is it possible to type in the wrong number without the computer discovering the mistake?

b What do you think might happen in TEAMSHIRTS' system if the wrong supplier number were typed in? (*R*)

As well as ensuring integrity of data, there are many other precautions which Dawn should include in the system. As one more example, consider what would happen if a supplier is slow in delivering new stock, and Mark runs out of blank small yellow T-shirts. Any order which comes in requiring these cannot be supplied immediately, and the team need to be clear what to do. It would be no good if, when the supplies of small yellow shirts were to arrive, everyone had forgotten about the orders which required them.

3.26

Suggest possible solutions to the problem described above, giving procedures for the people involved, and (if appropriate) systems flowcharts for the computer processing. (*D*)

How does Dawn produce the system?

Once Dawn has analysed the requirements of the system, and worked out what the computer should do and what the staff should do with the information as it flows through, she can move on to a more detailed *design* of the system. Only after the detail has been put down on paper does the program *coding*

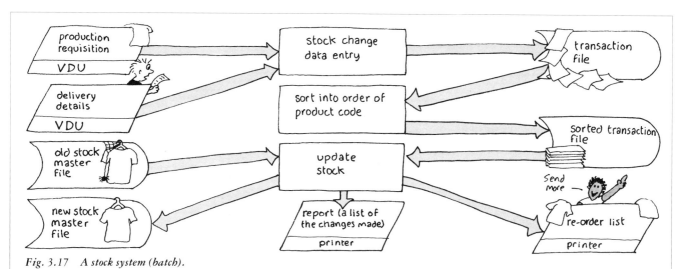

Fig. 3.17 A stock system (batch).

begin, turning the design into a working computer program.

In the stock update process, for instance, the systems design must specify:

— the structure of the stock file,

— the structure of the transaction file,

— the data to be input from the requisitions,

— the data to be input from the suppliers' delivery notes,

— the information to be shown on the screen at each stage,

— the information to be printed out.

It must also describe precisely what is to be done with the input data and files to obtain the output information and files. A set of instructions which can be converted into codes which the computer understands is called an *algorithm*.

Fig. 3.20 shows two source documents and the corresponding section of the transaction file.

An algorithm for the data input stage could be as simple as this:

> Ask the user what they want to do
>
> If they want to input a requisition or a delivery, ask them for details, check them, and put them on the transaction file
>
> Repeat the above until told to stop

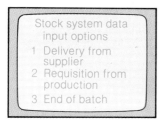

Fig. 3.18

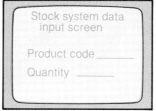

Fig. 3.19

Delivery note

Date 18/06/86

Product	Quantity
SMB	50
SMR	100
SLR	25

Hash: 180861

Requisition

Order no: 056
Customer ref: 10782
Date: 21/06/86

Message: Newport C C

Product	Quantity
SSR	2
SMR	3
SLR	1
TMY	5

Hash: 221535

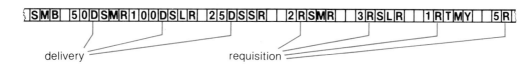

Fig. 3.20   delivery   requisition

Or it could be written in much more detail like this:

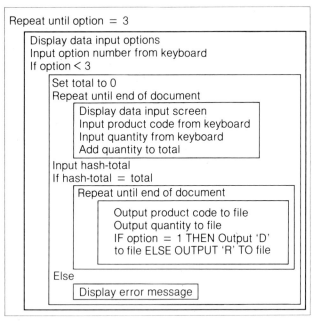

```
Repeat until option = 3
    Display data input options
    Input option number from keyboard
    If option < 3
        Set total to 0
        Repeat until end of document
            Display data input screen
            Input product code from keyboard
            Input quantity from keyboard
            Add quantity to total
        Input hash-total
        If hash-total = total
            Repeat until end of document
                Output product code to file
                Output quantity to file
                IF option = 1 THEN Output 'D'
                to file ELSE OUTPUT 'R' TO file
        Else
            Display error message
```

Fig. 3.21

This is just to give an impression of what an algorithm is; you will see how algorithms are designed from simple steps in later chapters.

3.27

Look back to where the stock master file is listed. Write out the new stock master file after the old one has been updated using the transactions shown in the *Delivery note* and *Requisition* on page 37 (Fig. 3.20). (*T*)

3.28

a Describe what would happen if Elaine had typed in 6 for the number of item TMY on the requisition.

b Explain why the computer is instructed to write D or R to the file for each transaction record.

c Copy the transaction file and continue it. These are the next two documents in the batch:

Delivery note		**Requisition**	
Date 18/06/86		Date 21/06/86	
		Order no. 064	
		Customer ref. 23450	
Product	Quantity	Product	Quantity
TSY	50	SMR	1
TMY	50	TMY	1
TLY	20		
Hash: 180806		Hash: 234202	

These instructions are quite precise, but before Dawn can ask a programmer to turn them into computer instructions, a little more detail is needed. For instance, she must write down how the operator is going to tell the computer when she has reached the end of a document.

One way they could do this is to type in something for the product code that they would never normally use, such as ZZZ. This is called a *rogue value*. Or Dawn may decide that it is easier for the operator to press the ESC key. It does not really matter, as long as the operator *knows* what the computer is expecting. For this reason, Dawn must write *documentation* for the user, as well as for the programmer.

User documentation will contain instructions on what the computer is going to do and how to put the data in. These instruction should be precise, but easy to understand, using diagrams wherever helpful. Even when many of the instructions to the operator are on the screen, with choices being made from clear menus, a handbook or *manual* should be provided which explains what each of the options means, and what to do in awkward situations.

Fig. 3.22 Manuals for an off-the-shelf package.

When all parts of the system have been designed and the programmer has produced the code to run on the computer, the system is almost ready to be put into operation, or *implemented*. One thing remains: *testing*. Dawn will provide the programmer with sets of test data — examples of all the documents and files which will be used to check whether the programs do what she specified without any errors. Dawn first works out what the output documents and the files should contain after the set of test data has been run. If the programs do not produce these results exactly, the programmer will have to make corrections to the code.

The test data will include *extreme* values (very large or small) and *incorrect* data as well, just to make sure that the system can cope with any problems which might arise when it is live. As well as testing each program separately, Dawn must also make sure that the system as a whole works correctly, checking that data stored by one program in the system can be accessed by the other programs which process it.

3.29
Look at this form:

Requisition	
Date: 25/06/88	
Order no. 034	
Customer ref. 176535	
Product code	Quantity
TMB	6
TMY	0
SL	2
SLB	9999

List the errors in the data, and say briefly what the computer should do in each case.   (*T*)

3.30
The system suggested by Dawn provides a check that the *numbers* have been input correctly, but does not check the *product codes*. Only certain product codes are to be allowed, and the computer must check whether a code which is typed in is one of those allowed.

a   What instructions would you include to tell the computer how to do this?

b   Would the input stage be the best place to carry out this validation? Explain your answer.   (*R*)

What if the system needs to be changed?

Dawn will then check that her user documentation matches exactly with what the programs do, and make copies of it for the staff of TEAMSHIRTS. She may also check that the staff can use the system correctly, and give them any necessary training.

She will also give them a copy of the technical documentation: system flowchart, file design, program designs, screen designs, error messages produced, etc. If TEAMSHIRTS need to change the system and Dawn is not available to do it herself, another programmer or analyst will need to understand what she has done.

Altering the system after it has been running for some time is called **maintenance**. For example, suppose that the team decide that the computer ought to be able to print out orders to the suppliers *automatically* when a stock update is carried out, instead of just printing a list of items that need ordering. A number of changes are needed.

In the stock system (see page 37 Fig. 3.17):

actual orders are produced instead of a reorder list; the suppliers' master file must be included, so that their names and addresses can be printed on the orders.

In the stock master file:

a reorder *quantity* as well as the reorder *level* must be included in each record, to be printed on the order.

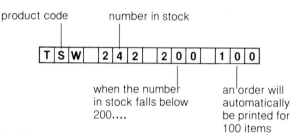

Fig. 3.23

In the stock update program:

the instructions for a reorder list must be changed to include the detail of the procedure for producing orders.

3.31
Redraw the stock system on page 37 (Fig. 3.17) to incorporate the changes described above.   (*F*)

3.32
Another possible change to the system would be to make the stock system interactive. Describe the changes that would be necessary.   (*R*)

What else do TEAMSHIRTS use their computer for?

There is another application for TEAMSHIRTS' computer which Dawn recommends. She thinks that it could help with Elaine's *financial planning*, that is looking at various possibilities for their sales and their pricing and investigating the likely effects on their profits.

This does not require a completely new program to be written specially for the purpose, however. They can buy a package called a *spreadsheet* from the dealer who has sold them the hardware.

This is the same type of program as a word processing or information retrieval package: users can type in whatever information they want to store. With a spreadsheet program, most of the stored data will be *numbers*, and, as well as the numbers, the program will store *formulas*.

To see how this works, consider one of the files (or sheets) that Elaine is going to set up. The following information will be stored for both T-shirts and sweatshirts (the data for T-shirts is shown):

	T-shirts	Sweatshirts
Cost of blank shirt	2.00	
Set up cost for printing	0.80	
Printing cost for each shirt	0.60	
Number of shirts	10	
Cost of post and packing	3.00	
Total cost	28.80	
Price charged per shirt	5.95	
Gross profit on sales	30.20	
% profit	105	

Fig. 3.24 Information laid out for spreadsheet analysis.

The gross profit has to pay for several things: the staff, rent and rates, electricity, etc. These costs need to be met before the business can begin to make money. Elaine needs to discover whether the sales they expect will give them enough profit, and what the effect of changing costs and prices will be.

She does not type in *all* of these figures; the total cost and the profit can be worked out from the other figures, using stored formulas:

total cost = (cost of blank shirt + cost of printing each shirt) * number of shirts + Set-up cost for printing + cost of post and packing

Profit on sales = price charged per shirt * number of shirts − total cost

(* means multiply)

Also Alan has found that it costs 80p to send one shirt, £1.20 to send two or three, £2.00 to send 4 to 6, £3.00 to send 7 to 12, and £5.00 to send over 12. This information can also be stored as a complex formula involving the programming word IF, so

that the postal costs, too, can be worked out by the computer from the number of shirts.

Elaine can now try changing some of the figures to answer questions such as:

— What if the cost of blank shirts goes up to £2.50?

— What if we increase the price to £6.25?

— What if we send them out by a cheaper but slower carrier?

— How many shirts must we sell a day to give a profit of over £200?

3.33
Copy the table of information which is stored in the spreadsheet (Fig. 3.24), but:

a Change the number of shirts to 20 and adjust other figures as necessary.

b Fill in the details for 5 sweatshirts if the cost of blank shirts is £3.50, printing costs are the same as for T-shirts, and postal costs are £1.20 for one or two, £2.00 for 3 to 5, £3.00 for 6 to 9, and £5.00 for over 9.

c Write down the percentage profit on 20 T-shirts and 5 sweatshirts.   (*T*)

3.34
Elaine thinks it might be a good idea to offer a discount for large orders of shirts.

a How could the sheet be changed to allow for a 15% discount on 10 or more shirts?

b What would the percentage profit then be on 20 T-shirts?   (*R*)

3.35
What other applications might there be for a spreadsheet at TEAMSHIRTS?   (*R*)

3.36
TEAMSHIRTS will be keen to have programs which are cheap, easy to use, and able to fit in with their procedures for handling the shirts.

Compare the advantages and disadvantages of specially written and off-the-shelf packages for

a stock control, or   *b* accounting   (*D*)

3.37
The computer dealer is also keen to sell TEAMSHIRTS a word processing package and an information retrieval package when they buy their system. What applications might they use these programs for?   (*R*)

End-of-chapter Questions

3.38

Briefly explain the difference between

a   batch and interactive processing,

b   hash total and batch total,

c   master file and transaction file.

3.39

Redraw the diagrams in Figs 2.22 and 2.23 using correct system flowchart symbols.

3.40

Draw diagrams similar to Fig. 3.8 for VIP's systems, described in Chapter 1, for:

a   hiring a tape,   b   returning a tape.

3.41

List the steps involved in systems analysis and describe briefly what tasks a systems analyst carries out at each stage.

3.42

List the documents used in TEAMSHIRTS' system, and briefly explain the purpose of each one.

3.43

Could computers, or computer-controlled devices, replace the work of people in any of the following aspects of the team's work:

a   deciding what prices to charge,

b   ideas for new designs,

c   printing shirts,

d   despatching orders?

3.44

If the stock control system is to be put on-line, Mark will need a workstation in the store to enter data concerning deliveries and the transfer of stock to the production area. State the advantages and disadvantages of:

a   installing a network system, on which Mark has a terminal,

b   providing Mark with a stand-alone system with disk drive and printer.

(*Advice:* consider cost, speed and ease of use.)

3.45

Do you think any of the documents used by TEAM-SHIRTS could be eliminated if they had a networked system with a central file backing store and terminals in each department?

3.46

Use computer and business magazines to make a list of manufacturers and models of hardware and software that could be suitable for TEAMSHIRTS.

3.47

Many mail order firms send out form letters to people they think might buy their products. As well as sending these circulars to previous customers, they could buy lists of names and addresses from other firms, or pick names from a telephone directory.

a   Do you think that TEAMSHIRTS should spend money on buying a list of names, rather than picking names at random?

b   If they do, do you think they should buy VIP's membership list, Mr Adams lists of house vendors and purchasers, or buy from another type of business?

c   Do you think the people on any of these lists would like to receive advertising material from TEAMSHIRTS?

3.48

TEAMSHIRTS' system will regularly carry out the following processes:

- Printing a *statement of account* for each customer who owes money to TEAMSHIRTS, showing the customer's name and address, the list of invoices not paid (include invoice number, date, and amount), and the total amount outstanding.

- Printing a list of items in stock (reference codes and quantities).

- Printing a list of how many of each item has been sold in each month for the last year (reference codes but not messages), and the total value of goods sold each month.

For each process:

a   Write down which files contain the data needed.

b   Draw a system flowchart.

c   Briefly describe the processing carried out by the computer.

Project briefs 1

1 TEAMSHIRTS require a software package which will display messages in different shapes and sizes.

Level 1 The user should be able to type in a short message, specify the height, width and colour of the characters, and have the result displayed on screen and printed if required.

Level 2 The message should be displayed in a rectangular shape, for example 12 characters wide and 6 lines high, with the user spacing the words to fit.

INPUT: VIP VIDEO LIBRARY VHS AND BETA

OUTPUT:

> VIP VIDEO
> LIBRARY
> VHS AND BETA

Level 3 The message should be spaced automatically, so that words are not split between lines.

2 The manager of a video shop wishes to obtain printed lists of the films in any category (comedy, war, romance, etc.) or price range. Statistics are also required concerning the members' hiring of films: how many of each of various types of film are out at any time, how many are overdue by more than a certain amount, etc.

Level 1 Produce a system which will enable the user to print lists of films of various types.

Level 2 Extend the system to enable the user to find how many of each type of tape have been hired out, how many are overdue, and any other useful information.

Level 3 Extend the system further to allow the user to find which tapes are more than a certain amount overdue.

3 A staff agency keeps records of a large number of office workers who have not got a permanent job, and they want to work as 'temps'. When a firm requires a temporary office worker, they ring up the agency and state the nature of the skills and qualifications required.

The Office Manager matches the firm's requirements as closely as possible to the staff she has available for work, and takes the personal preferences of her temps into account where she can. The Manager's secretary then sends a letter to the firm, giving them details of the person allocated. She also sends a letter to the temp, giving details of the job. When a temporary job finishes, the temp rings the agency to report that s/he is available for work again.

Level 1 Design and implement a computerised system to handle storage, retrieval and updating of staff records.

Level 2 Extend the system to allow printing of the standard letters required when a temp is allocated.

Level 3 Make the production of standard letters automatic when a suitable person is obtained from a search of the records.

Section B

We have looked at the way people use computers to handle information in business where previously only paper was used, and where the new technology has enabled new services to be provided. We are now going to examine the use of special microelectronic devices in industrial and household machinery to enable people to save time and have greater control over processes in their work.

CHAPTER

chips with everything 4

In this chapter we shall examine some of the ways that microelectronics have changed even our own houses. Ten years ago there were few devices in the average household that contained microelectronic parts. Today the situation is very different with many common household applicances being controlled by microprocessors. The main reasons for this are that microelectronic devices are cheap to produce and easily built into many products. In addition, microelectonics can provide smaller, better and more reliable control systems for a wide variety of equipment, including washing machines, cookers and heating equipment.

Fig. 4.1 *Many household appliances have microelectronic control systems.*

Central heating control

You may have dreamed of living in a magnificent mansion with many large rooms. This may not be the ideal world however; if the house was cold in winter and there was no hot water for washing, you would not be very happy. Our comfort depends on our environment being at the right temperature.

Central heating is not a new idea; it has been around since Roman times in various forms. Today we use gas, oil and solid fuel to heat water that flows through radiators, or to heat air which is then blown into each room. However, it is only very recently that microelectronic controllers have been used to keep the temperature of a house at the required level.

Mr and Mrs Johnson have just purchased a new house which has gas central heating and hot water radiators.

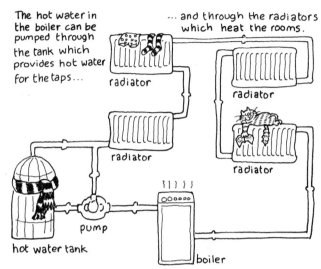

The hot water in the boiler can be pumped through the tank which provides hot water for the taps...

...and through the radiators which heat the rooms.

The gas burners under the boiler are automatically turned on if the temperature in the boiler drops below 58 °C and turned off again once it rises above 62°C

The boiler contains water which is kept at a temperature of around 60 °C while the heating system is running.

Fig. 4.2 *Hot-water central heating system.*

The Johnson's old house also had gas central heating, but the controller for the new system looks completely different from the old one:

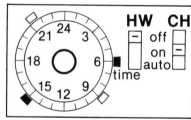

A controller using electromechanical methods: manual switches for electricity, and clockwork for timing. The black marks on the edge of the clock switch the system on, and the white ones switch it off. The time shown is 6 am, and the central heating is just about to come on.

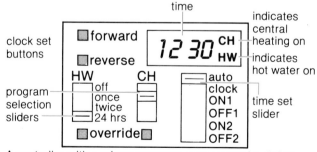

A controller with a microprocessor, memory and a digital electronic clock.

Fig. 4.3 *Central heating controllers.*

The purpose of the two devices is exactly the same: to switch on the heating and domestic hot water whenever the Johnson's want them.

How do the Johnsons tell the electronic controller what they want it to do?

They must decide at what times they want the central heating and hot water to be switched on. They can choose to have only central heating, only hot water, or both, at various times during the day. To select these times, they set the clock by moving the *time set slider* to the *clock* position and then they press the *forward* and/or *reverse* buttons until the correct time appears on the Liquid Crystal Display (LCD) — a display similar to that used on most digital watches. The Johnsons must now decide what combination of hot water (HW) and central heating (CH) is required.

Hot water (HW)	Central heating (CH)
OFF	OFF
ONCE DAILY	OFF
ONCE DAILY	ONCE DAILY
ONCE DAILY	TWICE DAILY
TWICE DAILY	OFF
TWICE DAILY	TWICE DAILY
24 HOURS	OFF
24 HOURS	ONCE DAILY
24 HOURS	TWICE DAILY
24 HOURS	24 HOURS

Fig. 4.4   Options available on an electronic controller.

The Johnsons select these options by using the *program selection sliders*. The word *program* is used here to describe a set of instructions used to control the central heating system, just as a computer program is a set of instructions that controls a computer.

4.1

Describe the positions you would have to set on the controller to have:

a   the hot water all day,

b   hot water on all day with heating on in the evening only,

c   hot water on all day and night with the central heating on in the morning and afternoon for a short time.   (*F*)

When they designed the electronic controller the makers decided to set certain times when the heating

and hot water would switch on and off. But the Johnsons can easily alter these default settings.

Fig. 4.5   Default ON/OFF times.

4.2

The default times listed here (Fig. 4.5) are set on the controller, and the *program selection sliders* are positioned at *twice daily* for HW and CH.

a   Describe when the central heating would be on and when it would be off over a 24-hour period.

b   Why do you think these defaults were chosen by the manufacturer?   (*T*)

4.3

The Johnsons notice that there are some combinations of slider positions that are possible but not shown in the table of options available (Fig. 4.4). Each slider can, in theory, be positioned in any one of the four positions: *off*, *once*, *twice*, *24 hours*. However, due to the way in which the Johnsons' central heating system was installed only ten programs are available.

Write out the other six combinations of hot water and central heating which could be chosen if the central heating was installed differently.   (*D*)

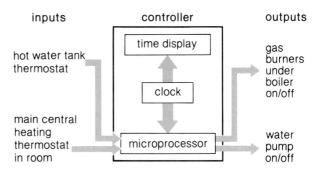

Fig. 4.6   Inputs to and outputs from the controller.

Suppose that the Johnsons decide to have the system switching on and off twice a day. To set the times required, they must move the TIME SET slider to ON 1, and then use the *forward* and/or *reverse* buttons to obtain the required time for the heating to come on at the start of the day. They repeat this using OFF 1 for when they want it to go off again, then ON 2 to come on a second time, then OFF 2 to go off finally. Once they have made all the adjustments to the times, they must return the *time set slider* to the *auto* position.

How does the system work automatically?

A device called a *thermostat* is used to switch on the boiler or a pump when the water temperature drops below a certain value, and to switch it off again when the temperature rises too high.

Fig. 4.7   Room thermostat.

4.4

There are many devices in the home which use thermostats; they may not be electronic at all.

a   List some of these devices

b   Which of your list are controlled by electronics? (D)

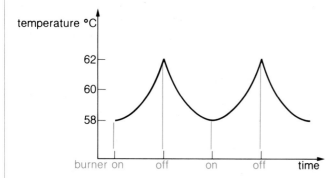

Fig. 4.8   Graph of temperature against time, showing when burner switches on or off.

The *hot water tank thermostat* is the Johnson's house is normally set to 60 °C, so that it switches the boiler on when the water is about 58 °C and off again when the water is about 62 °C. The Johnson may adjust it to suit their needs; if they decide to use the default

value, the following rule decides whether to heat the boiler:

IF the temperature of the hot water drops below 58 °C,

AND the hot water is set to ON at the controller,

THEN the boiler will heat the water.

The conditions can be shown on a **truth table**. This is a diagram used to represent the outputs from a system for *all* possible combinations of input.

Hot water below 60 °C	Hot water on at controller?	Gas boiler switches on?
No	No	No
No	Yes	No
Yes	No	No
Yes	Yes	Yes

Fig. 4.9

In our example, the controller is a system with inputs and outputs as shown in the table above (Fig. 4.9), but the table just shows two of the inputs and one output for simplicity. The gas boiler only switches on when the hot water switch is on AND and the water is below 60 °C; all the other possibilities shown would *not* cause the boiler to switch on.

Normally in a truth table the condition YES (or TRUE) is represented by '1' and the condition NO (or FALSE) by '0'. Our truth table becomes:

Inputs		Output
Hot water below 60 °C	Hot water on at controller?	Gas boiler switches on?
0	0	0
0	1	0
1	0	0
1	1	1

Fig. 4.10

We shall look at electronic components called **gates** which allow electric voltage to be connected to input wires, and allow current to flow through under certain conditions. The input voltage can be high (for the logic value 1) or low (for the logic value 0). If current flows, this produces an output voltage which is high (1) or low (0).

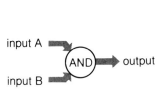

	Current at input A	Current at input B	Current output
input A → AND → output input B →	0	0	0
	0	1	0
	1	0	0
	1	1	1

An AND gate and its truth table

Fig. 4.11   Logic circuit for a two-input AND gate.

The component known as an **AND gate** produces exactly the result shown in the truth table above (Fig. 4.11). An AND gate is a circuit with two (or more) wires for input signals and one wire for output which gives an output of 1 only when *all* the inputs are 1, and an output of 0 otherwise.

4.5

The Johnsons have a *main central heating thermostat* as well as a hot water tank thermostat. They set the central heating thermostat to whatever temperature they require (eg 18 °C):

IF the temperature drops below 18 °C,

AND the central heating is ON at the current time,

THEN hot water will be pumped into radiators.

Copy and complete the truth table below using 1's and 0's to show how this part of the system works.   (*T*)

Temp below 18 °C	Central heating on?	Water circulates
0	0	
0		
1	0	
1		

Fig. 4.12

We can represent various other conditions in the Johnsons' central heating system with truth tables. For example, during the Christmas holidays the Johnsons are at home all day. The weather is very cold, and so they switch both central heating and hot water controls to 24 hours:

IF the water is too cold,

OR the house is too cold,

THEN the gas boiler will switch on.

The truth table for this is:

Water cold	House cold	Boiler switches on
0 (No)	0 (No)	0 (No)
0 (No)	1 (Yes)	1 (Yes)
1 (Yes)	0 (No)	1 (Yes)
1 (Yes)	1 (Yes)	1 (Yes)

Fig. 4.13

(Remember '1' means YES and '0' means NO.)

Again we have an electronic component which produces this kind of output: an **OR gate**.

An OR gate is a logic circuit, with two (or more) inputs, which gives the output 1 when any of the inputs is 1; otherwise it gives the output 0.

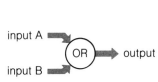

	Current at input A	Current at input B	Current output
input A → OR → output input B →	0	0	0
	0	1	1
	1	0	1
	1	1	1

An OR gate and its truth table

Fig. 4.14   Logic circuit for a two-input OR gate.

The Johnsons' central heating controller has two *override* buttons which are used to change the state of the controller when it is under timed control. If the heating is OFF, then pressing the override button will switch it to ON and vice versa. There is a similar button for hot water (see Fig. 4.3).

Suppose Mr Johnson comes home early on a winter's day: his wife is out, the house is cold and the central heating is not due to switch itself on for two hours. To switch on the heating, all he needs to do is press the override buttons (HW before CH).

An *override* button can again be represented by a truth table:

Hot water	Override button pressed	Hot water
OFF	→	ON
ON	→	OFF

Fig. 4.15

47

This effect can be achieved using a **NOT gate**.

A NOT gate is a logic circuit with one input that gives an output of 1 if the input is 0 and an output of 0 if the input is 1. This is also known as an *invertor*.

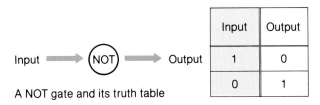

A NOT gate and its truth table

Input	Output
1	0
0	1

Fig. 4.16   Logic circuit for a NOT gate.

4.6

A switch where the same action is used to turn it on as to turn it off is called a *toggle*. Describe another situation in which a toggle is used.   (R).

The system is really more complex than we have described in so far as we have only looked at gates with a maximum of two inputs. For instance, if the Time Set slider on the Johnson's controller is not set to auto, then the controller will not function. Look again at the truth table for the state of the boiler as controlled by the hot water tank thermostat:

IF the time set slider is set to auto,

AND the temperature of the hot water drops below 60°C,

AND the hot water is on at the current time,

THEN the boiler heats the water.

This is an AND gate with *three* inputs and so there are *eight* possible combinations. The truth table and logic diagram for this would be:

4.7

When there are two inputs, there are four possible combinations of input values; when there are three inputs, there are eight combinations.

a   List the eight combinations for three inputs.

b   How many combinations would there be for a *four* input logic gate or circuit?

c   How would you calculate the number of possiblities for circuits with more inputs?   (D)

4.8

In the Johnson's kitchen there is an electrical fan that is controlled by a microprocessor with two sensors: one for humidity and one for temperature. There is also an override button.

Construct a truth table for controlling this fan so that:

IF the humidity is too high,

OR the temperature is too high,

OR the override button is pressed,

THEN the fan will switch on.   (F)

How can the logic gates be combined?

In some of the examples above we have set the program selection slider to a position and then not mentioned it further. However, we could include this slider position in our truth table.

One set of conditions for the boiler to switch on could be:

IF program selection slider is set to 24 hours,

AND the house is too cold

OR the water is too cold.

Inputs			Output
Auto set?	Hot water below 60 °C?	Hot water on at controller?	Gas boiler switches on?
0	0	0	0
0	0	1	0
0	1	0	0
0	1	1	0
1	0	0	0
1	0	1	0
1	1	0	0
1	1	1	1

Fig. 4.17

The truth table for this would be:

Selector slide at 24 hours?	House cold?	Water cold?	Boiler on?
0	0	0	0
0	0	1	0
0	1	0	0
0	1	1	0
1	0	0	0
1	0	1	1
1	1	0	1
1	1	1	1

Fig. 4.18

A special gate could be produced to give the same output as the truth table shown above. However, it is simpler to combine two (or more) gates to give this output.

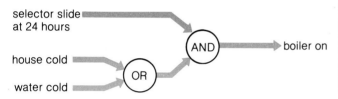

Fig. 4.19

4.9

Another type of gate which is often used is called an *exclusive OR*, with the symbol EOR or XOR. It has two inputs, and the output is 1 if either one or other of the inputs is 1, but not both. The output is 0 otherwise.

Draw a truth table to show all the possible results for an EOR gate. (T)

4.10

Inputs:

  room temperature less than 18°C
  heating on at current time
  heating override button pressed

Output:

  heating pump switched on

For the conditions above copy and complete the logic circuit below and truth table Fig. 4.20. (F)

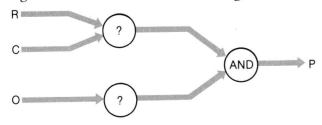

Room < 18 °C (R)	CH ON (C)	Override pressed (O)	Pump ON (P)
0	0	0	0
0	0	1	
0	1		
	1	1	
1	0	0	
1	0		
1		0	
1			

Fig. 4.20

4.11

For the inputs:

  boiler temperature more than 58°C
  heating ON at current time
  hot water ON at current time

and the output:

  gas burner switched on, the circuit would be:

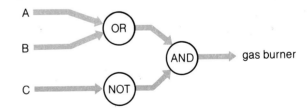

A	B	C	Gas burner ON

Fig. 4.21

a Complete the truth table for the circuit.

b Which of the inputs listed above correspond to A, B and C on the diagram? (F)

How is the controller built using logic gates?

We have just examined some simple logic gates that can be used to make up control circuits. Each of these gates or control circuits could be produced as a separate *silicon chip*. This is a single component which can contain a complex electronic circuit. It is produced by a special process to give a very compact form, replacing thousands of individual components which used to be needed in older electronic equipment: transistors, resistors and capacitors. The use of circuits based on silicon chips is called *microelectronics*.

Each of the 'legs' on a chip may be an input or an output and can be connected to another component in a device.

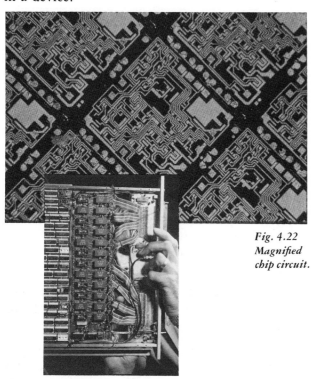

Fig. 4.22 Magnified chip circuit.

Fig. 4.23 A board containing several chips, indicating comparative size.

The controller of the Johnsons' central heating system could be made entirely out of simple chips each containing one logic gate, together with a chip used to control the clock. Instead, it could be made as a *dedicated* chip, specially designed for the purpose. Both these methods have disadvantages. An electronic central heating controller made from chips containing only one gate would be both expensive to produce and bulky, whilst a specially designed and manufactured chip would be *very* expensive unless a large number were to be made.

A more likely alternative to the above methods of constructing the controller is to use a *microprocessor*: a single silicon chip that performs all the functions of a computer's central processing unit. These are manufactured in very large quantities, and so are quite cheap.

A microprocessor would be used together with a memory chip to store all the controller's requirements as sets of instructions (programs), rather than 'hardwired' logic circuits. Programs stored permanently in memory chips are called *firmware*, as they are not quite either hardware or software. This method has another advantage: if a component fails, or if the software needs to be changed, it is easy to remove the old chip and insert a new one.

4.12

What features of firmware make it similar to:

a hardware? *b* software? (*T*)

4.13

Many electronic devices do not (yet) have chips in them.

a Make a list of electronic devices that you are familiar with, and write down which of these do not use microelectronics.

b Do you think any of these devices could be improved by using microelectronics? (*R*)

Other devices in the home

The central heating system that we have examined is just one aspect of modern home life that now uses microelectronics. Many other electrical devices now have automatic control, yet still allow the user to make decisions about how they are set.

The Johnsons' central heating controller performs only very simple tasks such as switching on and off the pump, depending on the time, the temperature, and the Johnson's chosen settings.

A microwave oven is used to cook food quickly, by using waves (similar to radio waves) to heat the food. One such microwave oven is controlled by a microprocessor, which can be programmed as follows:

IF a temperature sensor in the food indicates the food is cooked,

OR the time set on the oven clock is reached,

THEN microwaves are **NOT** produced.

Fig. 4.24 *A microwave oven.*

Here is the diagram and truth table for the circuit that controls the microwaves:

Food cooked	Time up	Microwaves produced
0	0	1
0	1	0
1	0	0
1	1	0

Fig. 4.25

4.14

The logic circuit for a burglar alarm is shown below. To save writing we shall represent the conditions by letters:

Alarm switched on = K
Door open   = D
Window open   = W
Alarm sounds   = A

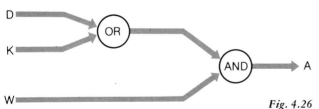

Fig. 4.26

a Write out in English the condition for the burglar alarm to sound.

b Draw the truth table for this circuit.   (*T*)

4.15

A video recorder will play a tape if it has a tape in, and the play button on the machine is pressed, and the pause button is not pressed.

Tape in   = T
Play button on machine pressed = P
Pause button pressed   = F
Video plays   = V

a Copy and complete the following truth table for the video recorder.

T	P	F	V
1	1	1	
1	1	0	1
1	0	1	
1	0	0	0
0	1	1	

Fig. 4.27

b Copy and complete this logic circuit for the above conditions.   (*T*)

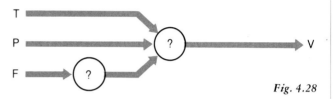

Fig. 4.28

4.16

A simple automatic camera has a built-in flash and it allows a picture to be taken if:

The flash is on

OR there is enough light

AND the shutter speed is correct.

a Write down the three inputs to the camera system.

b Write down the output.

c Draw the truth table for the system.

d Using single letters for each input and output, draw a logic circuit which would control the camera.   (*F*)

An automatic washing machine is a more complicated household system that often makes use of a microprocessor to reduce time spent on housework. In the washing machine the microprocessor stores details of many types of washing 'cycles'. One of these, for instance, might consist of filling the machine with hot water, washing for 5 minutes, emptying, rinsing in cold water for 5 minutes, emptying, and spinning for 2 minutes. These cycles are often called programs, as they consist of sets of instructions. The types of action which the user wants are:

open the door,

choose hot or cold water,

open and close valves, to let water in and out,

switch on and off the water heater,

start and stop the drum rotating,

change the speed of rotation.

4.17

Before automatic washing machines were common in the home, the tasks listed above had to be carried out manually.

a Describe the differences that users of manual machines would notice when they purchased an automatic.

b What effects do you think the automation of washing has had on family life? (*D*)

So far, washing clothes may seem to be a simple task. However, if clothes are to be washed as clean as possible without their colours running, a certain amount of care must be taken. Several years ago an International Textile Care Labelling Code was introduced, and most clothes today carry washing instructions using this code.

How does the washing machine know what to do?

The Johnsons have decided to purchase a washing machine for their new house. Having examined many different types of machine, they have chosen a push-button, microprocessor-controlled model.

The control panel of the model contains a display of the programs available, and these correspond to the washing instructions used in the International Textile Care Labelling Code.

	MACHINE hand-hot medium wash	HANDWASH hand-hot
4 / 50°		
	Cold rinse, short spin or drip dry	
(do not bleach symbol)	Do not use chlorine bleach	
(iron symbol)	Warm	
(P)	Dry cleanable	
(tumble dry symbol)	Tumble drying beneficial	

Fig. 4.29   An ITCL code label giving washing instructions.

Fig. 4.30   A control panel for an electronic washing machine.

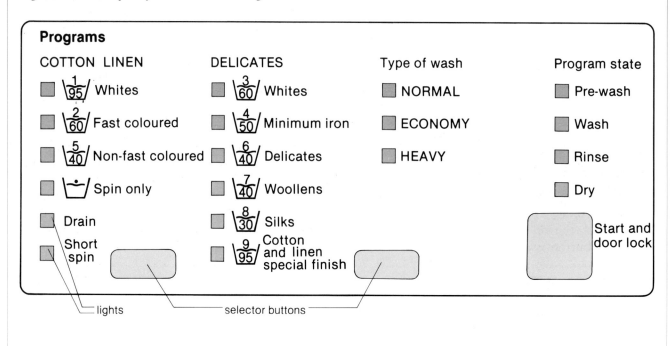

Programs

COTTON LINEN	DELICATES	Type of wash	Program state
□ \1/95/ Whites	□ \3/60/ Whites	□ NORMAL	□ Pre-wash
□ \2/60/ Fast coloured	□ \4/50/ Minimum iron	□ ECONOMY	□ Wash
□ \5/40/ Non-fast coloured	□ \6/40/ Delicates	□ HEAVY	□ Rinse
□ \·/ Spin only	□ \7/40/ Woollens		□ Dry
□ Drain	□ \8/30/ Silks		
□ Short spin	□ \9/95/ Cotton and linen special finish		Start and door lock

lights   selector buttons

Mr and Mrs Johnson first sort the washing into types requiring different programs, then place a batch of one type in the machine and close the door. To select the appropriate program they must then:

1 *Press the program select button until the light is on at the desired program.* If the select button is pressed once, the light moves on one place, to the next program. If the button is held down the light changes from one program to the next rapidly.

2 *Select the type of wash required:* normal (the default setting), heavy, or economy, depending on how dirty the clothes are.

3 Press the start button.

The machine will then automatically perform the appropriate series of actions to wash, rinse and spin the clothes without the Johnsons doing anything else. The sequence of instructions for the actions the machine actually performs is stored in the firmware. In fact, this is really a computer program.

4.18

If the Johnsons followed the set of instructions described above for doing their washing, they would not be very pleased with the results.

a What is missed out?

b Do you think that a microprocessor could help them avoid mistakes like this? Give a reason for your answer. (D)

The programmer (ie the person who writes the programs) must fully understand the working of the machine and be able to describe the step-by-step procedures to complete each of the different wash cycles. As we saw in Chapter 3, a step-by-step procedure for solving a problem or performing a specific task is often called an *algorithm*.

We use algorithms all the time, without thinking; when we want someone to do a job we have to put an algorithm into words, and we often write them down. When we want an electronic device to do a job we have to turn our algorithm into a computer

program or, if the task just involves making decisions, a logic circuit may be used.

An algorithm can be used to describe any series of actions and can appear in different forms:

Heat the oil in the pan and fry the chicken until brown.
Remove the chicken and add the vegetables, stir well, cover the pan and cook over low heat for 5 minutes.
Stir in the tomato puree, the bran and the stock and return the chicken to the pan.
Cover and cook over low heat, stirring frequently, until the chicken is tender.
Add a little more stock if the sauce becomes too dry.

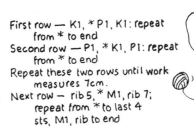

With the locknut free, insert the feeler into the gap between the rocker pad and the valve stem and turn the adjuster until the feeler will just turn in the gap.
Leave the feeler in place, hold the adjuster, and nip down the locknut.

First row — K1, * P1, K1: repeat from * to end
Second row — P1, * K1, P1: repeat from * to end
Repeat these two rows until work measures 7cm.
Next row — rib 5, * M1, rib 7; repeat from * to last 4 sts, M1, rib to end

Fig. 4.31

The designer of an algorithm must be careful not to miss anything out, or else anyone who uses the instructions will have the same problem. If the algorithm is stored on a chip, or on a computer disk, the problems will be even worse. The Johnsons could only blame themselves if they failed to add washing powder. But they would not be very happy if their automatic washing machine failed to close the valve that lets water in, just because someone had forgotten to put that instruction on the chip!

Here is an algorithm to do the washing:

Place clothes in washing machine
Add soap powder.
Fill with water to correct water level.
Switch on agitator

Switch on water heater.
If water is not hot enough, heat it until it is.
Switch off washing machine

Drain water from washer.
Transfer washing to spin drier.
Spin to remove soapy water
Repeat until the water is no longer soapy.
Rinse washing.
Spin washing.

Fig. 4.32

The programmer, who works for the washing machine manufacturer, has prepared algorithms and written programs to completely control the machine. These programs are stored in the machine's memory and, once the program has been selected by the Johnsons and the start button pressed, everything is taken care of. The way instructions are stored and the way they control the mechanical parts of a machine are described in Chapter 5.

4.19

Many tasks which you carry out follow an algorithm. These tasks may be at home, at school, or elsewhere.

a   Choose one of these tasks and write out briefly the instructions involved.

b   Name three devices not described in this chapter which follow an algorithm automatically. (*F*)

4.20

Write out an algorithm describing one of the following tasks:

a   operating a video or audio cassette recorder,

b   selecting a TV program and watching it,

c   cooking a piece of meat in a ordinary (not microwave) oven.   (*T*)

An algorithm describing the wash cycle for 'white cottons and linens' on the Johnsons' washing machine is:

Wash at 95°C (water at normal level)
Rinse 4 times (water at high level)
Drain
Spin

This algorithm only gives an outline of the processes, and will need to be broken down into smaller steps.

For the 'white cotton and linens' these smaller steps would be:

Lock door to drum
Fill washing machine with hot water to normal level
Heat water up to 95 °C rotating drum occasionally
Operate drum in washing motion for 20 minutes
Drain water
Repeat the following 4 times

> Spin for 2 minutes
> Fill with cold water to high level
> Operate drum in washing motion for 2 minutes
> Drain

Spin for 5 mins
Unlock door

Fig. 4.33

Most instructions need to be broken down further before they are ready to be converted into electronic form. **Heat water** can be written as:

> Repeat until temp is 95 °C
> Switch on heater for 2 mins
> Rotate drum for 2 mins

Fig. 4.34

Notice that some instructions are very similar to others in this and in other programs, for example *Spin for 5 minutes* and *Spin for 20 minutes*. The 'woollens' wash will have an instruction *Heat water to 40°C*, written as (see top of next page):

```
Repeat until temp is 40 °C
Switch on heater for 2 mins
Rotate drum for 2 mins
```

Fig. 4.35

The only difference between the two algorithms above is the temperature. This is called a *parameter* for the procedure **Heat water**. We can write *Heat water (95)* or *Heat water (40)*.

In writing an algorithm the amount of detail used will depend on who will be using the information. We need eventually to consider details such as when to operate valves to let water in or out, details of washing motion for the motor, choice of spin speeds, and so on.

Chapter 3 illustrated a more complex algorithm, for data processing rather than control. Chapter 13 includes a summary of the way algorithms have been set out in this chapter, and this method will be used in the rest of the book.

4.21

When the Johnsons' washing machine performs a 'fast coloureds, heavy-soil wash' it performs the following procedures.

   Prewash in water at 40 °C (normal level)
   Main wash at 60 °C (normal level)
   4 cold rinses (high level)
   Spin

a Break down this algorithm into smaller steps.

b Name all the parameters that you have used in your expanded algorithm.   (*F*)

4.22

Write an algorithm that could be used to control the Johnsons' central heating system if it is set to auto and twice a day for central heating and for hot water. (Use the default on on/off times).   (*R*)

Some more chips?

The Johnsons have become concerned that, with such an easy life, they are becoming overweight. They decide to start a calorie-controlled diet. A calorie is a measure of the amount of energy that a particular food contains. If we do not use up the calories in the food that we eat, our bodies turn these calories into fat.

Mr and Mrs Johnson want to be sure how many calories are in each portion of food they eat. Slimming magazines often publish charts of calorie tables, showing how many calories are contained in one ounce or gram of a particular food. They must therefore weigh the food and then multiply the weight in grams by the number of calories per gram. This can be most inconvenient when other people are sharing the same meal and it is difficult to cook individual portions. It is also impossible to work out how much of each food type is in a meal without complicated tables.

Mrs Johnson decides an easier way is to buy a new device which looks like a simple weighing scale. It is a little more complex than this, however.

Fig. 4.36
An Avery domestic scale.

There are several buttons on the front, and these are used to select:

   weighing
   calorie calculation
   food analysis.

There is a scale that displays the values using an LCD, using characters created using a 7-segment display.

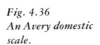

The figure 8 uses all the seven lines (segments) which can be lit up on a seven-segment display. Other figures just use some of them.

Fig. 4.37 A seven-segment LCD display showing both letters and numbers.

The Johnson's new scale can be used as a simple weighing machine, by pressing the lb/kg button to choose the units they want. If they want to analyse the food on the scale, they can select the type of food by using the ≫ and > buttons to display the food code. They look these up in a booklet supplied with the machine.

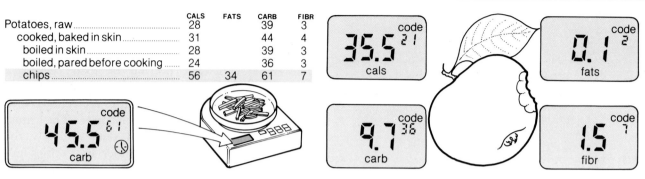

	CALS	FATS	CARB	FIBR
Potatoes, raw	28		39	3
cooked, baked in skin	31		44	4
boiled in skin	28		39	3
boiled, pared before cooking	24		36	3
chips	56	34	61	7

Fig. 4.38

Fig. 4.40

4.23

Any digit shown on the LCD display is made up of some or all of seven lines, called segments. Some 7-segment displays are designed to show some of the capital letters as well as the decimal digits.

7 SE6 DISPLAY

Fig. 4.39

a Draw each letter and digit as it would appear on such a display.

b Which capital letters cannot be shown using this type of 7-segment display?

c List pairs of characters which could be confused.

d If one segment was not working, describe the problems that would arise when reading a number from the display.

e How many different symbols can be produced on a 7-segment display? (Include the blank display.) *(F)*

4.24

Look at the codes shown in Fig. 4.38.

a What do you notice about the order of the foods in the list?

b Why do you think they are in this order?

c Do you think that they would be stored in this order in the machine's memory? *(D)*

Suppose Mr Johnson wants to check a portion of chips that he has brought in. He first selects the food code, then presses a button and the calorie display appears. If he presses it again, the fat content appears, measured in grams or ounces depending on which scale he chose. Many people are also concerned that the type of food they eat does not contain sufficient fibre, or protein; if Mr Johnson presses the button again the protein and fibre content are displayed in turn.

How does the weighing scale work out the values?

The inputs to the machine are:

- the weight of the portion of food
- a code representing the type of food.

The weight of the food is sensed by a device called a *transducer*. This is a means of turning an input from the outside world into an electrical signal, such as a direct current. The transducer for the weighing scale is a special metal device that will bend when weight is placed on it and thus produce a current. The heavier the weight, the larger will be the current. This current can have any value in a certain range, and changes continuously as food is put onto the weighing pan. This means that it is an *analogue* signal.

All of the processors in the computers we have seen so far have been *digital* devices. This means that they can only work with distinct values, or digital signals, with which it is much easier to calculate electronically. There *are* machines, called *analogue computers*, that could take the analogue signal from the transducer and process it, but these are large and difficult to use. Another disadvantage of an analogue machine is that the *output* will also be analogue, and the display of the results would be on a meter or drawn as a graph.

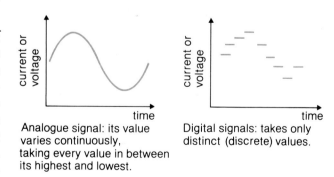

Analogue signal: its value varies continuously, taking every value in between its highest and lowest.

Digital signals: takes only distinct (discrete) values.

Fig. 4.41 Analogue and digital signals.

The designers of the weighing scale decided to use a digital processor to calculate the number of calories, and so the analogue input has to be changed to a digital value. There are various methods of doing this, but the simplest is to use an *Analogue to Digital Convertor (ADC)*. This can be a special chip that accepts the varying direct current signal and changes it to a series of distinct values. These are represented by codes formed by switching on and off the current in eight separate wires; this is explained in Chapter 5.

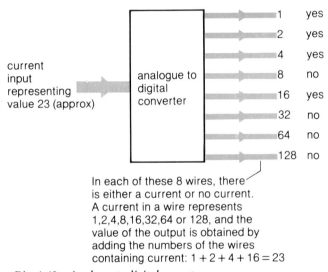

In each of these 8 wires, there is either a current or no current. A current in a wire represents 1,2,4,8,16,32,64 or 128, and the value of the output is obtained by adding the numbers of the wires containing current: 1 + 2 + 4 + 16 = 23

Fig. 4.42   Analogue to digital converter.

A special processor chip was designed to accept an analogue input from the transducer, convert it into a digital signal, and then calculate the weight. This microprocessor also controlled the display and could do the other calculations.

The way in which the machine works can be summarised in an algorithm:

Input analogue signal from transducer
Convert to digital signal by ADC interface
Store weight value
Input signal from front panel for food code
Multiply weight by code to calculate calories
Output weight and/or number of calories on LCD panel

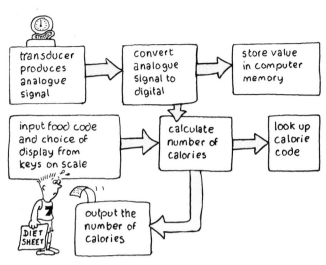

Fig. 4.43   Producing calorific values.

The manufacturers designed one processor chip to carry out all these functions. The first stage was to write down the algorithm required, breaking it down into more and more detail as the design team made decisions about exactly how it should perform. Although the program was to be placed on the chip as firmware, the instructions were first tried out using a full computer system. This made it easy to change the program during development.

When the team were sure that the program was correct, the computerised development system produced a circuit design which was then sent to the processor manufacturer for production. The particular circuit design was chosen because not only could it perform the simple calculations needed, control the display and do the analogue to digital conversion, but also it had a very low power consumption which allowed a small calculator battery to be used.

Many devices in the home and in factories produce analogue signals, so these ADC's are widely used devices. This application in domestic scales has been a simple one, but the principle of conversion of input signals can be applied to more complex machines.

4.25

The following devices can be linked to a computer system: traffic lights, thermometer (electrical), joystick for a computer game, monitor, keyboard, flow meter (detects the speed of liquid in a pipe), lift in a building.

Which of these would need an analogue to digital convertor?

Before digital microelectronics were so common, most devices used analogue output, such as a clock or a car speedometer. Most humans find it easier to judge the size of a value quickly by reading a mark on a scale rather than looking at a number on its own. In cases where an analogue output is required, the idea of an ADC can be used in reverse to give output in analogue form after processing.

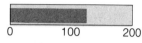

digital display   analogue display

Fig. 4.44 Analogue and digital displays.

A *Digital to Analogue Convertor* (*DAC*) does this job.

As well as linking analogue devices to digital equipment, digital devices can also be linked. The technique of linking one microelectronic device to another so that signals are sent and received correctly is called *interfacing*, and this is described in Chapter 13.

4.26
A scientist sets up an experiment in which a chemical is melted in a test tube using an electrical heater. Heat is supplied at a constant rate.

An electrical thermometer is placed in the chemical and connected to a computer. The temperature is displayed on the screen so that the scientist can see how it changes over a period of time.

a   Which one of the following is a false statement concerning the temperature readings:

i They must be taken frequently.
ii They must be taken regularly.
iii They must be verified.
iv They must be converted to digital values.

b   Suggest two ways that the value of the temperature could be displayed on the screen.

4.27
A 'mouse' or joystick that you may have used as an input device to a computer is an analogue device, and the input signals must pass through an ADC before the computer can process them.

a   Write down any other devices which will need conversion from analogue to digital signals before processing. (*Advice:* these may be computer input devices, transducers for control systems, or anything else you can think of.)

b   Can you think of any devices which use a DAC to produce analogue output after processing?   (*R*)

End-of-chapter Questions

4.28
Explain what is meant by:

a   transducer,
b   logic gate,
c   microprocessor,
d   algorithm.

4.29
What is the difference between

a   analogue and digital signals,
b   a microprocessor and a dedicated chip?

4.30
a   What is the name of the device that the central heating system described in this chapter used as a transducer?

b   Explain why you think that the central heating system has such a complex controller rather than one switch to turn the hot water on or off, and another switch to turn the central heating on or off.

4.31
If the two controllers shown in Fig. 4.3 (page 44) do the same job, what are the main advantages that the electronic controller has compared to the old type of controller?

4.32
Draw a logic circuit using AND, OR and NOT to do the same job as an XOR gate (see Question 4.9).

4.33
Which of the following household devices would benefit from microprocessor control? Give reasons for your choices.

a   washing machine,   *e*   electric drill,
b   video recorder,   *f*   toaster,
c   food processor,   *g*   dish washer.
d   burglar alarm,

4.34
For each of the following activities which apply to machines, write down any advantages and disadvantages of having microelectronic components:

a   repair and service,   *c*   use by consumers.
b   manufacture,

4.35

The manufacturer of a particular household machine might claim that the use of microelectronic components improves his product in several ways. Choose any domestic appliance that could contain a microprocessor, then copy and complete this table. Tick the boxes to show which claims you consider to be important for the appliance you have chosen.

The microprocessor makes it:	significant	not significant	not true
smaller			
cheaper			
more versatile (it can do more things)			
less likely to breakdown			
longer lasting			
easier to use			
easier to repair/service			
cost less to run			

Fig. 4.45

4.36

Write an algorithm for the procedures that Alan of TEAMSHIRTS had to carry out before despatching an order, referring to a requisition, some shirts and an invoice.

4.37

a VIP's stock file (see Chapter 1) had the following record structure:

Field 1   Tape code
Field 2   Tape title
Field 3   Number of member hiring tape
Field 4   Date due back

Arrange these instructions into an algorithm to make a list of the numbers of those members who have overdue tapes:

If contents of field 4 is less than today's date
Read next record of stock file
Repeat until end of stock file
Ask user to type in today's date
Print Field 3

b Write a similar algorithm to search Mr Adams's House File (see Chapter 2) and list the reference codes and addresses of properties under £50 000 which have more than 3 bedrooms.
(*Advice:* refer to Figs. 2.15 and 2.16)

4.38

In a commercial greenhouse it is necessary to keep the temperature and the humidity (amount of moisture in the air) as constant as possible. Windows should be opened if the temperature rises above 25 °C or the humidity rises above 95%. Gas should be switched on for heating if the temperature falls below 10 °C.

In the present control system, a thermometer in the greenhouse and a hygrometer (which measures humidity) are connected as input devices to a logic circuit. There are two outputs from the circuit: one to the motor which opens the windows, one to the heating switch.

A new control system is devised, with the logic circuit replaced by a microprocessor and an outside thermometer connected as another input device. The computer uses the outside temperature to calculate the heating power needed, and sets the gas supply accordingly.

a Explain the advantages of the automatic system compared with manually controlling the windows and heating.

b Draw a truth table for the present system with inputs:

A temperature above 50 °C
B temperature below 10 °C
H humidity above 95%

and outputs:

W window motor on
G gas on for heating

c Draw a system diagram for the microprocessor-controlled system, showing all the inputs and outputs.

d Explain why ADCs may be needed in the microprocessor-controlled system, and indicate on your diagram where they would be placed.

e Write an algorithm for the program which will control the devices.

f What advantages would the new system have, compared with the old automatic system?

cows, control and the countryside

Many jobs in industry take a lot of time but little skill. Even jobs which require skilled workers often just consist of repeating the same task over and over again. Computers and microelectronic control devices can be designed to do many of these jobs, giving more control over the tasks, but needing fewer people to do the work. Again we shall looking at a manual system, and then consider the application of microelectronics.

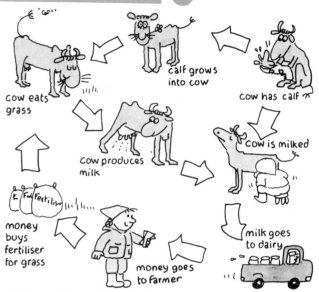

Fig. 5.2   Milk production cycle.

Fig. 5.1

A dairy farm and its computers

Grovewood dairy farm is a business with the main aim of producing and selling milk. They use cows to 'manufacture' the milk, and there are a number of other things which the farm needs:

* grass for the cows to eat,

* fertiliser to make the grass grow,

* winter feed,

* people to look after the cows and milk them.

You may be able to think of more.

There are other aspects to the business as well: the farm may grow other crops, calves may be reared for beef, etc. But we shall concentrate on the feeding of cows and production of milk.

Cows do not normally give as much milk in winter time, when they have only stored food to eat instead of fresh grass. But consumers tend to want the same amount all the year round, so farmers have to buy expensive extra food for those cows which they know will give the most milk.

If this extra food is placed in a general feeding trough, most of it will be eaten by the strongest and the greediest, and they may not benefit from it nor give any extra milk. Alison is the herd manager, and she will know which cows *should* have extra, and

will want to avoid wasting food on those which will not benefit. Each cow is stamped with an identification number to avoid confusion.

Fig. 5.3

5.1

a   Using the information given above, explain why Alison will want to give extra feed to certain cows.

b   How do you think she might decide which cows should have extra, and how much they should have? (D)

5.2

Suppose you have a herd of 100 cows, of which 25 need extra feed at any one time.

a   Try to devise a procedure or system to solve the problem of giving extra feed to those cows which should have it.

b   What problems might in practice stop your system from working?   (R)

Fig. 5.4 A cow wearing a transponder.

How can new technology help?

There is, of course, a microelectronic solution to the problem of giving extra feed to certain cows. The cows wear a collar containing a device called a **transponder**. This transmits a small **signal**, a sequence of radio waves which can be picked up by a receiver. But whereas an ordinary radio would turn this signal into *sound*, a special receiver can recognise the pattern of waves as a *code* and convert it to a *number* using electronics. Each transponder emits a *different* signal, and so each cow has a different number.

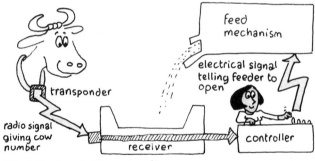

Fig. 5.5 Cow feeding system diagram.

Special feeding stalls contain receivers which are linked to a control device. This contains a microprocessor and a certain amount of memory. When a cow lowers her head into the feeding trough, the controller receives a signal from the transponder and checks to see whether the cow wearing this device is due to have a 'meal'. If so, a portion of feed is automatically dropped from a hopper into the trough.

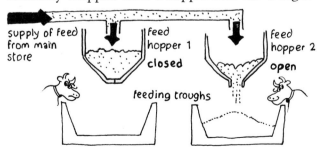

Fig. 5.6 Feed is dispensed to the cow in the stall on the right.

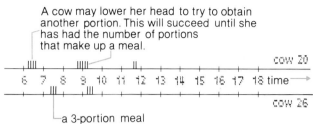

A cow may lower her head to try to obtain another portion. This will succeed until she has had the number of portions that make up a meal.

a 3-portion meal

Fig. 5.7

The cow may lower her head again to try to obtain another portion. This will succeed until she has had the number of portions that make up a meal. She will not be able to get any more until a certain amount of time has passed, so that she cannot eat all her rations at once. Different cows have different daily rations.

5.3

The automatic feed system is made up of the controller, the receiver and the feed dispenser.

a List the input devices for the system.

b List the output devices.

c Would you describe the system as a *computer*? Explain your answer. (D)

5.4

For each of the following, write down whether it is an *analogue* or a *digital* quantity:

a sound,

b a cow number,

c a daily ration of extra food for a cow,

d a radio signal. (R)

Knowing when to feed the cows?

Alison can look at a display on the controller at any time. For any cow, she can look at the cow number, the number of feed portions allocated to that cow and the amount the cow has not yet eaten today. She can type in the number of a particular cow that she is concerned about, or she can look through all the records, one at a time.

Alison can also change certain numbers which are stored in the controller's memory. She can use the keypad to type in any of the following:

the maximum number of portions per meal
(we shall shorten this to **portions_per_meal**)
how many seconds between portions in a meal
(we shall use **seconds_between_portions**)
how many minutes between meals
(we shall use **minutes_between_meals**)

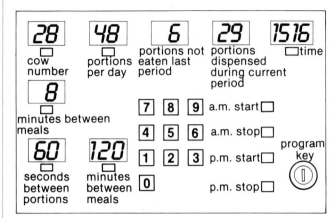

Fig. 5.8 Front panel of controller.

Each of these values is the same for all cows. One value can be set differently for each cow, however:

the number of portions per day
(we shall use **portions_per_day**)

This special data can only be altered by turning a key, which only the farmer and Alison have. If she decides that cow number 29, for instance, should have 48 portions per day, she first presses the button labelled *cow number*, and types 29. She then presses the button labelled *portions per day*, and types in 48. The number of portions per day will change, so this quantity is called a **variable**. Portions_per_day is the *name* of the variable.

The controller keeps a record of the following information for each cow as time passes. These numbers will also change, and so they too are variables:

the time when the previous meal was finished
(variable name **last_meal_time**)
the time when the previous portion was dispensed in the current meal
(variable name **last_portion_time**)
the number of portions eaten in the current meal
(variable name **eaten_this_meal**)
the number of portions eaten during the day
(variable name **eaten_today**)

The time is also a variable, but it is split into three separate values, with names **hours, minutes** and **seconds**. Thus if the time is 16 minutes and 23 seconds past 3 in the afternoon, it will be written as 1516.23 in the 24-hour clock system and stored as

hours = 15
minutes = 16
seconds = 23

The controller is plugged into the mains electricity supply, but it has a battery as automatic backup power, so that the clock is always right.

5.5

At 12.00 one day, values are set as follows:

portions_per_meal 6
seconds_between_portions 60
minutes_between_meals 90

For cow 20 the value of portions_per_day is 30, and for cow 26 the value of portions_per_day is 36. Use the diagram on page 61 (Fig. 5.7) to work out:

a the values of the variables last_meal_time, last_portion_time, eaten_this_meal, eaten_today, for cows 20 and 26,

b how many portions cow 26 has left in her current meal,

c when cow 20 can start another meal,

d how many portions cow 20 has left from her daily ration.   (*F*)

5.6

At another time of the year, values are set as follows:

portions_per_meal 8
seconds_between_portions 60
minutes_between_meals 120

For cow number 29, portions_per_day is set at 48 and the current values of other variables are:

last_meal_time 1436.32
last_portion_time 1652.46
eaten_this_meal 6
eaten_today 32
time 1653.34

a If number 29 goes into the stall, will she be able to obtain food?

b Explain how the controller decides whether to dispense a portion of feed when it receives a signal from a transponder.   (*T*)

How does the controller work out when to feed the cows?

A particular storage location used for a special purpose is often called a **register**. One register in the controller indicates whether a signal is to be sent to switch on the motor which opens the feed hopper. This *output* register will contain the value 0 most of the time, indicating no food is to be dispensed. But when the controller decides to dispense a portion of feed, the register will be set to 1. This register thus stores the value of a variable, which we shall call **open**. There is also an *input* register which holds the number of a cow as she lowers her head. This is also 0 the rest of the time.

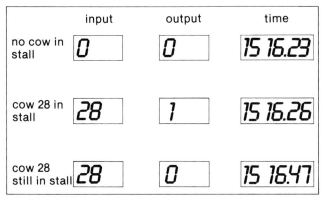

	input	output	time
no cow in stall	*0*	*0*	*15 16.23*
cow 28 in stall	*28*	*1*	*15 16.26*
cow 28 still in stall	*28*	*0*	*15 16.47*

Fig. 5.9   Contents of registers at three instants.

We can write down a step-by-step procedure (an algorithm) to decide whether to set **open** to 1 so that a portion of feed is dispensed. To keep this simple, we shall assume that each cow is allowed just *one* portion per meal. The variables involved will be **portions_per_day**, **eaten_today**, **last_meal time**, **minutes_between_meals**, and also time (variable names **hours**, **minutes**, **seconds**), the input **cow_number** and the output **open**.

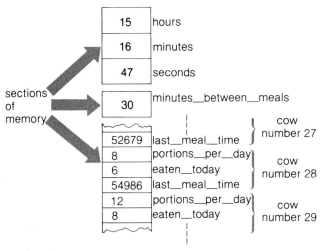

Fig. 5.10   Contents of memory locations.

5.7

The variable 'time' is going to represent the total number of seconds since midnight.

a   Calculate the value of the variable **time** at 1516.23.

b   Write an algorithm to work out the value of **time** from the variables hours, minutes, seconds. (R)

5.8

Suppose the minimum time between meals is set at 2 hours, the maximum portions per meal is 1 and the minimum time between portions is 40 seconds.

a   Draw up a table with the following headings:

Time	last_ meal_ time	last_ portion_ time	eaten_ today	eaten_ this_ meal

b   Work through the algorithm for cow number 28, which is allowed 8 portions per day. She puts her head in the trough at 0645.43, 0657.12, 0839.52, 0851.05, 1113.47, 1456.09, 1634.18, 1639.52, and 1841.26

c   How many portions remain uneaten at the end of the day? (T)

5.9

When **open** becomes 1, the controller must send a signal 20 metres to the hopper mechanism.

a   Write down ways of sending this signal.

b   Explain which you think would be the best way of sending the signal. (R)

Here is the algorithm for one day, written in sentences first, then using our special layout (Fig 5.11):

If the cow with her head in the trough is wearing a transponder, has not eaten all her daily ration, and the time since the last meal is more than the time between meals, then open the hopper, set the time of last meal to the current time, add 1 to the number of portions eaten, and close the hopper. Repeat continually until the end of the day.

```
open: = 0
last_meal_time: = 0
eaten_today: = 0
REPEAT UNTIL time = 2400.00


   IF cow_number > 0 AND eaten_today
                         < portions_per_day
      AND time — last_meal_time
                    > minutes_between_meals *60


         THEN
             open: = 1
             last_meal_time: = time
             ADD 1 TO eaten_today
             open: = 0
```

Fig. 5.11   Cow-feeding algorithm.

5.10

Look back to the algorithm in Fig. 5.11 (page 63).

a Why do we need to set open to 0 again after a portion of feed has been dispensed?

b Why does the algorithm start with:
eaten_today: = 0?

c What else needs to be added to the algorithm to make it continue to work over several days? (D)

Where there are *several* cows wearing transponders then, instead of just *one* memory location for each variable **eaten_today, portions_per_day, last_meal_time**, there will be a block of locations, called an *array*. Each location in the array holds data about one cow.

| | cow numbers | | | | |
	1	2	3	4	5
portions_per_day	12	8	8	0	8
eaten_today	6	6	2	0	5
last_meal_time	51670	54118	38623	0	49908

Each row of this table is an array variable, with an entry for each cow. In memory, the values are really stored one after the other, in sections of memory, as in Fig. 5.10.

Fig. 5.12

Alison can also obtain details of cows which did not eat all their food yesterday. This information can be displayed on the controller or it can be printed out, if there is a printer attached. She can also get a detailed list of all the cows and the feed they have not yet eaten if she wishes. A printer will also record automatically at midnight (when farmers are asleep!) a list of all cows with feed left uneaten, the total of feed allocated, and the total of feed dispensed.

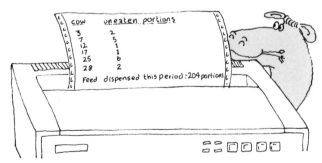

Fig. 5.13 Print-out at end of feeding period.

5.11

Why will Alison find it useful to print out each of the lists and totals described above? (D)

5.12

It is possible to allow for more than one portion per meal. The algorithm in Fig. 5.11 could be adapted by changing one of the decision conditions, adding two extra decisions, and adding two extra steps to the procedure when the cow is to be fed.

a Extend the algorithm to work when there is more than one portion per meal.
(*Advice:* think of a cow which is trying to get as much food as possible.)

b Check your algorithm for cow 15 which is allowed 24 portions per day, and lowers her head into the trough at 0634.25, 0634.48, 0635.24, 0636.12, 0643.04, 0644.31, 0932.56, 0936.47, 1020.03, 1146.28, 1405.26, 1406.09, 1406.32, 1425.14, 1426.52, 1809.14, 1812.43. The maximum number of portions per meal is 4, and the other variables have the same values as in Question 5.9.

How the controller works

We have seen what is needed to control the feeding of the cows and how the controller can decide to dispense food at certain times. We shall now look in more detail at how the algorithm is carried out by means of microelectronics.

We have seen that Alison can change the way that the controller makes decisions: she can alter the number of portions per meal, the timing of meals, etc. The manual (a reference book which arrived with the system) refers to this as 'programming' the controller. But as we saw in Chapter 3, *programming* means something special to people whose business is computers: it means working out the detailed *instructions* which make the computer do what the user wants.

The feed controller has already been programmed when it leaves the factory. Its memory contains all the necessary instructions in what is called *Read Only Memory (ROM)*. This term is used because the processor only 'reads' instructions from it, and the user cannot change what is in this part of memory.

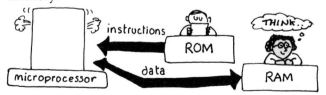

Fig. 5.14 Connections between parts of controller.

The controller also contains some **Random Access Memory (RAM)** which stores the data which may change, for example the data for what individual cows have eaten that day. The processor can read values from RAM, and 'write them back' again if they are altered. Some data change quite often, such as **eaten_today**, other data only change now and again, such as **portions_per_meal**.

We have seen the algorithm outlining the instructions which control the dispensing of feed. The controller can carry out other tasks, such as displaying the total feed dispensed since midnight. Here is an outline algorithm for this process:

```
REPEAT UNTIL all cows have been processed
       ADD next cow's feed TO total
DISPLAY total
```

Fig. 5.15

How can we tell the microprocessor in the controller how to do this? The instructions must be converted to codes, which the processor can use to switch signals through the circuits. These codes are stored in the computer's memory as sequences of 1's and 0's (binary digits).

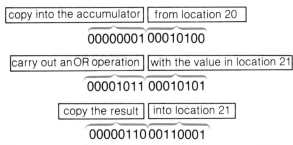

This sequence of codes makes a microprocessor do the same job as a simple OR gate as described in Chapter 4. The processor's circuit is very much more complicated than an OR gate, but it can do many other things as well.

*Fig. 5.16 **Typical instruction codes.***

We first need a more detailed algorithm for the task, specifying:

● how to find the value in memory which represents the next cow's feed,

● how to tell when all cows have been processed.

The farm has only 30 transponders, and so there is a block of 30 memory locations containing values for the feed dispensed. The REPEAT UNTIL structure

could not be used if all these locations had separate variable names, so we shall call them all **feed_dispensed** and put the cow numbers in brackets. Thus we can think of the section of memory as:

variable	value	meaning
feed_dispensed (1)	24	feed dispensed to cow 1
feed_dispensed (2)	18	feed dispensed to cow 2
.	.	.
.	.	.
.	.	.
feed_dispensed (30)	12	feed dispensed to cow 30

Fig. 5.17

The algorithm becomes:

```
total: = 0
FOR cow: = 1 TO 30
       ADD feed_dispensed (cow) TO total
DISPLAY total
```

Fig. 5.18

5.13
Explain the difference between ROM and RAM. (*T*)

5.14
Why does the first step in the algorithm above (Fig. 5.18) set the total to 0?   (*T*)

5.15
Adapt the algorithm (Fig. 5.18) to:

a list the numbers of the cows for which no feed has been dispensed,

b calculate the average amount of feed dispensed,

c count how many cows have eaten less than the average amount of feed.   (*F*)

We therefore need the processor to do the following things:

● add whole numbers

● subtract whole numbers

● test whether one stored value is more than another

● test whether one stored value is the same as another

Instructions for these actions will be stored in the ROM as codes. The instructions will have two parts: the *operation code* and the *operand*. The operand is either a value to be used by the operation, or the address of a location in memory where the value can be found. They will be in the form shown in Fig. 5.16 on page 65, and we shall assume that each part of the instruction uses 8 binary digits.

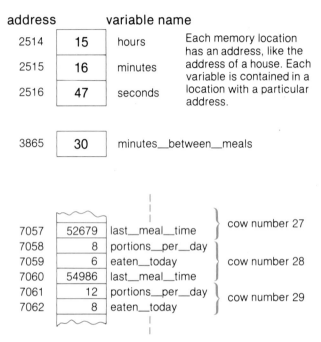

Fig. 5.19

order to *repeat* a section of instructions, or *miss out* a section, a *jump* instruction will be needed as well. You may have noticed too that sometimes we need to add a fixed number, and at other times we need to add a variable.

So this list of instructions should do all we need:

operation code	typical operand	meaning
ADD	52	add the value stored in location 52 to the accumulator
SUB	52	subtract the value stored in location 52 from the accumulator
ADN	52	add 52 to the accumulator
SBN	52	subtract 52 from the accumulator
LDA	52	copy the value stored in location 52 to the accumulator
STA	52	copy what is in the accumulator to location 52
LDN	52	place the value 52 in the accumulator
JMP	2	jump 2 instructions forward
JGR	2	jump 2 instructions forward if the accumulator is greater than 0
JLE	2	jump 2 instructions forward if the accumulator is less than 0

Fig. 5.21

To simplify the codes, all instructions are designed to work on the number stored in one special register, called the *accumulator*. But this does mean that extra instructions are needed to copy a number from RAM into the accumulator and vice versa.

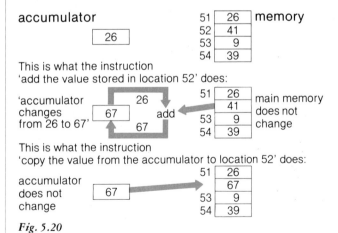

Fig. 5.20

The processor will normally work through the instructions in the order in which they are stored in memory. This is called *executing* the program. In

With this simple set of codes, *one* instruction in our algorithm language may need *several* coded instructions.

For example, suppose location 52 stores **eaten today**, 57 stores **portions_per_day**, and 49 stores **feed**, as in the diagram Fig. 5.19. The instruction:

IF **eaten_today** < **portions_per_day** THEN **feed: = 1**

would look something like

LDA 52	puts eaten__today into accumulator
SUB 57	subtracts portions__per__day
JGR 2	if result is less than 0, ie eaten__today is less than portions__per__day jump to the second instruction after this
JMP 3	otherwise, jump to the third instruction after this
LDN 1	place the number 1 in the accumulator
STA 49	copy it to the location feed

Fig. 5.22

66

5.16

Suppose the accumulator holds the number 23 and location 48 holds the number 11. The contents of these stores may be altered when an instruction is executed.

What would be the contents of the accumulator and location 48 if the instruction executed is:

a ADD 48,

b ADN 48,

c LDA 48,

d STA 48. (*T*)

5.17

Explain the difference between the instructions

a JMP 3,

b JGR 3. (*T*)

5.18

a What do you think JMP −2 would mean?

b Describe what will happen to the number in location 26 when this procedure is executed:

    LDN 0
    ADN 1
    STA 26
    JMP −2 (*D*)

5.19

a Can you think of any other instructions that would be useful?

b Could they be written as procedures using the codes we already have? (*D*)

How does the processor work all this out?

We have looked at registers which can be set to 1 or 0, and how decisions are carried out electronically using sequences of these digits as codes. But it is no use just being able to store the numbers 0 and 1. *Larger* values, such as cow and transponder numbers, must be stored as well, and calculations need to be carried out on values such as the number of portions. The digits 0 and 1 are referred to as **binary digits** (often shortened to **bits**), because there are only two of them. A larger number is stored in a register made up of several bits (usually 8), often called a **byte**.

| 0 | 0 | 1 | 1 | 0 | 1 | 0 | 1 |

Fig. 5.23

In the decimal system that people normally use, the digits in different positions are worth units, tens, hundreds, etc. Each position can be 0, 1, 2, 3 . . ., 9. In binary notation, the largest digit in the units position is 1, and so to represent *two*, we need another digit. Three can be stored with two digits, but to store the value four, we need another digit again, and so on.

These are the first eight numbers in binary:

one	1
two	10
three	11
four	100
five	101
six	110
seven	111
eight	1000

Fig. 5.24

5.20

a Continue the list above (Fig. 5.24) up to thirty-two.

b What is the largest number that can be represented by seven bits?
(*Advice:* look for a pattern in the values which need a new digit. Try to work it out without writing them all down.)

c How many different values can be represented by a byte? (*F*)

5.21

a How would the decimal number 45 be written in binary?

b What decimal number is represented by 1101011? (*T*)

5.22

It is a great advantage when dealing with electronics to have only two different digits to store.

Give one *disadvantage* of this when large numbers have to be stored. (*D*)

Here is the diagram of the register (Fig. 5.23) showing the decimal value of each digit.

64	32	16	8	4	2	1
0	0	1	1	0	1	0	1

Fig. 5.25

The decimal value of the number stored can be found by adding the value of each bit which contains 1:

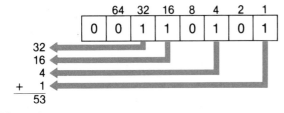

Fig. 5.26

Larger numbers can be stored by grouping several bytes together to make what is called a *word*. This term is used because one *byte* is the storage space needed for one *character* (for example, a letter), so a word stores several characters. We shall look at codes for characters in Chapter 10. The number of bytes in a word depends on the type of CPU.

We can also store fractions by deciding that part of the word indicates how far the decimal point should be moved, like the display on a scientific calculator.

If you multiply 177000 by 22000 the answer is 3894000000. This is displayed:

$$3.894 \quad 09$$

Fig. 5.27 *Calculator display of 3 894 000 000.*

To *add* decimal numbers, you need to know the answer to many simple sums, such as 6 + 2 = 8, 3 + 9 = 12, etc. But to add *binary* numbers, you only need to know that 0 + 0 = 0, 1 + 0 = 1, 0 + 1 = 1, 1 + 1 = 10. This is a great advantage when designing electronic circuits to calculate automatically; we will need a lot of them, but each one can be fairly simple.

To add two seven-bit binary numbers and store the answer in 8 bits, we also need to 'carry'. We can work out each digit in the answer in two stages — first add the digits given, then add the carry from the last position.

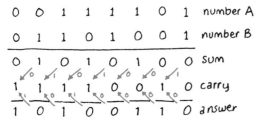

Fig. 5.28 *Binary addition.*

5.23
Convert to decimal the values shown above (Fig. 5.28) and check the result.   (*F*)

5.24
a Write the values twenty-two and nineteen as eight-bit binary numbers.

b Add them together in binary.

c Check your answer by changing it back to a decimal value.   (*T*)

5.25
a Add together 01110011 and 01011101 in binary.

b Convert these values to decimal, add them as usual and see what the answer should be.

c Why might the computer think the binary answer is a different value? (*Advice:* look at the left-hand bit).

d Why do you think this is called *overflow*?   (*T*)

When the instructions, values and addresses are stored in the controller, they are in binary form (called *machine code*).

code		binary value
ADD	becomes	00000001
SUB	becomes	00000010
ADN	becomes	00000011
SBN	becomes	00000100
LDA	becomes	00000101
STA	becomes	00000110
LDN	becomes	00000111
JMP	becomes	00001000
JGR	becomes	00001001
JLE	becomes	00001010

Fig. 5.29

The whole task of translating lists of instructions like this is carried out by a special computer program (called an *assembler*, because it 'assembles' the machine code from our instructions). The language we have used for the detailed instructions is called an *assembly language*, and each instruction gives *one* instruction in machine code. For instance, if **eaten_today** is stored in location **52**, **portions_per_day** in **57**, and **open** in **49**, the section of code on page 66 (Fig. 5.22) becomes

00000101	00110100
00000010	00111001
00001001	00000010
00001000	00000011
00000111	00000001
00000110	00110001

Fig. 5.30

5.26

a How many different memory locations can you refer to, if you have 8 bits for each address?

b What is the memory size of the computer you normally use?

c Can you explain how it can have different addresses for all these locations? (*R*)

Here· is some code for the complete totalling algorithm:

```
LDN 1     Location 42 stores count, 43 is used
STA 42    to build up total, and feed dispensed
LDN 0     is stored in location 44.
STA 43    In the real program, feed dispensed
LDA 43    would be stored in 30
ADD 44    successive locations, but we would
STA 43    then need extra instructions to
LDN 42    move through the memory. These
ADN 1     are too complex to study at present.
STA 42
SBN 30
JLE −7
```

Fig. 5.31

5.27

a Work through the program coded above, writing down the contents of each memory location at each stage (including the accumulator), and crossing out the old value when a new one replaces it, like this:

```
acc.  42   43   44
4̶     1    0    6
0̶                        (after the first 6 steps)
6
```

Fig. 5.32

b Assemble this program into binary machine code.

c Explain what the two instructions SBN 30 together with JLE −7 are doing to the value in the accumulator. (*T*)

5.28

a Write similar assembly code for the feed algorithm on page 63 (Fig. 5.11).

b Assemble the code you have produced.

c Write down algorithms for other tasks that the controller performs, and code them as far as possible in our assembly language. (*R*)

Other uses for computers on the farm

The type of feeding mechanism described is just a small part of the full computer-controlled system installed at many farms. The farm is a business, and a computer can help keep financial records in the same way as for VIP video and TEAMSHIRTS.

Fig. 5.33 The milking cluster being placed on the cow.

Fig. 5.34 Milk being pumped into a jar.

Several activities in the milking parlour can also be automated:

```
• identifying cows
• removing the milking machine 'cluster' from the
  cow's udder
• recording the milk given by each cow
• feeding cows while they are being milked
• recording the date when a cow last had a calf
• instructing the herd manager to stop milking a
  cow, a certain number of days after calving
```

Fig. 5.35

The feeding systems, the milking records and the accounting procedures can all be linked together by software which accesses the same data.

5.29

For each item in the list above, state whether the main activity of the computer is input, output or storage.   (*T*)

5.30

Each cow has its number on a label attached to its ear, and stamped on its back. If all the cows also wear a transponder, describe *two* ways that the computer might discover which cow is in a particular stall.   (*F*)

How can a computer help in the milking parlour?

To milk a cow, Alison or her assistant first cleans the udder, and then attaches the cluster of tubes shown in the photograph (Fig. 5.33). This device squeezes the milk out with the same sort of regular action that a person would use when milking manually. It must be removed shortly after the milk runs out, or else the cow will suffer. Alison can see the milk flowing into the jar which stores it temporarily, and can judge when it has stopped if she watches carefully. She will also know from experience how long afterwards it is best to remove the cluster — this varies from cow to cow.

In order to make the farm more profitable, she needs to be able to milk more cows at once than she can watch by herself. Instead of paying an assistant to work with her all the time, the farmer may decide to install more automatic machinery.

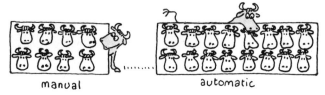

Fig. 5.36 *Automatic parlours can have more stalls.*

5.31

An automatic cluster remover can tell when a cow's milk has finished, it can stop the squeezing shortly afterwards, and it can turn on a small red light to let Alison know that the cow has finished.

a   What sort of device tells the computer whether milk is flowing?

b   What sort of device tells the computer when a certain number of seconds have elapsed?

c   What sort of device gives a small red light?

d   What sort of device tells the pump to start?

e   Write an algorithm which inputs the cow number and whether milk is flowing, and outputs whether to pump or not.   (*R*)

Cows sometimes fall ill, and Alison has to give them drugs. It would be disastrous if milk from cows who were having drugs or who had infectious diseases went into the main tank, as this goes straight to the dairy to be bottled. The dairy tests each tanker as it arrives, and any batch which is contaminated has to be thrown away. The farmer responsible would be fined heavily. Sick cows have to be milked for their own good, however, but the milk must be kept out of the main tank.

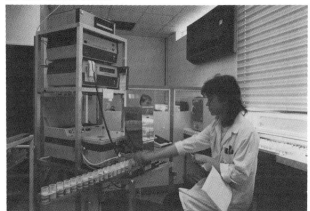

Fig. 5.37

So when Alison gives a cow drugs, she keeps a careful record of how long the effect will last. As each cow comes in to be milked, she checks the list. These records can be stored in a computer system, of course. Up to 8 messages, such as:

DUMP MILK
COW OFF FOOD
DUE TO STOP MILKING

can be displayed at a milking position for any cow that comes in.

5.32

The DUMP MILK message is displayed when the computer recognises a cow that is ill.

a   Describe what else the program would ask Alison to do, to make sure that the message stops appearing when the cow has recovered.

b   How do you think the system would work out when to display the message DUE TO STOP MILKING?

c   How do you think the system would work out when to display the message COW OFF FOOD? (*R*)

5.33

Describe the effects of automation on:

a the cows, in terms of their general well-being,

b the herd manager, in terms of working conditions and job satisfaction,

c the farmer, in terms of business profits and quality of life,

d society, in terms of animal welfare and effects on the countryside,

e farm workers, in terms of employment prospects.   (D)

What else may be possible in the future?

There are many developments which may lead to very different methods of farming in the future. As far as dairy farming is concerned, there are likely to be changes in the area of business analysis, for instance, weighing cows over a period of time and calculating the value of the feed and the grass, and in how the animals are treated.

It may be possible to have 'milking on demand': whenever a cow feels like being milked, she will walk up to a heat-seeking robot arm which attaches the cluster, monitors the milk for drugs/disease, detects dirt and cleans if necessary, and milks the cow, despite being kicked! The subject of robots is looked at in some detail in the next chapter.

Herd managers could then look after cows in fields, with more time to give personal care. They would study reports from the computer to decide what balance of feed is needed for each cow to improve the amount and quality of milk. Automation may, however, lead to dairy farming becoming more like a production line, with the computer system controlling all aspects of the work. We shall look at how this idea in used in factories in the next two chapters.

5.34

Describe the problems you might find in designing a robot to milk a cow.   (D)

End-of-chapter Questions

5.35

Explain the meaning of the following terms:

a bit,

b accumulator,

c operand.

5.36

For each of the following ranges of whole numbers, write down whether you would need a bit, a byte or a word to store a number in the range:

a 0 to 1 inclusive,

b 0 to 9 inclusive,

c 0 to 999999 inclusive;

d −273 to 999 inclusive,

e 1 000 000 to 2 000 000, storing the numbers correct to the nearest 1000

5.37

a Explain the difference between *instructions* and *data*.

b Could you tell the difference if you looked at the binary values in memory?

5.38

There are two main security problems which might cause the data stored in the controller to be corrupted:

a an unauthorised person could change the preset values, deliberately or by accident;

b a break in the supply of electricity, by a power cut, for instance, could affect the memory locations.

For each of these cases, describe how the designers of the controller have minimised the danger of corruption.

5.39

a Explain what is meant by the term *array*.

b What is the advantage of using an array, compared with using several variables with different names?

5.40

Design an algorithm for milking a cow which could be used as instructions for a robot.

5.41

The system in the parlour where cows are milked and fed has several variables. List as many of these as you can.

5.42

A new version of the out-of-parlour feeder has certain differences:

a two microprocessors, one for cow identification, one for feed control,

b touch-sensitive buttons on the display,

c a built-in stock control facility for feed,

d security code instead of a physical key,

e no printout option.

For each of these changes, explain why you think the manufacturers made them.

5.43

The details of cows stored by the controller can be thought of as a file, with fields:

> cow number,
> portions per day,
> etc.

a List the other field names.

b Write down which is the key field.

c Explain why this file is held in RAM rather than on backing storage.

5.44

Some farmers who installed early types of automated feed systems stopped using them after quite a short time.

a Why do you think they might have abandoned these expensive systems?

b Do you think that these farmers would be more or less likely to install the more advanced systems now available than farmers who have not used microelectronics before?

5.45

A portable traffic light system is designed for places where road works allow only a single line of traffic at a time.

The following sequence is repeated throughout the day:

Phase 1: TL1 red   TL2 red
Phase 2: TL1 red   TL2 green
Phase 3: TL1 red   TL2 red
Phase 4: TL1 green   TL2 red

The controller uses microelectronics to switch the lights on and off to give this pattern. The road works supervisor can set the length of time that each phase lasts, stored in variables time1, time2, time3 and time4. Thus if time1 is 5, time2 is 20, time3 is 5 and time4 is 30, then phase 1 will last for 5 seconds, phase 2 for 20 seconds, phase 3 for 5 seconds and phase 4 for 30 seconds.

a Explain the need for phase 1 and phase 3.

b Suggest why the supervisor might have decided to set different time periods for phases 2 and 4.

c Describe how the colour of the two lights could be represented as binary values in an output port.

d Using instructions such as:

> WAIT (10) meaning 'keep the lights as they are for 10 seconds.'
> SWITCHLIGHT (1) meaning 'switch traffic light 1 to the opposite colour'

Write an algorithm to display the sequence described above for 2 hours. (Assume both lights are red to start with.)

e Explain the advantages and disadvantages of this microelectronic method, compared with the manual method using a sign with STOP on one side and GO on the other.

(*Advice:* consider the drivers, the road workers and the council's Highways Manager.)

f Describe how the microelectronic system could be made more flexible with an extra type of input device and a more complex program.

Fig. 5.38

C H A P T E R
quality control 6

We shall now look at the use of microelectronics to control and check processes in larger manufacturing systems, and we shall see how computers can be used to link various aspects of control and ensure efficient production to give customers exactly what they want.

Recycling waste paper

Paper is made from wood, and this involves cutting down trees. So a lot of the paper and card we use these days is made by *recycling* waste.

Old boxes, newspapers, etc., can be turned into fresh paper to be used for wrapping things and for making corrugated board. Ideally, a factory which does this runs continuously, 24 hours a day, seven days a week, 50 weeks a year.

water
waste paper
pulper
filter
pour onto flat wire mesh
pressing and drying
rolling and cutting
paper

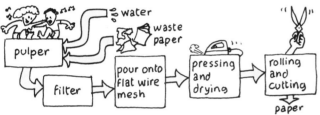

Fig. 6.1

There are three main factors which affect the success of the business:

- the rate at which paper can be recycled,
- the quality of the product,
- the energy used.

The use of computers in process control has improved all three of these considerably.

How have these improvements come about?

The production of recycled paper starts with the mixing of waste paper and water to form a pulp.

The drying cylinders are enclosed in an insulating hood to reduce the amount of heat wasted. Because the paper dries by evaporation, the moist air produced must be blown out of the hood and fresh, dry air drawn in.

To prevent too much *heat* being lost with the moisture, a heat exchanger is used. The pipes taking hot air out are wrapped around the pipes bringing cold air in. The air coming in is thus heated up, so less steam is needed for the drying cylinders, and less fuel needs to be burned to produce the steam.

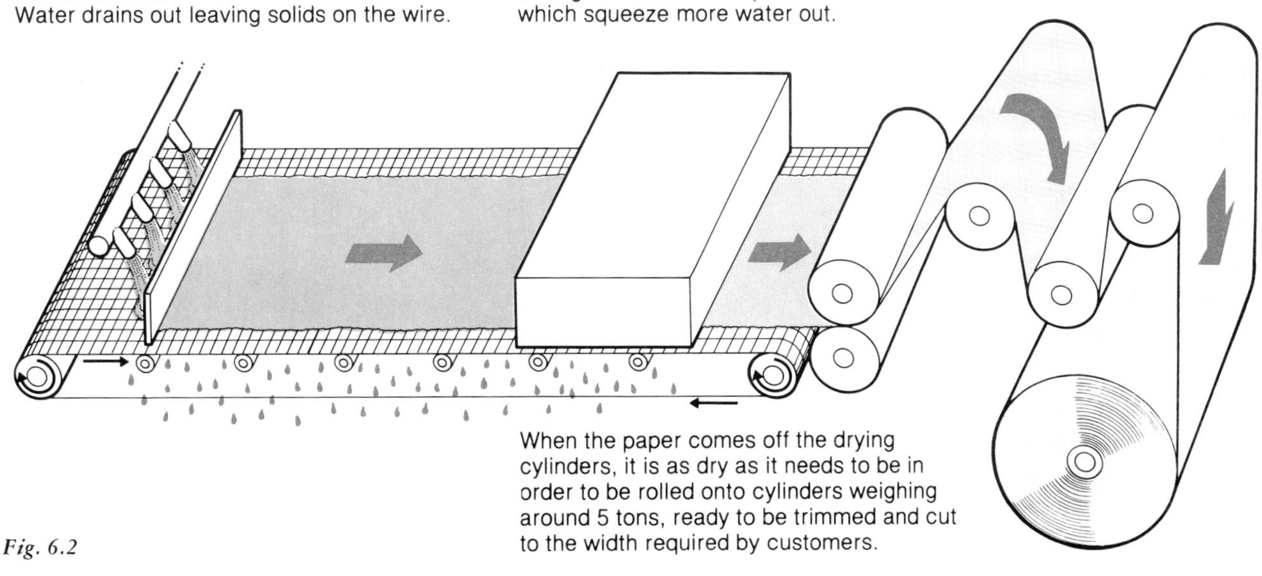

The waste paper is mixed with water to form a liquid pulp with about 5% solids. This is poured out of nozzles onto a flat screen made out of fine wire mesh. This is called the *wire*. Water drains out leaving solids on the wire.
At the end of the wire, it passes through a box heated by steam where more water is sucked out. It is now about 20% solid, and passes through steam-heated presses which squeeze more water out.
The paper then passes over a series of steam-filled cylinders. Several tons of moisture per hour are removed from the paper.
When the paper comes off the drying cylinders, it is as dry as it needs to be in order to be rolled onto cylinders weighing around 5 tons, ready to be trimmed and cut to the width required by customers.

Fig. 6.2

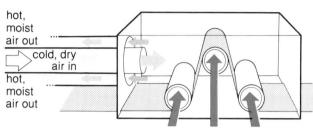

hot,
moist
air out

cold, dry
air in

hot,
moist
air out

steam heating into drying cylinders

Fig. 6.3

The temperature of the air coming in will vary, of course. This is measured by a type of thermometer which produces an electrical voltage which is proportional to the temperature (the higher the temperature, the bigger the voltage). This electrical signal is converted to digital form, so that the value for the temperature can be stored in an input register for a control computer. The procedure is similar to that of the weighing scale in Chapter 4.

6.1

a What type of signal is the voltage which depends directly on the temperature?

b What is the name of the device which converts this signal to a form which can be input to the computer?

c What number system will be used to represent the value in the input register? (*T*)

The connection where the signal enters the computer system is often called a *port*. The computer's CPU can obtain this value whenever the program asks for it.

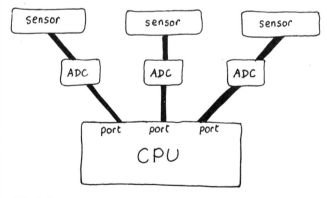

Sensor   sensor   Sensor

ADC   ADC   ADC

port   port   port

CPU

Fig. 6.4

A value for the moisture content of the paper at the *start* of the process is input from another sensor in the same way. The requests for input, called *polling* the ports, are usually repeated very rapidly. The

computer calculates with these two values to work out the rate at which steam should flow into the drying cylinders. The aim is to keep the machine speed, and the moisture content of the paper at the *end* of the drying process, at the values set by the manager.

There should be around 6% moisture in the paper at the end of the process. All measurements are collected continuously by the computer system and displayed on screens so that the supervisor can check the working of the system. The supervisor is *monitoring* the process, so the screens are often called *monitors*.

An algorithm for this would be something like:

    REPEAT indefinitely
        Ask port for temperature
        Ask port for moisture
        Calculate rate of steam
        Set steam flow
        Display temperature
        Display moisture
        Display rate of steam

Graph plotters are also used to keep a permanent record of the variation in values, and the supervisor can ask for a printout of the variables at any time. This information is important; if anything goes wrong with the system — a breakdown, or too much power being used — the manager needs to see what the values were over the period of time leading up to the problem. The process of recording values at regular intervals is called *logging* the data.

Fig. 6.5 A graph plotter.

This display is in analogue form, but is produced from the digital outputs which tell the pen how far to move. The values are checked very frequently, so the jerks of the pen as the values change are very small and the graph looks quite smooth.

6.2

Why do you think a plotter is used for most of the logging rather than a printer?

6.3

Instead of output to the plotter and to the printer when required, the values of the important variables in the system could be written to a magnetic tape or disk at frequent intervals. These values could then be printed, plotted or processed later if required.

a   What would be the advantages of using magnetic backing store for the purpose of logging?

b   What would be the disadvantages of magnetic storage media?

How are different papers made?

To find out how different papers are made we must first go back to the part of the process where pulp is poured onto the wire. Paper is produced in different *widths* and in different *weights*. The weight is the number of grams in a square metre of the paper. The rate at which pulp should be poured on to the wire depends on the weight of paper being produced, as well as the speed of the wire.

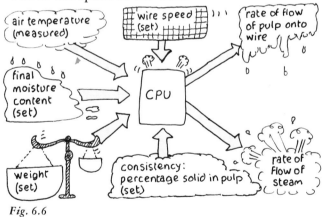

Fig. 6.6

It is important to check that the weight and moisture content that have been *set* are actually *achieved*. If the errors are greater than a certain amount — the *tolerance* allowed in the variable — then adjustments must be made.

The weight and moisture are checked by sensors at several points across the paper as it comes off the wire. If the weight is wrong at a certain point, then

the nozzle pouring pulp onto the wire at that point must be adjusted. If the moisture is wrong, then the steam pressure in the box at that point must be adjusted.

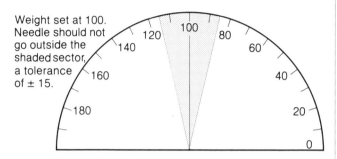

Weight set at 100. Needle should not go outside the shaded sector, a tolerance of ± 15.

Fig. 6.7

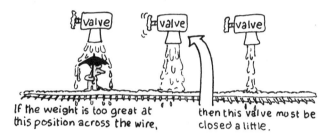

If the weight is too great at this position across the wire, then this valve must be closed a little.

Fig. 6.8

The person who is machine supervisor for the shift watches screens showing diagrams of the 'profile' of the paper.

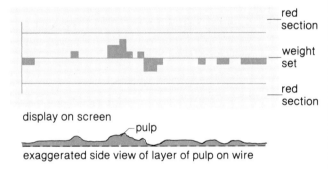

display on screen

exaggerated side view of layer of pulp on wire

Fig. 6.9

When part of the profile goes into the red section, the supervisor makes an adjustment, based on his experience and knowledge of the equipment. This is an unpleasant job, as both the air and the machinery are hot, wet and dirty.

The computer system could do automatically the same tasks as the supervisor by signalling to an *activator*. The activator could be a small motor which opens or closes a valve slightly to alter the flow of pulp or steam. A short signal would just turn the valve a little, and a longer signal would give a larger adjustment.

The valve is closed a little by sending a short signal from the computer to turn the motor on for a brief time.

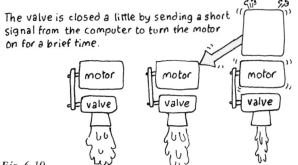

Fig. 6.10

6.4

Write an algorithm which specifies what the supervisor does to maintain the weight and moisture content of the paper within the tolerance allowed. (T)

6.5

If the adjustment of the valves was made automatically by the computer:

a   What would be the advantage of keeping the supervisor?

b   How do you think his job would change?   (D)

6.6

List the possible advantages of:

a   manual control,

b   computer control,   (D)

This part of the control system uses the idea of **feedback**: the values of the outputs of the process are used to affect the inputs. For example:

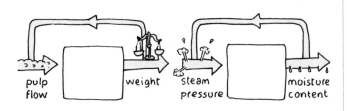

Fig. 6.11   Feedback loops.

6.7

Look back to the drying cylinder system. Describe where feedback can be found.   (T)

6.8

Draw similar diagrams to those above (Fig. 6.11) for the central heating system in Chapter 4:

a   for the room heating system,

b   for the hot water tap system.   (F)

How is production of pulp controlled?

Going back one stage further in the paper-making process, we can find another example of computer control. The composition of the pulp made from waste paper and water is set to be around 5% solids.

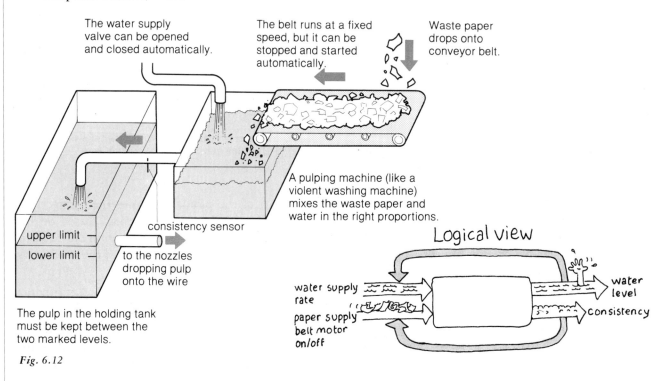

The water supply valve can be opened and closed automatically.

The belt runs at a fixed speed, but it can be stopped and started automatically.

Waste paper drops onto conveyor belt.

A pulping machine (like a violent washing machine) mixes the waste paper and water in the right proportions.

consistency sensor

to the nozzles dropping pulp onto the wire

upper limit

lower limit

The pulp in the holding tank must be kept between the two marked levels.

Logical view

water supply rate

paper supply belt motor on/off

water level

consistency

Fig. 6.12

The control procedure, then, has to switch off the water coming in when the water level on the tank reaches the upper level and switch it on again when the level gets low.

6.9

For the pulping control system:

a List the inputs and outputs needed.

b Write down whether feedback is involved, giving reasons for your answer.

c Draw diagrams similar to those above (Fig. 6.11) to show the connection between the inputs and outputs.   (*D*)

6.10

There are two water level detectors in the tank, lower (L) and upper (U). Each outputs logical 1 when covered, 0 when uncovered. The water supply valve (V) is open when V is 1 and closed when V is 0. It is switched on and off by an activator (A): when A is 0 nothing happens; when A is 1, the switch changes from on to off or off to on.

a One of the four combinations for L and U cannot possibly happen. List the three possible combinations for L and U in a truth table.

b Draw up a truth table with 6 rows for output A with inputs L, U and V.

c Draw a logic diagram for the process. You will need at least 4 gates.   (*F*)

In the same way, the control program must start the waste paper belt if the consistency drops below 5% and stop it when it rises above 5%. The use of a computer means that this can be done by periodically polling the sensors, say 10 times every second, and following an algorithm which is repeated indefinitely.

6.11

a Design the algorithm for the mixer control, using the phrases 'upper level covered', 'lower level covered,' 'valve open,' 'belt running,' 'switch water valve,' 'switch belt.'

b What advantages has this system over a simple logic circuit?   (*R*)

Further aspects which benefit from computer control are the actual production of energy and its use to produce steam, and the order processing and accounting systems which are also handled by computer, using the standard types of software that we have seen in Chapter 3.

But what we have looked at is a piecemeal system: parts of the process have been changed over to computer control one at a time. Each part uses a different computer, and it would be difficult to link them. It would be possible to install a complete new computer system which would control every part of the business. The computer could work out from the customers' orders how much paper to produce of different weights, what widths to cut it into, and which lorries to load it onto.

6.12

Why do you think the control processes have been installed one part at a time?   (*D*)

6.13

It would cost a great deal of money to install an up-to-date control system, and a lot more paper would have to be produced to pay for this investment. This means that new paper-making equipment would also be required, and probably a new factory building to house the larger machines. The factory is currently on a small site near the centre of a large city.

a Do you think the new factory would be built in the same area as the present one? Give reasons for your answer.

b If all paper mills were faced with the same decision to expand and modernise or close down, what would be the effects on the industry?   (*D*)

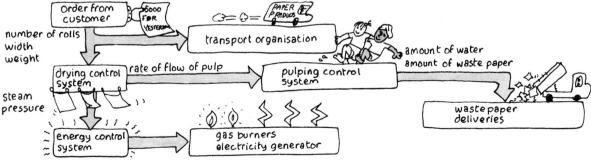

Fig. 6.13

Fig. 6.14   An engineering drawing.

Fig. 6.15   The Morris 1000, designed by hand.

Computers have also changed the actual manufacturing process itself. Very powerful computers are used in the design of products, and machines can be directly controlled by microprocessors to make a product designed in this way. We shall look at computers helping to design motor vehicles and robots helping to make them. We shall also consider a general system for moving parts around automatically.

Car manufacturers have made great advances in recent years and models are designed and manufactured using many processes controlled by computer.

Vehicles used to be designed by a team of engineers using drawings of each item, such as doors and seats. These were then collected together, and if any of the parts did not fit or changes were needed, then the design had to be redrawn. This was a very lengthy and expensive process, often taking up to four years before even the prototype of a new vehicle was available for testing.

To design a product as sophisticated as a new car, a very powerful computer is needed. It must be able to display complex diagrams on the screen, and must also be capable of calculating very quickly to produce the shapes needed in these displays.

The use of a computer to display designs, accept changes and calculate effects is called *Computer Aided Design* or *CAD*. Each designer has a terminal linked directly to the main computer, and all their changes are stored centrally.

The changes that the designers make are shown immediately on the screen. This requires a huge number of calculations, and the display screen needs to be updated very rapidly. This needs a computer

system with a processor powerful enough to show the results immediately. We will look at these large, powerful computers in other applications later in the book.

Fig. 6.16   The designer uses one VDU to design a car panel.

When the design is complete all the figures for the car shape are stored in the computer and can then be fed to the welders and cutters.

These welding and cutting operations that used to be done by hand are then performed by machines controlled by the figures supplied to them. This process is called *Computer Aided Manufacture* or *CAM*, Thus the whole manufacturing process is called CAD/CAM; we shall see how it works by following the design and manufacture of a modern saloon car.

How does the design start?

Designers sketch out their ideas, which are based on surveys of what customers want, together with safety features, 'drag', and other factors affecting performance.

The design team now produce a full size clay model of the car. This is shown to influential people, such as dealers, and, if the style is acceptable, the rough outline is ready for input to the computer.

The clay model is used to obtain precise measurements for the body shape. These are stored in a computer file called the *engineering master database*. From these figures the computer will calculate all the parts and components that are required to produce the final car. This is only one use of a database and we shall look in more detail at how databases are used in Chapter 8.

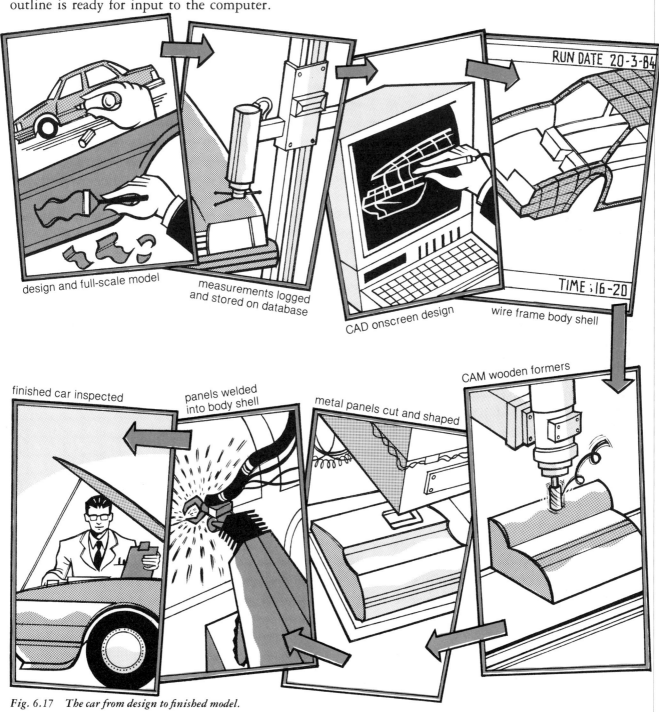

Fig. 6.17   *The car from design to finished model.*

How does CAD help the designers?

The CAD system is very complex, requiring a powerful computer and skilled users. The designers work at terminals connected on-line to the computer, so that editing the database is *interactive*. The terminals used for this graphics work are **Graphical Display Units**, which give more accurate displays of lines and shapes than ordinary monitors.

6.14

The figures in the database are prepared *off-line*, but the design is edited *on-line*.

a Explain the difference between on-line and off-line working.

b Describe how the procedures would change if alterations to the design had to be made-off-line. (*D*)

We shall look at some design problems and illustrate how the computer helps the designers. Firstly, the body shell:

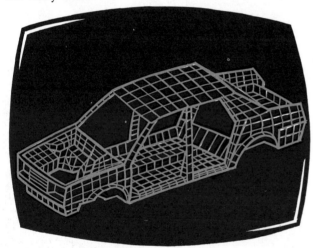

Fig. 6.18 *When all the panels have been designed, they can be assembled on screen to show the final body shell.*

Each panel can be displayed as a wire-frame diagram calculated from the figures in the database. A panel can be modified as in Fig. 6.16 using a **light pen**. Any changes made on that particular panel cause changes in the numbers in the database. Any other panels that will be attached to this one will also be changed so that they will still fit accurately.

Each section of the frame is displayed in different colours, showing the stress on various parts. If a lot of stress is expected at a certain point, extra reinforcing panels and struts can be built in. In the past this would have had to be done by testing an actual vehicle.

6.15

The old process of building and testing a car required actual prototypes to be built. These were tested for stress and extra struts and panels added.

a What advantages have been gained by using the CAD process?

b Suggest how the use of the CAD process might affect employees of the company, other than the designers. (*D*)

6.16

a The designer of the doors of a car decides that the front door is too narrow. He decides to enlarge the door. Explain how this change could affect the other panels on the car.
(*Advice:* refer to Fig. 6.18.) (*F*)

b What advantage is gained by having the database available when a designer is working on a door panel? (*F*)

The moving parts of the car, like the boot lid, need to move in relation to the body shell. It is essential that the moving parts of the car function correctly. The database can be used to simulate the movement of these parts.

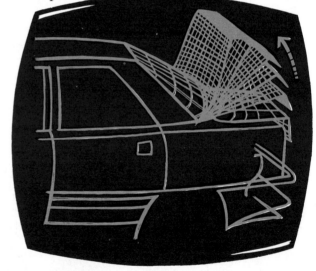

Fig. 6.19 *The computer can use the database and an algorithm to calculate all possible positions of the boot lid. It will then display these on the screen, making it easy for the designer to check that it misses the rear window.*

If problems occur, the shape of the opening section or the position or style of hinge can be changed. It would cause immense problems if the boot shape had to be changed on an actual model, as the rear section of the car would also have to be changed. Using the database these changes are made automatically.

It is clear that a change in one panel affects other panels. This used to require alterations to many drawings, but now this merely means the computer changing a few figures on the database.

6.17

a Write down other components that could be tested in the same way as the boot lid.

b The computer itself can be programmed to work out whether the boot lid misses the rear window. Why do you think the designer checks the movement on-screen?

c What are the advantages of using this design process over the older system of actually building prototypes and working from engineering drawings? (D)

How can the car be made from the database figures?

These final figures on the database are now used to control metal cutting and milling machines that will produce large wooden shapes. These are used in turn to produce the metal panels. The panels are *precisely* what was designed on the screen, as they are cut using the same figures.

All the panels needed in the production of the car (often up to 350) have been designed on the screen and cut using the set of measurements stored in the engineering database. The cutting of these panels is directly controlled by the computer and this process is an example of *Computer Aided Manufacture* (*CAM*). The whole body panel has been designed, tested and manufactured using the computer. This is the *CAD/CAM process*.

When all the sections of the car body have been manufactured, they have to be joined together to form the full shape. This is achieved by using machines called 'spot welders' that join the panels together at several spots along the edges of each panel. The spots are fairly close together, but have to be accurately positioned. Some of the joints are in places which are very awkward to reach, and this work used to be done by men holding the large spot welders and moving the jaws into position. Other joints are easy to weld: around the door panels, for instance.

The welding process has been automated by using two types of spot welding machine. Large static machines are used for the main assembly.

Fig. 6.21 A static welder.

For the awkward parts of the body shell, robot arm welders are used. These machines have welding heads attached to the end of arms that move in all directions. They can reach any part of the body shell, but in practice, many identical machines are used, each programmed to do a different job on the production line.

The use of these automatic machines, controlled by programs to carry out these repetitive tasks, is one example of *robotics*. This term covers all types of

Fig. 6.20 A milling machine cuts wooden panels, using figures stored on the computer's database. Metal panels are cut using the same figures by a Computer Numerical Control (CNC) machine.

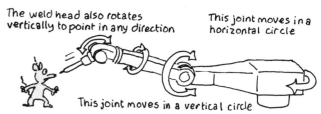

Fig. 6.24 *The robot arm moves in all directions.*

This process happens very quickly so the arm appears to move rapidly and accurately. It can be precisely controlled and, as the body shells are fixed on the production track, the position of the panels can be calculated directly from the engineering database. This allows the robot arms to be programmed easily.

6.18
What are the advantages of using robots to weld the body shells of motor cars? *(D)*

6.19
The production track now makes many different styles of the same model of car, changing easily from one to another. Previously, cars of a particular type were produced in batches, because everything had to stop for a changeover. Explain:

a how it is now possible to have different types of car on the track, one after another,

b what the advantages are for the manufacturer.

Robots are also used to assemble goods that are made from a lot of small parts, such as electronic circuits. These machines, called 'pick and place' robots, simply pick up each part and place it in the correct position. When all the components are placed, the circuit board is floated across a pool of molten solder and all the components are permanently fixed in place. This is an important method in modern manufacture, resulting in fewer mistakes and wastage. This also means that the components are much cheaper.

The robots we have looked at so far are intended to work in one place for a period of time. But most people have a vision of robots as things which move around, finding their own way from one place to another. This is very difficult for a computer-controlled machine, which can neither 'see' like humans, nor work out what it is touching.

6.20
The advantages listed at the top of the next page have been suggested for robots, compared with humans, in industry:

Fig. 6.22 *Robot arm welders on the production line working on different parts of the body shell.*

computer-controlled machine which can be programmed to perform a variety of tasks.

The way these robot arms move may seem almost human, but in fact they are simple joints moved by motors under the control of instructions from computer programs in the CPU.

At each of the joints in the arm there is a device called a *stepper motor*. These motors move a fixed number of degrees every time a pulse of electricity is received along the control line; they do not turn in analogue fashion.

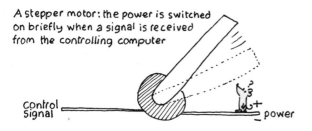

Fig. 6.23 *Controlling the movement of the joint.*

A digital signal moves the motor a fixed distance. If there are stepper motors at each joint, a combination of signals can be sent which will move the arm to any required position. The rotating head can also be controlled by another stepper motor to position it accurately on the joint.

- 24-hour operation is possible.

- They can work in extremes of heat, cold, dust, fumes, radioactivity.

- They produce items of exactly the same quality every time.

- They are very precise in their movements.

- They can be built to lift heavy weights.

Write down a similar list for the advantages of humans. (D)

6.21

Many of the stages in the manufacture of motor cars now incorporate the use of computers and robots. These include:

    component delivery,   windscreen fitting,
    paint spraying,   safety testing.

Choose one of these stages and descirbe how robots or computers could help the process. (R)

6.22

Design a robot that will follow a trail around an office. Describe the method you would use to guide the robot, what the trail would be made of and why you would choose your method rather than some other alternatives. (R)

Can robots move around the factory?

Many industrial processes require things to be moved regularly from one area of the factory to another. For example, in the paper mill, rolls of finished paper are carried to the warehouse; in the car factory, doorhandles, lights, and other parts are carried from the warehouse to the production track.

In some factories, it has been possible to automate this sort of movement by installing wires under the

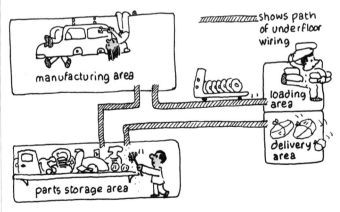

Fig. 6.25

floor along the path where the parts have to be carried, so that a truck can follow the path.

6.23

a Describe what would happen if there was something in the truck's path.

b What could be done to solve this problem? (*Advice:* think of a sensor and an activator.)

c Describe what would happen if the item to be picked up was in the wrong place.

d What could be done to solve this problem?

e If the factory manager decided that the parts should be stored in a different part of the building to make delivery easier, what would have to be done to the truck system? (R)

6.24

Do you think a computer or microprocessor is needed in a truck that follows a wire under the factory floor? Explain why. (D)

Computer control techniques can make this a much more flexible system.

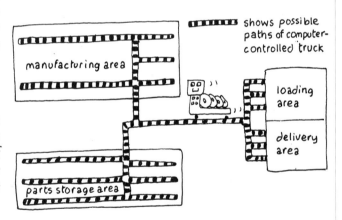

Fig. 6.26

There are a number of problems to be solved, however.

- How does the computer know where the truck is at any particular time?

- How does the computer know where the truck ought to go next?

- How does the computer signal to the truck?

- How does the system deal with unexpected obstacles?

- How does the computer make sure that the truck picks up the right item?

Three main ideas are used in the system. Firstly, **barcodes** are used to identify places and objects, together with laser scanners. This input system is just like the one used in many supermarkets.

Secondly, the truck contains a *computer of its own*, in addition to the central computer. Thirdly, *radio communication* is used between the truck and the central computer.

How do the bar codes give information?

Fig. 6.27

If you pass a piece of paper with a small hole in it over a bar code, you will see a sequence of white and black flashes. The wider the bar, the longer the flash. The laser scanner sees the same effect, and converts the flashes into a sequence of pulses. These can represent a binary number, as we saw in Chapter 5.

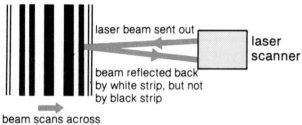

laser beam sent out

laser scanner

beam reflected back by white strip, but not by black strip

beam scans across the black and white strips

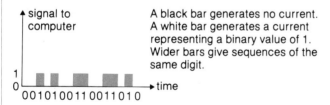

signal to computer

A black bar generates no current. A white bar generates a current representing a binary value of 1. Wider bars give sequences of the same digit.

time

00101001100011010

This gives two 8-bit binary numbers — the two coordinates of the truck.

Fig. 6.28

The computer on the truck has been programmed with a plan of the factory floor in the form of co-ordinates, and the position on the plan of different bar codes (Fig. 6.29).

The scanner can always see two bar codes. These represent coordinates, and from these the truck can work out its *own* coordinates. The truck has also

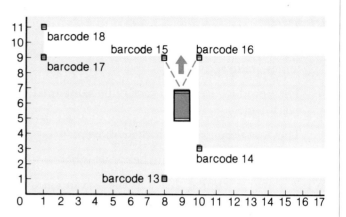

Fig. 6.29

been programmed with the route that it must take, using algorithms made from instructions such as:

IF position = (9,10) THEN
SET HEADING west

How does the system cater for human error?

Systems just involving people have many problems, because people make mistakes. Systems just involving machines also have problems, because machines break down. Machines with moving parts can break or wear out; purely electronic parts do not tend to wear out, but are useless if the electric power fails.

Systems involving *both* can have the worst problems of all, or they can give the best of both worlds. To succeed, such a system requires that the people involved understand what the machines are doing, and that they learn to use them properly. In addition, the machines must be programmed to take account of people's mistakes.

6.25

List the problems caused by human error which could arise with the automatic truck system.   (D)

Some of the problems which are catered for are:

● *Obstacle in the way of truck:* the truck is programmed to turn and find its way around the obstacle, using bar codes to find its way.

● *Bar code covered up:* bar codes are positioned so that a third one will always be visible; the truck still has two to work from if one is obscured.

● *Item to be picked up is in the wrong place:* the items themselves can also be labelled with bar codes, and the truck can be instructed by the central computer to search out a particular code.

6.26

Copy Fig 6.29 and mark where extra bar codes should be placed to make sure that there are always three which the scanner can 'see'.   (*F*)

6.27

Suppose the central mechanism of the truck fails.

a   What problems could be caused by a runaway truck?

b   How do you think the designers of the truck tried to prevent such problems occurring?   (*R*)

It is possible, of course, for the programmers to make mistakes. Such errors can take three main forms, and these are illustrated with reference to Fig 6.29 and the example instruction:

IF position = (9, 10) THEN
SET HEADING west

- *Syntax error:* when the computer cannot make sense of an instruction when converting it to machine code.
  Example: a comma may be missed out of a pair of coordinates

     IF position = (9 10) THEN
     SET HEADING west

- *Execution error:* when the computer cannot carry out the instruction while it is being *executed*, that is when the program is running.
  Example:

     IF position = (9, 10) THEN
     SET HEADING north
     MOVE FORWARD 3

- *Logical error:* when the computer carries out all the instructions, but does not achieve the results expected.
  Example: assuming the truck is intended to reach the door between bar codes 17 and 18,

     IF position = (9, 10) THEN
     SET HEADING east

A common logical error is to put the right instructions in the wrong order.

A common term for such errors is *bug* — so called, apparently, because someone working to put right a fault in an early computer suggested that it might be caused by an insect in the circuits! Anyway, the idea spread, and we even have a completely new word to mean the correction of errors: *debug*.

What sort of computers are used in control systems?

We have looked at microcomputers used in small businesses, and microprocessors used in fairly simple devices. The processing units in these are slow and can access only a limited amount of memory. Many small, cheap microcomputers used in the home and school are 8-bit machines: this means that all instructions and memory addresses are either just 8-bit bytes or combinations of bytes which have to be dealt with one at a time. Most small business machines (desktop computers) are 16-bit machines. These are more powerful than 8-bit machines, as they can handle more complex processes in one machine code instruction, and can address a larger amount of memory.

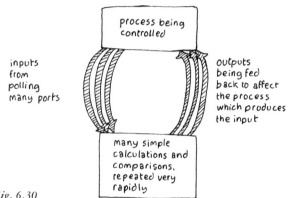

Fig. 6.30

But a system such as the paper mill control needs to compare and calculate with a large number of different inputs in time to affect the process that it is controlling. This is referred to as *real time processing*, and is a mode of operation common in data processing as well as control applications. Not even 16-bit microprocessors can work with sufficient speed to deal with this sort of operation. Nor can they provide a quick response to several different users, all expecting results at the same time, if they have many terminals connected for interactive processing.

For these types of computing, a *minicomputer* is usually used: the next step in speed, power and cost from a micro. For systems requiring fast processing of very large quantities of data for many purposes at once, such as the CAD/CAM system at the car factory, a system called a *mainframe* computer is needed. This type of computer usually handles a wide range of different applications. Many have several other processors to help, in addition to the main CPU.

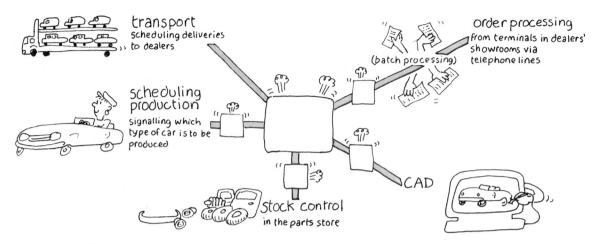

transport
scheduling deliveries
to dealers

scheduling
production
signalling which
type of car is to be
produced

order processing
from terminals in dealers'
showrooms via
telephone lines

(batch processing)

CAD

stock control
in the parts store

The possible uses of a mainframe computer for a car manufacturer. The main processor
and storage is 'surrounded' by smaller processors to handle communication with interactive users.

Fig. 6.31

The use and working of this type of system is considered in the next section.

6.28

Which of the following would most likely be a microcomputer, which most likely a minicomputer:

a the computer on the truck fetching components,

b the central computer controlling the truck,

c the computer controlling the paper-drying process,

d a CAD system in school,

e a CAD system in car seat manufacture? (*T*)

6.29

Using a diagram like Fig 6.31, explain how a large paper-making company might use a mainframe for all its control and data processing systems. (*F*)

End-of-chapter Questions

6.30

Explain what is meant by:

a robotics,

b bar code,

c minicomputer,

d real time system.

6.31

Explain the difference between:

a polling and logging,

b sensor and activator,

c plotter and printer,

d CAD and CAM.

6.32

a Could the control of the pulp mixer described in the chapter be done manually?

b Could it be done by mechanical means?

c What hardware is needed for the computer system?

d What is the advantage of using a computer rather than manual or mechanical methods?

6.33

The factory runs for fifty weeks a year. The other two weeks are used to shut down the works for maintenance. Which are likely to need more attention — the mechanical or the electronic parts of the mill?

6.34

Do you think more or less paper is used now than 20 years ago, when there were few computers?

6.35

Do you think that validation of input is necessary when it is obtained from sensors? Explain your answer.

6.36

What plans should the manager of the paper mill have prepared in case the control computer breaks down?

6.37

For each of the following inputs to the system, say whether it is analogue or digital in nature:

a steam pressure, *c* weight of paper,

b pulp flow, *d* width of paper,

e the length of time for which the waste paper conveyor belt runs.

6.38

a Give examples of systems in the home or elsewhere which use feedback.

b Which of these are controlled by microelectronics?

6.39

A car manufacturer can now develop a new vehicle from just an idea to the production line in 2–3 years, whereas the process used to take 6 or 7 years.

a List the stages in the development of a new car.

b Describe briefly which stages are assisted by new technology.

c What advantages does this faster development give the company?

d What effects has this change had on the general public?

6.40

Products which are made in large quantities are usually assembled on a production line, with each machine or person along the line doing exactly the same thing to each item. Each type of product would have a different line, working continuously through the day.

An alternative would be to have work stations all around the factory, each of which could assemble completely any type of product required.

a What effect does the use of a production line tend to have on the products available to the consumer?

b Why do you think a production line is usually preferred by management?

c Which method do you think the employees would prefer?

d As programmable robots replace single-task machines, do you think the organisation of production will change? Explain your answer.

6.41

Some robots, such as those which are used to spray products with paint automatically, are programmed by a human leading the robot arm through the path that it is to follow, and the robot's computer remembers the movements.

a What are the advantages of this, compared with programming a robot by means of codes and numbers?

b What are the disadvantages?

c Describe how the same idea might be used with

Fig. 6.32   A robot paint sprayer.

the factory truck.

d Why do you think that this method is not used for the truck?   (D)

6.42

Some farmers have experimented with robot tractors, for ploughing, harvesting, and similar tasks in the fields.

a What advantages would these machines have for the farmer, compared with conventional tractors?

b What problems do you think the experimenters would have found?

6.43

a Choose an occupation which you might like to do in the future; for example, this could be paid employment, a leisure activity, or raising a family.

b List the aspects of it that could be performed by computers and robots.

c Which aspects could *not* be automated?

6.44

Some passenger trains (on the London Underground, for example) can now be controlled completely automatically and no driver is needed. In other countries, such trains often operate without a driver, yet in Britain (at the time of writing) there is always a driver as well.

a Describe briefly some of the decisions made by a driver which would have to be programmed for the computer system.

b What data would be needed to make these decisions?

c Suggest what types of hardware would be required in each train, along the line, at stations, and at the transport headquarters. Include input, output and storage devices as well as processing equipment.

d Describe the effects of introducing driverless trains on the railway management, the railway employees, and the travelling public.

e Why do you think Britain has been slow in adopting driverless vehicles?

Project Briefs 2

1 Design and implement an automatic baby soother system. When a baby cries loudly, the system should automatically start up an entertaining activity, such as a sequence of screen pictures, a tune, or a moving toy. The activity should continue while the baby is crying and until a certain amount of time after the crying stops.

2 A system is required to control traffic at roadworks as described in Question 5.45.

Level 1 Design and implement a system which will allow the supervisor to set the time for each phase.

Level 2 Improve the system so that the lights will remain green at one end even after the time set by the supervisor, unless a car is waiting at the other end.

3 A firm which supplies fitted kitchen units offers a design service. They want to make this service flexible, with customers given choices of various items to place where they like on a plan of their kitchen drawn to scale. The items are

cupboard units (standard or double width length),
drawer units (standard width),
sink units (double or triple width),
electrical goods, such as a cooker and washing machine
work surfaces to go over any number of units, other items, or spaces.

They should be able to change their minds easily, and quickly calculate the cost of any combination.

Level 1 Design and implement a system which allows the designer to specify the number of each type of unit and the length of each work surface. The total cost should be displayed automatically, and it should be possible to alter easily any figure and instantly see the revised cost.

Level 2 The designer should also be able to draw on screen a room plan to scale, choose from a range of symbols representing kitchen items drawn to the same scale as the room plan, position them where required on the plan, and print out a copy.

Section C

The computer systems we have looked at so far have been relatively small. They have been very useful for the particular tasks for which they have been used, but microprocessors, microcomputers, and minicomputers cannot handle all the business of a large company nor the services provided by local councils and central government.

Large manufacturing companies, banks, health authorities and the police are amongst the users of very powerful and expensive computer systems. Such systems have many more peripherals, each of which is larger and faster than similar devices used with micro-computers. They usually have many terminals, often linked over long distances. Large computer users may well have several computers linked together, with each one used for a special purpose and perhaps one which is not used at all unless the main one breaks down.

In this section, we shall look at three examples of these large systems, and see why the work needs such powerful and expensive computers.

the computer takes the biscuit

Many of the products that we buy every day are manufactured by large companies. Their factories are often spread over different parts of the country, and multinational companies have factories and depots all over the world. The managers of these companies need to organise their various branches so as to make their products cheaply and to distribute them to their customers as efficiently as possible.

We shall look at one such company which makes food products on a large scale, and concentrate on just one of its many hundreds of products. The computer is used for many tasks in large companies, and many people are needed to operate powerful mainframe machines.

Producing chocolate biscuits

If you like chocolate biscuits, you may have wondered how they are made, and perhaps you have tried to make something similar yourself. It is unlikely, however, that you have thought about how a computer system can help to make biscuits.

Fig. 7.1   Biscuits for sale.

Fig. 7.2   The production control room.

One large company that manufactures chocolate and confectionery employs 35 000 people all over the world, but we will look at just one of their factories.

How is the production of biscuits planned?

The company uses a computer to control the production at the factory and this computer is linked to another one at the company headquarters.

The factory will only manufacture biscuits that have been ordered by shops, so they need to work quickly and have available all the ingredients that they need. The computer is used to control this and organises the production in a manufacturing system.

7.1

Even a simple chocolate-covered biscuit will need several ingredients.

a   Write down a list of ingredients you think the company will need.

b   How many different companies will be involved in supplying these ingredients?   (R)

The system of production is shown as a diagram in Fig. 7.3.

The centre of the whole system is the *sales plan*. This shows the quantity of each product that has been ordered by customers. As with many large companies, this one only produces goods that have actually been ordered.

7.2

The company only produces biscuits which have been ordered by shops or other distributors.

a   Estimate the number of shops across the whole country which sell biscuits.

b   Suggest two reasons why the company only produces biscuits to order.   (D)

The quantities of each product ordered are collected by sales representatives who visit shops and supermarkets. The orders are sent to head office where they are collected together. All chocolate biscuit sales, for instance, are totalled, and this is repeated for each other type of product.

When the company launches a new product, or starts a special advertising campaign, the numbers of items which will be sold are estimated by the Marketing Department. The product must be in the shops ready for customers to buy, so that the effect of the advertising is not lost.

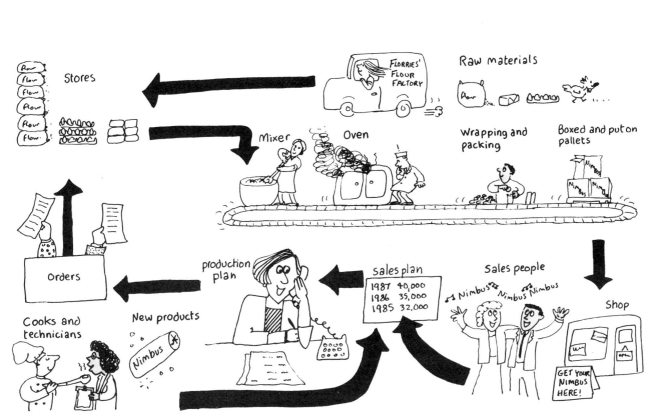

Fig. 7.3 Biscuit manufacture.

Fig. 7.4 How many biscuits to make.

The sales plan therefore contains orders for the new product as well as familiar ones. These orders cannot be produced until the factory knows the recipes and what packaging is being used; this is decided by the Research and Development Department. To obtain the *production plan* the ingredients and packaging needed for all the items in the sales plan must be calculated and ordered. Some of the work will be sent to other companies, such as printing wrappers

Fig. 7.5 The production plan.

for the bars and labels for the boxes. This work must be coordinated and all the people involved must cooperate to make production efficient.

7.3

Using Fig 7.3 to help, decide what information you would need in the factory to manufacture a new product called the 'Nimbus Bar'.   (D)

What will affect sales of the biscuits?

The sales plan can also be changed in the light of unforeseen circumstances. The food industry is very competitive and, for each company to survive, it must try to increase its market share. The market share is the proportion of total sales of a particular item that the company obtains:

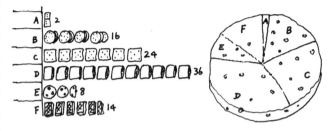

Fig. 7.6   *The company's product share.*

Every company is trying to make its products more attractive than those of its competitors. The customers have a wide range of items to choose from, and they tend to become bored with familiar products. A company must continually review its product lines, for if they become less popular a competitor could take more of the market share. This will cause production to fall, the company will lose profits and there is less work, so people are made redundant and the company could even go out of business.

A company's sales figures are essential information, so these figures are kept as very closely guarded secrets. Knowledge of the sales trends, the new products and possible advertising would be of great value to a competitor, and so security is of the utmost importance.

7.4

A rival company would be interested in the number of biscuits which are being sold by its competitor.

a   Describe how the rival might discover these figures.

b   Suggest how computers could help with this task.   (*D*)

How many biscuits must be made?

Once the sales plan is complete, a production plan is produced (see Fig 7.5). This consists of a list of the products that need to be produced. Each factory will be given their portion of this list, so they can organise the day's work. Biscuits are used in many other products, some coated in chocolate, some half covered and some iced.

Before a computer was used to control production in the factory, a storeman controlled the issue of raw materials. Pieces of paper were used to pass information about the amounts of material to be issued. The storeman who looked after the stocks did not know exactly what was going to be drawn from his stores each day, so he had to keep large stocks to ensure that production would not be stopped.

In a large factory there are hundreds, even thousands, of employees. Each person has a specific job and must be supplied with the correct materials so they can perform that job as well as they can. The system used to organise all these activities is called *production control*. We will look at the section of this organisation which controls the raw materials.

All raw materials are delivered by trucks and tankers and then sent around the factory as they are needed. To organise and control these materials a *store* is used. In a manual system, the storeman's job is to make sure that the production lines have all the materials that they need, the correct quantities are delivered to the factory, and that his stores have the expected quantities of each material.

Fig. 7.7   *Re-ordering stock.*

7.5

Food materials deteriorate rapidly. How would you suggest the storeman makes sure that he keeps the materials in his store for the shortest time possible? (*R*)

7.6

The storeman cannot remember all the materials and quantities that are in the store. He needs a form that can be used to issue materials from the store to

92

the production line. He will compare these with the delivery notes, so he can check what is in stock at any one time.

Design a form that he could use. (*Advice:* he deals in *tonnes* of flour, fat, etc.) (*F*)

7.7

a Describe a method that the storeman could use to *reorder* any materials that were out of stock.

b Design the *order form* he would use. (*Advice:* production must continue, so the stores must always have materials that might be required on the production line. The quantities used per day are in tonnes, and delivery may take 3–7 days.) (*F*)

How does the computer help with production control?

In the previous system, orders for raw materials were made by posting order forms to company headquarters, where they were collected together. The company had a central mainframe computer which was used for totalling the various quantities of materials and compiling bulk orders which were sent to the suppliers. These order forms were printed directly by the computer.

Orders from shops show how many cartons of packets of biscuits are required. These cartons are called *outers*. The number of biscuits required to meet the order has to be calculated and then the quantities of materials worked out. In the old system the data had to be collected together from all the various orders and totalled manually. The order totals for each product were combined with the figures for any new products being launched before being entered on a special form.

The data was arranged on this form so that it was easy for the clerk to type it into the computer. This process is called **data preparation** and is performed by **data preparation clerks**.

The form had the data arranged so that the next item was ready as the computer program asked for it. The data was arranged so that it was convenient to the computer, not the people involved in collecting it.

This process of data preparation was lengthy and often created problems when data was wrongly input. Data verification was used to help prevent numbers written by the storeman being copied wrongly by the data preparation clerk.

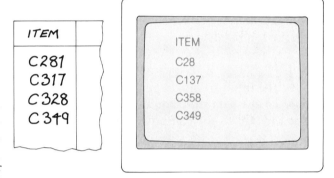

Fig. 7.9 Errors in preparation.

7.8

Using the hand-written numbers in Fig 7.9 give examples of the following types of error,

a transposition,

b transcription,

c omission. (*T*)

7.9

The data being input by the data preparation clerk can be checked for errors using the processes of verification and validation.

a Describe how the data could be verified.

b Describe two typical validation checks that could be carried out on some of the data items being input.(*F*)

Fig. 7.8

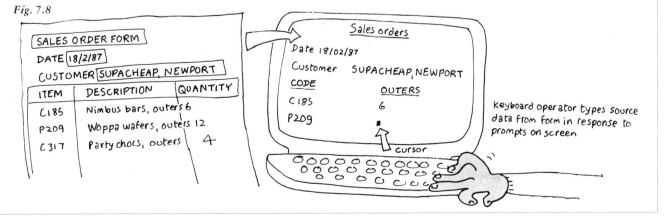

93

First operator enters data, to be stored on disk.

SALES ORDER FORM

SALES ORDER FORM

Second operator types the **same** source data again, and the key-to-disk controller checks with the original data stored on disk.

Fig. 7.10 Data verification.

A *key-to-disk* system enabled a data preparation clerk to enter data from source documents using a visual display unit (VDU), comprising a keyboard and monitor screen. When the keyboard operator had typed in the data from a form, he or she checked the data on the screen, and then pressed a button labelled SEND. A dedicated minicomputer controlled the input from a large number of VDUs and organised the data stored on disk so that it could be input directly to the computer when required.

Because the data preparation equipment is not connected directly to the mainframe computer, this mode of working is referred to as *off-line*. In some situations, it is convenient to input the data from magnetic tape rather than disk, and a key-to-tape system could be used for data preparation.

The whole computer installation was in one building and comprised a large data preparation area and the processing, storage and printing equipment.

Fig. 7.11 The computer room.

7.10

Problems could arise with the old method of ordering and storing materials.

a What difficulties could be caused by postal delays?

b What precautions must be taken when storing perishable materials?

c What effect would Easter and Christmas demand have on the system?   (*D*)

The company realised however that there were problems with the old system of generating the production plan from the sales plan.

The company decided to expand their use of computers. It was still important to keep the central mainframe computer to coordinate all the activities of their factories, but each factory was in addition provided with a minicomputer, and microcomputers connected to the mini placed all around the factory.

The company decided to use this new *distributed system* with computers in each factory, rather than one big central computer with *dumb terminals* in each factory which could only be used for typing data into the central mainframe. Each factory manager would then have control over the way the factory was run. This was possible because small computers had become quite cheap, but the decision was made mainly because the management realised that employees preferred to have more control over local affairs.

How did the new computer system improve production control?

Production control is divided into two main functions:

● Managing the supply of materials

● Controlling machinery

To replace the old ordering system, a completely different approach was introduced. Each product was analysed into its components, giving a product structure (see page 95 opposite):

Information about the structure of every product is stored on the mainframe computer. Some of the ingredients for one product may be needed for several others, and it is usually cheaper to obtain all the supplies of an ingredient from the same supplier, who will give a discount for bulk purchase.

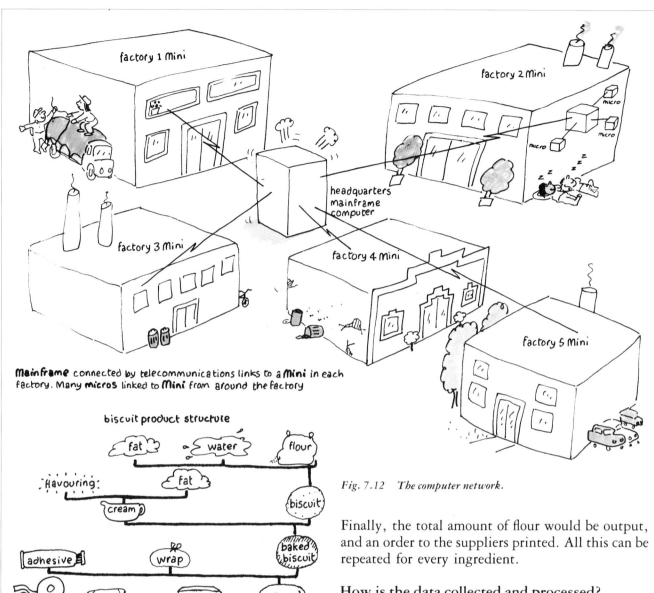

Factory 1 Mini

Factory 2 Mini

micro

micro

micro

headquarters
mainframe
computer

Factory 3 Mini

Factory 4 Mini

Factory 5 Mini

Mainframe connected by telecommunications links to a **Mini** in each factory. Many **micros** linked to **Mini** from around the factory

biscuit product structure

fat   water   flour

flavouring   fat   biscuit

cream

baked biscuit

adhesive   wrap

Sellotape   film   box   wrapped biscuit

Outer (carton)

Fig. 7.13   A product structure.

The computer uses the product structures to calculate the total quantities of each ingredient: flour, for instance. To do this it must have a set method (algorithm) for searching each product structure to find out how much flour is needed.

For each type of biscuit, the number of biscuits would be input and the following procedure would be carried out:

```
Repeat for each level of the product structure
     Repeat for each item
          If item = flour then

               multiply number of biscuits ordered
               by amount of flour needed
               add to total flour needed
     Repeat for each pointer
          move to next level down
```

Fig. 7.14

Fig. 7.12   The computer network.

Finally, the total amount of flour would be output, and an order to the suppliers printed. All this can be repeated for every ingredient.

How is the data collected and processed?

Orders will be received from large stores, and salesmen who travel round visiting smaller shops. These are collected together so that the computer can process the orders from customers using the product structure of each item. It can then calculate the quantities of raw materials needed by each factory, print orders to suppliers for these materials, and print a list of products to be manufactured.

7.11

The procedure listed above deals with the amount of flour required for one type of biscuit on an order.

a   Modify the algorithm listed to find the total amount of *fat* required.

b   Extend the procedure you have written to calculate the total amount of fat needed for *all* types of biscuit on the order, and include the input and output stages.   (*F*)

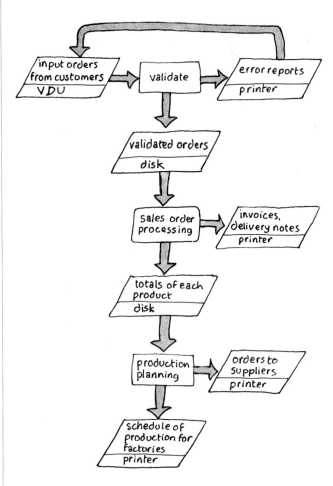

Fig. 7.15   *A system diagram of production planning.*

This method of collecting data from all the orders and dealing with them all at once is an example of **batch processing**. The job of calculating supplies is carried out at a regular time each day so the computer can be used for different jobs at other times. A major disadvantage of a simple batch processing system is that the whole computer system is tied up for a long time with just this one job when other departments may have urgent needs for processing.

7.12

The time taken to transfer a customer order from disk to the CPU for processing is 15 milliseconds (ms) and the time taken to process it is 3 ms. The printer will output 1000 lines a minute, and an order to suppliers is output on preprinted stationery with an average of 10 lines to be printed on each one. The production list for each factory takes up 500 lines on average.

A typical run would require 200 customer orders to be input, produce 20 orders to suppliers, and print out the production list.

a   What is preprinted stationery?

b   How long would it take for the printer to output the 20 orders to suppliers?

c   How long would it take to print the production list?

d   What is the total time taken to input the customer orders from disk?

e   What is the total time for input and output?

f   For what percentage of the time is the CPU actually processing?

(*Advice:* refer to Fig 7.16 and note that 1 millisecond is 1/1000 of a second.)

Normally the orders for the raw materials are sent straight to the suppliers' computers and the materials can be instantly despatched. Each factory will receive the correct quantity of the materials that it needs to meet all the orders. The number of each item that the factory needs to produce each day is sent to the factory's own minicomputer. This is checked against the deliveries and the despatch of finished product. One advantage of this system is that the factory does not need to keep large quantities of raw materials, and can use for other purposes the money that used to be spent on these stocks.

These orders are sent directly from one computer to another through private cables, in the same way as the estate agent in Chapter 2 used public telephone

Fig. 7.16

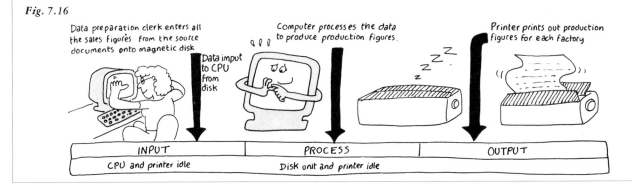

lines. The minicomputer in the factory uses the information from the mainframe computer to list the quantities of raw materials to be drawn from the stores, and how they should be mixed according to the correct recipe. It will also list the items to be despatched to each of the customers. The system allows automatic stock control, ordering and sales.

Fig. 7.17   Stock in the warehouse.

7.13

The cost of keeping materials in warehouses is £2 per month for every £100 of stock. The company keeps £1 000 000 of stock at any one time.

a   What is the cost per day of keeping this stock?

b   How much could be saved in a year if the stock could be halved?   (F)

7.14

This new computerised method of production control has advantages for the company at head-quarters and for each factory.

a   List the advantages that HQ gains from the new system.

b   What advantages are there for each factory? (D)

7.15

There are many ways in which computers can aid a company, including robotics, process control, transport scheduling and safety.

The company would like to have a perfect factory where the lorries deliver their materials straight to the production line, and the finished products are loaded straight onto lorries going to the customers.

Describe what other steps they would need to take to automate this process completely.   (R)

The other means of production control is the use of the computer to control machines directly. We have seen one use of this idea in Chapter 6, and the same techniques are used in the biscuit factory.

Fig. 7.18   Biscuits in production.

How is the baking controlled?

At present, separate microcomputers are used to control directly the various stages on the production line. These computers receive signals from the production line and can immediately send out a signal to change any process on the line.

7.16

The microcomputers in each factory are used to control directly different sections of the production line. Using Fig 7.3 to help:

a   List the possible inputs that each microcomputer could receive.

b   Describe for each input what control these computers would exercise over the process involved. (R)

This form of computer control cannot be carried out by means of batch processing. Immediate response directly to the line is needed, so this processing is done in real time.

If the temperature of the ovens baking the biscuits rose too high, the biscuits would burn. If it fell too low the biscuits would be uncooked. It is essential to keep the temperature between certain limits. The temperature is polled continually, along with many other readings. If the temperature has fallen, the heaters are turned on again; if it is too hot they are turned off.

7.17

Part of the production line for a biscuit is a baking oven. The biscuits have to stay in the oven for an exact time at a particular temperature. The temperature is polled regularly by a microcomputer.

a   What is meant by *polling*?

b   What sort of signal would be received from the oven by the microcomputer?

c What device would this computer be controlling in order to change the temperature?

d What sort of signal would be output to control this device?

e Draw a diagram showing the control system for one of the baking ovens. (*Advice:* refer to Chapter 6.)

f Write down an algorithm for this control process. (*F*)

7.18

Choose another process carried out by the control microcomputers and draw a diagram showing how the control system could be organised for the process you have chosen. (*F*)

The mainframe computer system

The computers in the factory have been chosen for the control of production, but clearly they can do many other things for this company. The mainframe computer at headquarters would probably work out all the employees' wages; it will do all the accounts, it can produce sales figures for all the products and supply statistics to managers to see the effect of advertising campaigns. We shall now look at some of the special software needed to control all of these data processing tasks and the people trained to operate the system.

7.19

Direct control of the production line and the creation of production plans are two processes carried out by computer.

a Suggest three other processes that the computer could carry out.

b Describe briefly the output that would be produced for each process.

c Explain who in the company would need to see the output in each case, and what use they would make of it.

d What precautions could be taken to ensure that people from rival companies did not see the output? (*R*)

To control all of the input and output, and to perform processes on several jobs, it uses a complex program called an *operating system*. This is a machine code program and is loaded into the computer when it starts running. Since the program contains the instructions for loading itself in, this is called *bootstrapping*, or *booting* ('pulling itself up by its own bootstraps').

All computers need an operating system, and as different computers have different jobs to do, they also have different operating systems. The more complex the role of the computer, the more complex the operating system has to be. We shall see some of the functions of an operating system in the rest of this chapter, and other operating systems will be introduced in the next two chapters.

How was the new system introduced?

As we have seen, the mainframe computer at headquarters was purchased before the new computerised production system was introduced. It was expensive, and its processing power has to be used to maximum benefit. The incorporation of the mainframe at the centre of the new system had to be carefully planned by the team of systems analysts who devised the system.

To see how the mainframe is used and what the operating system does, we shall look at three particular jobs that are required. These are the tasks, in simplified form:

- Production planning
  Input of sales data
  Calculations of quantities
  Output of orders to suppliers and production figures for factories

- Wages calculations
  Input of hours worked
  Calculate wages
  Output of payslips and transfer money to bank computers

- Sales forecasts
  Input sales records from disk
  Calculation of future sales using complex formulas
  Output of screen displays and printed charts

These operations can be divided into the separate sections of input, process and output. Each of these will take different lengths of time. If we ran the three jobs in the order shown, as a batch process, each will be done in turn. When the first is finished, the second can start; when the second is finished the third can start.

The computer is not actually processing for most of the time. This is clearly very wasteful of the expensive processor. It would make sense for the com-

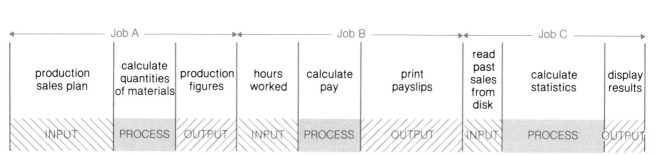

Job A			Job B			Job C		
production sales plan	calculate quantities of materials	production figures	hours worked	calculate pay	print payslips	read past sales from disk	calculate statistics	display results
INPUT	PROCESS	OUTPUT	INPUT	PROCESS	OUTPUT	INPUT	PROCESS	OUTPUT

Fig. 7.19 The jobs for the computer.

puter to share its processing time between these jobs. When the *processing* is finished for one job, because input or output is required, the operating system could switch the CPU over to work on another job. One way of achieving this is shown below in Fig. 7.20.

Maximum use has been made of the computer's expensive processing time and internal memory. Instead of storing just *one* program, it uses all of its internal memory to store many programs while they wait for processing. It is not idle while a lot of sales orders are read in, or waiting for all the wage slips to be printed out. It partly overcomes the problem of having peripherals which work much more slowly than the processor.

7.20

List the peripherals used in the mainframe computer system, with the slowest first and the fastest last. (*Advice:* the fewer mechanical parts, the faster a device will work.) (*R*)

How does the computer control all the different jobs?

The type of processing shown in Fig 7.20 was introduced on the mainframe computer at company headquarters. The operating system for this computer is a special one because it can organise many different jobs. As we have seen, it can run batch processing for production control as well as organising communications to each factory and each supplier.

This operating system that can run many different jobs at the same time is called *multiprogramming*. It can decide how to divide the processing time between jobs, and can deal with input and output from the peripherals which work more slowly than the CPU. A multiprogramming operating system makes it seem that the various programs are all run at once, but in fact each is run in short bursts. Although this is a complex and therefore expensive piece of software, the company realised that it would

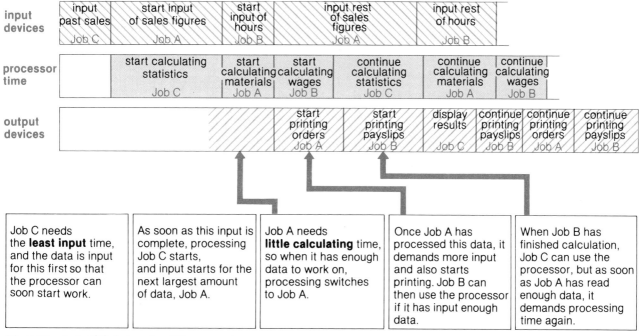

Fig. 7.20 A simplified view of multiprogramming.

allow them to gain more benefit from their expensive mainframe.

This system has great advantages over the operating system that can only do one job at a time, often called a 'one-job' operating system: these kinds of system are most often found on microcomputers. The organisation of one-job and multiprogramming systems is shown below (Fig. 7.21).

The multiprogramming operating sytem has to make decisions as to which programs to run and in which order. Each job is given a priority. In our example, Job A has top priority, Job B has second priority and Job C has the lowest priority. Whenever Job A needs the processor it will take over from either of the others. Job C will only be able to use the processor when neither of the others needs it. The highest priority is usually given to a job which does very little processing and has a lot of input and output.

7.21
Describe the advantages to the company of using a multiprogramming rather than a one-job operating system on their mainframe computer.   (D)

7.22
At the top of the next column are three jobs which might run at the same time in a multiprocessing system:

- reading data from customers' orders stored on disk, and printing invoices,

- calculating the wages for the employees from the times they clocked in and out, and printing payslips,

- reading the sales figures for a particular product from different regions over the last ten years, and calculating which place would be the best to build a new factory so as to reduce transport costs to the minimum.

a   Which of these should have the highest priority?

b   Which should have the lowest?   (R)

7.23
Spooling is a common technique used by complex operating systems for organising printout.

a   Explain why spooling is essential when only one printer is available for a multiprogramming or network system.

b   Explain how spooling can reduce the time needed to complete the processing of a job, even when several printers are available.

7.24
Explain why a job which transfers a lot of data between peripherals and does very little processing should have highest priority.   (R)

Fig. 7.21   *A one-job operating system compared with multiprogramming.*

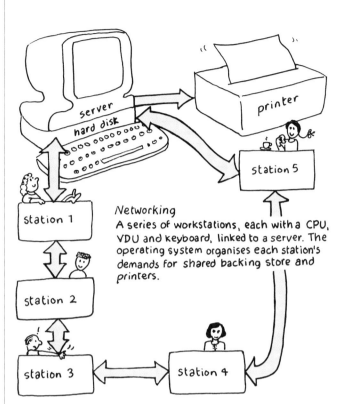

Networking
A series of workstations, each with a CPU, VDU and keyboard, linked to a server. The operating system organises each station's demands for shared backing store and printers.

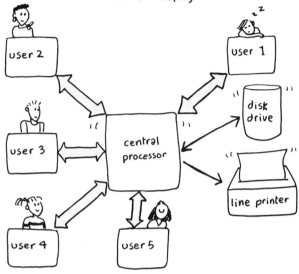

Fig. 7.22   Computers link together.

There are other types of operating system which are commonly used, including the *multiaccess* systems which are described in Chapter 8 and the networks of microcomputers as described in earlier chapters.

How is the new computer system managed?

Fig. 7.23   The system analysts.

The company employed computer specialists to set up the new system. As well as systems analysts, they also paid programmers to write their own applications software, as there were no suitable packages available.

Some of the *systems software* which performed basic operating tasks such as,

- controlling disk drives and tape units
- organising and indexing files on disk
- outputting files from disk or tape to the printers
- accepting data from VDUs and storing it systematically on disk
- sorting and merging files
- giving messages to operators

was provided by the computer manufacturer. Other systems software was purchased from *software houses*. These are firms who employ specialist programmers to write efficient systems software, such as the programs to handle the communications with branches, which would not be needed by every company buying the computer system.

The systems analysts designed, installed and implemented the new system, and the programmers wrote the *applications software*. Although these programs carry out specific tasks for the company, such as working out the production plans, or scheduling deliveries from warehouses to shops, they are very complex. The systems analysts specify what the programs are to do, and then Senior Programmers

Fig. 7.24 *Modular programs.*

will split each one into modules. They write down exactly what each module needs as input, what it should produce as output, and how it should work. A junior programmer would then work on writing the code for one module.

When each module is fully tested on its own, the senior programmer tests all the modules of the program together; if the analysts and programmers have done their jobs well, the full program should work immediately!

These programs will not be written in machine code, but in a programming language such as **COBOL** which was specially designed for writing programs for business data processing.

```
OPEN INPUT EMPLOYEE-HOURS
OPEN OUTPUT PAYSLIPS
READ EMPLOYEE-HOURS AT END GOTO FINISH
COMPUTE GROSS-PAY =
              HOURS-WORKED * RATE-PER-HOUR
```

Fig. 7.25 *COBOL instructions.*

COBOL is one example of a **high-level language:** such a language is easy for *humans* to understand, but it must be translated into machine code so that the *computer* can execute the instructions. This translation is difficult, but the designer of the language can write an algorithm for translating it into machine code for any processor. The computer can thus be programmed to do the translation for us: this is called **compiling** the program.

Whereas different makes of computer need different *assembly codes*, high-level languages are much more standardised. A programmer can write some source code, and compile it for various computers without making changes: the compiler for a particular computer takes care of producing the correct machine code.

It is much easier to write and debug programs written in high-level languages compared with the low-level assembly languages like the one we saw in Chapter 5, but the programs produced might not be as efficient as those written in assembly code. In assembly code, one instruction translates to one

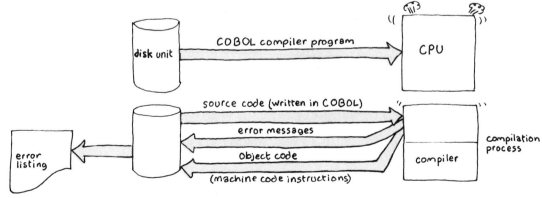

Fig. 7.26 *Compiling the COBOL program.*

machine code instruction, but in COBOL one instruction may need several machine code instructions. The compiler follows a fixed procedure for the translation, whereas a good assembly programmer would be able to see short ways of achieving the same results.

To help high-level programmers further, however, most languages, are designed to be particularly good for certain types of work, such as *FORTRAN* for scientific work requiring many accurate calculations, *ALGOL* for describing complex algorithms, *CORAL* for real-time control, and *BASIC* which is easy to learn. Newer languages such as *ADA* and *PASCAL* try to combine the strengths of other languages.

The programmers will also write ***maintenance documentation*** (giving a detailed explanation of how the code carries out the tasks specified) and ***user documentation*** (instructions to the operators on how to make the programs do what is required, and to data preparation staff on how the data should be typed in and verified).

7.25

In the modular structure of the program for the production plan (Fig 7.24), each box represents one module of the program.

a Give reasons why a different person would produce each module of a complex program rather than one programmer produce the whole package.

b Describe the work that a senior programmer or analyst would carry out on the overall program specification before each module could be written by a junior programmer.

c Explain what other work would be needed from each junior programmer and by the senior programmer before the package could be implemented. (*D*)

7.26

Each programmer has to write detailed maintenance documentation for each module.

a Explain why the systems analyst insists that this detailed documentation is produced.

b How would another programmer make use of this documentation?

c Would other staff need to see this type of documentation? Explain your answer. (*R*)

7.27

Computer languages used in education and homes are often translated using interpreters rather than compilers. An *interpreter* translates each instruction reaching it while the program is running, rather than translating them all first.

a Explain why an interpreter makes debugging short programs quicker than with a compiler.

b What are the disadvantages of interpreters for professional programmers? (*R*)

The ***computer operator*** performs the more routine tasks needed to keep the computer running. He or she will obey instructions produced by the operating system on the ***console*** terminal, such as prompts to load a new tape or to change the pre-printed forms in the line printer.

```
> LOAD DISK FOR FACTORY-PAYROLL PROGRAM
    ON DRIVE 2
ACCEPTED
> LOAD TAPE FOR EMPLOYEE-HOURS FILE WEEK 34
    ON UNIT 3
ACCEPTED
> LOAD PAYSLIP BLANKS ON PRINTER 1
```

Fig. 7.27 Instructions on the operator's console.

The computer is not making up these instructions itself; they are written into the operating system software. In a batch processing system, the operators will use a ***job control language (JCL)*** to describe to the operating system which devices and software modules will be needed for each batch of data to be processed, and the computer system will then proceed automatically through its jobs, pausing only while the operators carry out the few manual tasks. This will have been documented by the programmers, and the operator's job, although it needs skill and training, is relatively routine.

```
PAYROLL WEEK 34
RUN FACTORY-PAYROLL PROGRAM USE DRIVE 2
FILE£1 EMPLOYEE-HOURS USE UNIT 3
FILE£2 EMPLOYEE-DETAILS USE UNIT 5
FILE£3 PAYSLIPS USE PRINTER 1
```

Fig. 7.28 Job control language.

The chief operator must keep a log of all computer operations, recording the timing and nature of each job processed.

Job code	Start time	Finish time	Department	Devices
A34	0900	0955	S	T3,D1,P1
A35	0906	0932	R	D2,P2
A36	0915	1008	P	T1,T2,D3
A37	0935		S	T4,P2
A38	1017		P	D2,D3,P1

Fig. 7.29   Control log.

With simple operating systems, this would have been done manually, but with modern multiprogramming and multiaccess systems, the operating system itself has to keep the records, and print out, on the console, information that the operators need.

The day-to-day management of the computer system is the task of the *operations manager*, and there will be a *data processing manager* in overall control of training, development and maintenance, as well as data preparation and operations.

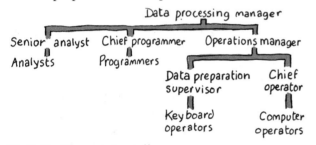

Fig. 7.30   The computer staff.

7.28

Some of the jobs that the computer system requires humans to do are listed below:

- type in the sales figures for each product,

- load the data disks containing the product structure data when the computer requests them,

- decide how the computer would calculate what quantities of raw materials should be ordered,

- ensure the preprinted order forms are supplied to the line printers,

- correct any mistakes in the computer programs that occur as the system is being commissioned,

- organise who should be allowed to see particular pieces of information,

- keep records of which files are on which tapes, and what generations they are.

Suggest which personnel would be most likely to perform each task.

7.29

A lot of jobs have been created by introducing the new computer. Many of the jobs use new skills, and some of the jobs that were done before are not needed any more. Retraining courses could be held for these new jobs.

a   Suggest some jobs that could disappear.

b   How would you help the people involved so that they would not be made redundant but would continue working for the company?   (D)

Has the use of computers been of benefit to the company?

The company makes use of computers in many parts of their business, from production control, where the use of computers is still being developed further, to accounting and financial planning.

The whole of production planning is now under the control of a central computer, while local control is conducted by the factory-based minicomputer. Each data logging or control application in each factory is controlled by a specific microcomputer. The management intend to link the control computers to the minicomputer so that production will be totally automatic, from receiving orders to despatch of products.

The major advantage gained is in the speed of response of the system to changes in the requirements of production and sales. The new computer system performs tasks that were impossible before; production costs have been reduced, and product quality has been increased.

7.30

The company has gained many advantages from the introduction of their new computer system. Describe the advantages they have gained in:

a   control of stock,

b   raw material purchasing,

c   quality control,

d   centralising of data.   (D)

The type of computerised management system that the company created is used widely throughout industry. If the company were to introduce computers *now*, starting from a completely manual system, they would buy standard software rather than pay people to write it specially. A software house would supply the system, and would customise the software to suit the needs of the particular company.

7.31

a   Explain what is meant by *customising*.

b   What would be the benefits for the company of using customised standard packages rather than producing their own system from the beginning? (*R*)

Can the computer see the future?

As well as controlling the production and despatch from day-to-day on the basis of orders received, the mainframe computer's processing power could handle another important task — helping to make plans for the future.

In Chapter 3, we looked at a spreadsheet package on a microcomputer which could store formulas for the profit on sales of shirts, according to how many shirts had been sold. TEAMSHIRTS could use this to type in the number of shirts they expected to sell, and work out what their profit would be. They could also investigate what the effect on the profit would be of changing their prices or an increase in their costs.

In the case of a large company with many factories, warehouses, vehicles, products and employees, the task of calculating the effect of changes is vast. As sales of various products change, the company regularly needs to answer questions such as:

- Which is the best firm to supply each of the raw materials?

- Which factories should be used to make each product?

- How many vehicles will be needed for transport?

- How many staff will be needed at each branch? What skills will be required?

- What investment is needed in equipment, transport and materials?

- And, of course, will the company make a profit, taking into account sales, purchases, labour costs, transport costs, loan repayments, and so on?

The procedure for answering these questions will be very complex; there will be millions of calculations and comparisons. *Without* a computer, the questions would be answered by managers carrying out rough calculations, drawing graphs, and making guesses. *With* the computer *simulation*, managers still make guesses, but their decisions can be based on much more comprehensive and reliable information. Other factors, such as inflation, tax rates, and currency values can also be taken into account in the *model*. This is the algorithm that has been programmed so that the computer can work out what might *really* happen.

Fig. 7.31   The computer helps in many ways.

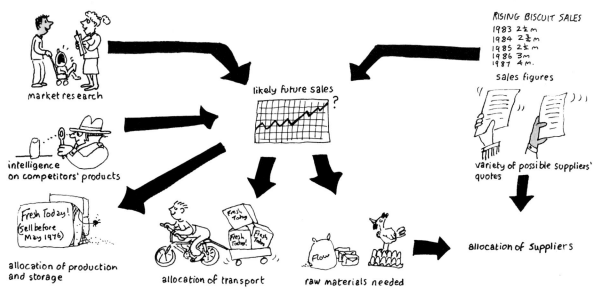

market research

intelligence on competitors' products

likely future sales

RISING BISCUIT SALES
1983 2½m
1984 2½m
1985 2½m
1986 3m
1987 4m.

sales figures

variety of possible suppliers' quotes

allocation of production and storage

allocation of transport

raw materials needed

allocation of suppliers

7.32

a Explain why the company could not use a microcomputer with a spreadsheet package for their models.

b The company wrote their own software. If they were starting again now, they say they would buy in the software as the processes they want are widely used in industry. Write down the advantages and disadvantages of these two methods of obtaining software. (D)

End-of-chapter Questions

7.33

Explain what is meant by:

a modem,

b multiprogramming,

c console.

7.34

Explain the difference between:

a COBOL and JCL,

b line printer and dot-matrix printer,

c systems software and applications software,

d compiler and interpreter.

7.35

The company in this chapter uses computers for:

— stock control in the factory,

— data logging and process control in the factory,

— production planning at head office.

a What type of computer is used for each of the jobs above?

b Explain briefly why the company chose the types of computer given in your answer to (a) above.

7.36

The company would like to link the data logging computers to the minicomputer so that production could become almost completely automated. List the steps and procedures that the systems analysts would have follow in order to implement such a change.

7.37

Some processes are better performed by real-time processing, while other are better suited to batch processing. Listed below are some processes already mentioned in this chapter and in earlier chapters:

— updating records of tapes hired out,

— listing members who have overdue tapes,

— enquiring about houses for sale,

— keeping records of stocks,

— maintaining the temperature in a room using a central heating system,

— feeding cows,

— ensuring that paper pulp has the correct moisture content,

— designing vehicles,

— guiding a truck around a factory,

— processing the orders from biscuit salesmen,

— controlling ovens,

— calculating employees' wages.

a List those processes which *must* be real-time operations, giving reasons.

b List those which are best suited to batch methods, giving reasons.

c For the others, explain why you think each is more suited to on-line operation.

7.38

a Write down the names of several companies with factories in many parts of the country.

b Write down the names of some 'multinational' companies.

c Suggest what extra difficulties a multinational company might find in trying to link the computer systems for factories in different countries.

d What extra advantages would a multinational company gain if all their factories around the world were linked in this way?

7.39

At present salesmen take orders during the day, then post their returns to the computer department at head office.

a Suggest alternative methods that these salesmen could use to speed up the process.

b Indicate any problems that there might be with your new system.

desirable CPU to let, timesharing available. . . 8

Chapter 7 dealt with a large mainframe computer system used by a manufacturing company to carry out many different tasks. This chapter also looks at a mainframe system, but this one is used in providing public services, and works in a rather different way.

In Chapter 2 we looked at the work of an estate agent, and the use he makes of computers in selling houses, given that he may have several hundred houses on his books at any time. Birmingham City Council is also involved in housing, but they own 140 000 houses. The estate agent's interest in a house ends when it is sold, whereas the City Council rents houses, and has to keep records on them all for as long as they remain standing. So they need a rather bigger computer . . . . . .

Fig. 8.1   Mary Taylor and Suzy Smith.

A City Council's computer

Mary Taylor lives in a flat on the fourth floor of a block in a suburb of Birmingham, which she rents from the City Council. If she finds that a repair is needed to her flat, such as a blocked drain, or a wall needing some replastering, she walks down to the Council's local office, one of 45 around the city. There, she would find Suzy Smith, one of the clerks who works for the Council. Her office is not like the traditional long desk, with a grille separating 'customers' from the Council's clerks.

Instead, Mary sits down alongside Suzy, at a desk containing nothing but a VDU, with its screen and keyboard. She explains her problem, whereupon Suzy types her address on the VDU's keyboard, and a fraction of a second later some of the details of her flat appear on the screen. Suzy adds the repair

details, by typing on the keyboard, and the necessary repairs for Mary's flat are recorded in a computer. In another office elsewhere in the city, later that day, a computer printout will tell the Council's works department about the problem at Mary's flat, and within a few days the repairs should be done.

8.1

Explain briefly what a VDU is, and what it is used for.   (*T*)

8.2

Describe some other reasons for Mary Taylor to visit Suzy's office, apart from reporting the need for repairs.   (*R*)

8.3

What details do you think would be stored concerning a council house or flat? Design a suitable file structure.   (*F*)

Where is the computer?

When Suzy Smith types something on her keyboard, the response appears on her screen very quickly, usually within a second. The same is true of the other VDUs in her office. Some offices have just two VDUs, others in the busier parts of the city have thirty or forty.

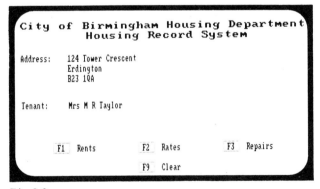

Fig. 8.2

To a person like Mary Taylor, the VDU looks like one of the microcomputers she has seen in shops, other offices and her children's school. However, Suzy's computer has to send messages to other departments of the Council; it has to record payments of rents and rates and transmit them to the City Treasurer's office; and it must be capable of doing this rapidly. It must therefore be capable of retrieving information about any house or flat in the city very quickly.

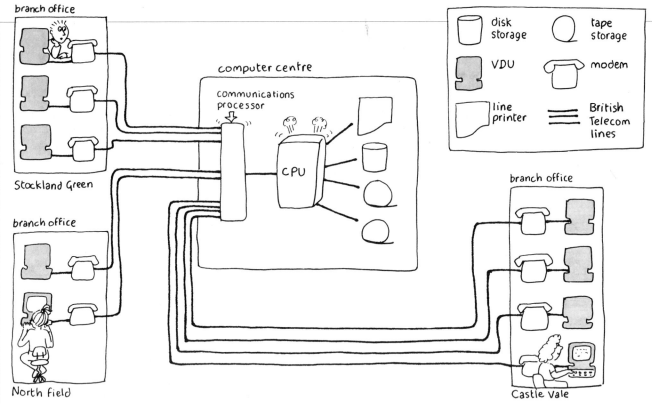

Fig. 8.3   Remote mainframe processing — a small part of the city system.

In fact, Suzy's VDU is not a computer at all. It is just one of about two hundred *terminals*, all connected via telephone lines to a massive IBM computer located near the city centre. All the data which Suzy needs to carry out her work is kept by the central computer on disk drives which hold many millions of characters. This is a **multiaccess** system: hundreds of users can link simultaneously to use the same CPU's processing power.

8.4

a   What is the unit of storage required for one character?

b   What term is used for a million of these units? (*T*)

8.5

Why do you think the data on houses is kept on disks and not on magnetic tapes?   (*T*)

8.6

The housing file contains 140 000 records (one for each Council house or flat). Each record in the housing file contains about twenty screenfuls of information. A screen has 24 lines of data, each of which can hold up to 80 characters.

a   Assuming that an average line contains 20 characters, work out how many characters make up an average record.

b   Use your answer to (a) to estimate the size of the housing file, in megabytes.   (*F*)

8.7

A record in the housing file contains around 10 000 characters.

a   Time yourself while typing 100 characters on the keyboard of the school's microcomputer. From this, estimate how long it will take to enter one complete record in the housing file.

b   Work out how long it would have taken one person to set up the file.

(*Advice:* there are 140 000 records, and a typist would average around five hours actual typing in a working day, five days a week. Work in round numbers!)   (*F*)

Such a huge central file is usually referred to as a **database**. This term is used for a large file with a complex structure which is used by many different people in an organisation for different purposes. A database can also be several related files, where each one acts as an index to records in others.

The task of creating the housing database began in 1976. From your answers to the questions in this chapter so far, you will have seen that such a huge database would have taken many man-years to set up (even allowing for the difference in typing speed between you and a professional). Ten man-years means that it took one person ten years, or a team of ten people one year, or a team of twenty people six months.

During this period, the Council would have been running two systems *in parallel*: the old system using pieces of paper, taking a long time to send to other offices, and the computerised system. This means that more staff would have been needed during the changeover period, some to enter all the data into the new system, and some to train the clerks, like Suzy, who would be working the new system. If someone like Mary made an enquiry, she might get a quick reply, if her record had been entered into the system. She might receive a much slower service, if her record were one that had not yet been entered into the computer.

8.8

Another way of changing over to a computerised system is to wait until the whole system is ready, and then change over to the new system overnight.

a What are the advantages and disadvantages of sudden changeover, compared with parallel running?

b Explain how the disadvantages could be reduced by having a 'pilot' scheme in operation, where one or two offices use the new system for a period of time before the big changeover. (D)

What else does the Council's computer do?

Birmingham City Council, like all other local authorities, has much more to deal with than housing. To pay for all its services (social services, education, libraries, parks, refuse collection, and many more), it levies *rates* on every property in the city. This means that the owner of each property must pay a certain amount to the Council each year (many householders in fact pay in monthly instalments).

The Council's computer is also used to keep records of rates payments. This is an even bigger task than the housing records, since it involves *every* property in the city, not just those which the Council happens to own. The list includes houses, flats, shops, offices, factories, schools, car parks, waste ground, advertisement hoardings, a railway museum and a BBC television transmitter — over half a million properties in all.

8.9

If all half million ratepayers pay in instalments (ten a year), how many transactions involving rate payments will the computer process in an average working day? (*Advice:* the computer works five days a week, fifty weeks a year.) (F)

8.10

Find out about the payment of either rent or rates by householders, and design a file structure for the records of payments. (*Advice:* it should be possible to write an algorithm to find out from your file whether the payments are up-to-date for any house.)

What hardware makes up the system?

Fig. 8.5

Each terminal in the City Council's system consists of a VDU with keyboard and a modem. At the other end of the phone line, the signals from all the VDUs are received by a device called a *communications processor*. Each signal is given some extra codes, to identify which terminal it came from. The communications processor must ensure that the signals are not mixed up with each other. It has some memory, which is used to remember the signal until it is complete, when it can be sent to the CPU.

The communications processor also has to receive replies from the central processor and route them to the appropriate terminal. In fact the communications processor is more complex than many small computers. You will find more about how computers and terminals communicate in Chapter 13.

Fig. 8.4

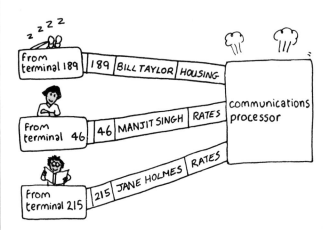

Fig. 8.6

8.11

Many small microcomputers are now used with '*dial-up*' modems, which, when needed, will automatically dial a number and connect themselves to the British Telecom network. Why would modems of this kind not be suitable for the City Council's system? (*D*)

The lines used by the council's computer system are *dedicated* — they permanently connect the terminals to the computer, and do not use the public BT phone network. The terminals are switched on every morning and off again in the evening, and in between they are working continuously for ten hours. It would not only be inconvenient to keep dialling numbers, but the equipment would wear out more rapidly — and the phone bills would be tremendous!

How does the computer do so many things at once?

Suzy Smith and all her colleagues expect the computer to give them instant answers to their requests for information. Thus the computer must give the appearance of doing several hundred things at once. Not only that, but Suzy wants the answers to her questions, not someone else's — so somehow the computer has to keep all the jobs separate from each other.

This remarkable feat is due to a very large and complex operating system. We met one version of an operating system, using multiprogramming, in Chapter 7. The form of operating system used in the City Council's computer is a *time-sharing* system. To illustrate how it works, we will first think about a different form of time-sharing, also connected with housing: holiday homes.

8.12

What is the purpose of an operating system? (*T*)

What is time-sharing?

You may have seen adverts for time-share holiday homes, in Spain or in holiday resorts in this country. Suppose Mr and Mrs Jones, Mr and Mrs Stuart, and Miss Carruthers all want a regular holiday, in a house or cottage they own themselves. They probably cannot afford it on their own, but if they pool their resources, they can buy the cottage between them. The company selling the cottage will probably sell it to a dozen or more families altogether, who between them would occupy the cottage for the whole holiday season each year.

July				August		
Week 1	Week 2	Week 3	Week 4	Week 1	Week 2	Week 3
Mr & Mrs Jones		Ms Carruthers		Mr & Mrs Stuart		

Fig. 8.7

Mr and Mrs Jones therefore have the exclusive use of the cottage during their particular fortnight, every year. On the other hand, they cannot change to a different week one year; if they wanted their holiday in August, for example, they would find the Stuarts in residence. Each family has the right to the whole cottage for their time, but no right during other weeks. Thus each family has the advantage of a cottage of their own without the expense — but they no longer have control over when they use it or what else it is used for.

Birmingham City Council's computer uses exactly the same idea, but with a rather quicker turnover of users! The system works something like this: when the CPU receives a request from Suzy for some information, the operating system of the computer finds the program needed and loads it into the immediate access memory of the CPU. It then starts to obey the instructions in the program to retrieve the information Suzy wants.

After a certain time, Suzy's time-share comes to an end. The length of time is, in fact, only a small fraction of a second — but remember that a powerful mainframe computer can obey several million instructions in a second, so that it can get through a lot of work in one *time-slice*.

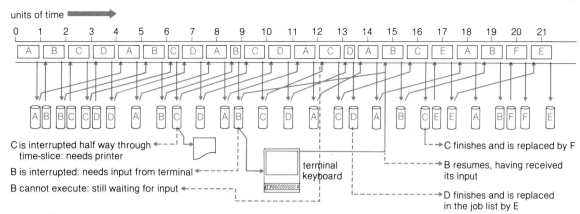

Assume four programs are operating at once — in practice there are many more

Fig. 8.8 A time-sharing operating system at work.

When the time-slice ends, the program is shunted out of the CPU onto a disk, together with the values it has worked out, and another task, probably connected with a different office, takes its place, just as the Stuarts replace the Joneses when their time is up. This job may load another program, which will then run for the same length of time as Suzy's before suffering the same fate.

After a while, when the CPU has carried out many other tasks, Suzy's program and data are loaded back into the CPU again, and execution carries on from where it left off. Eventually, the program will have had enough CPU time to find out the information Suzy wanted, and send it down the phone line to her VDU.

It sounds as if it takes a long time to run a program. But the computer works so fast that each program gets its time-share several times a second. The replies from the computer therefore come out on the VDU screens just as fast as the operators can read them — so that each terminal appears to have the CPU all to itself.

8.13

If a time-slice is 1/100th of a second, and a task is required to produce a guaranteed response within four seconds, what is the largest number of users that can be handled at any time:

a if any task can be completed within 1/100th of a second?

b if tasks may take up to 1/20th of a second in total? (*F*)

What about the furniture?

The operating system, then, has the task of swapping one program for another at frequent intervals. It must do many other tasks, however.

When the Stuarts move into their cottage each year, they would take all their clothes with them, as they would not expect to wear the Jones' clothes! On the other hand, they would not take furniture with them, expecting that the Jones would have left the beds for them to sleep in.

The programs in the time-sharing computer system have similar problems. The computer's operating system includes some *public* software, which is available to all programs using the system. This might, for example, include sections of program to search a disk, or to send a line of print to a printer; there is no point in saving instructions like these every time and then reloading them, since every program will use them. These are like the furniture of the time-shared cottage. On the other hand, some of the data for each program is private; the people dealing with the Northfield office, for example, would not be pleased if their rates payment record suddenly appeared on a screen in Castle Vale!

It is obviously vital that (like the Jones' clothes) the private data of one program are kept separate from the private data of another, while allowing both access to public software. The programmers who write and maintain the operating system must take great care to ensure that it always does this.

8.14

a Manjit Singh receives a rates bill for £600 000 for one year, yet he is just an ordinary householder. Explain how this could have happened.

b Give some examples of what might happen if the private data of one program were mixed up with the private data of another. (*D*)

In fact the operating system is even more complex than so far described. Most of the terminals like to have four jobs permanently running. At the start of the day most of the operators in the offices, such as

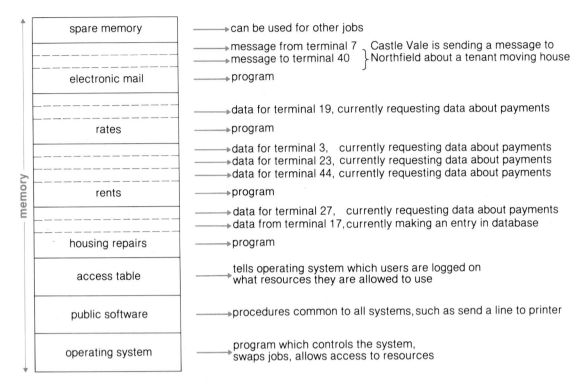

Fig. 8.9 *One way of partitioning CPU memory for a multi-access system.*

Suzy Smith, will start four jobs going (usually housing repairs, rent payments, rate payments and messages to other departments). Through the day they can select one of these jobs with a single key-press, and then type in the data needed. The operating system at the other end of the telephone link has to keep all the necessary programs running all the time, as it would be inefficient if the most frequently used software was being shunted continually between disk and CPU.

A way of doing this is to 'partition' the mainframe's memory, giving some of it to the repairs programs, some to rent payments and so on, and leave some memory spare for other occasional jobs which any particular terminal might want to do. Within each job, the processor deals with all requests for information from whichever terminals have requested it, constantly swapping data from disk to immediate access memory and back, each time-slice.

Who can get into the system?

Apart from entering queries about housing repairs, and payments of rent, Suzy can also enter payments of rates, which are stored on an even bigger database on a different set of disks. However, because these databases involve large amounts of public money, there are problems in allowing so many terminals access to them.

8.15

a Explain briefly the difference between rent and rates.

b Why do the records of rates require a bigger database than the records of rents?

c Describe the difference in the way payments are made.

d Could the same program handle the payments for both rents and rates? (*F*)

8.16

Many problems could arise if every terminal in the city could access and modify all of the databases in the computer. Write down as many different problems as you can. (*D*)

When Suzy *logs on* in the morning, she has to type in a code number; the computer then asks her for a password which she also types on her keyboard. If she types these correctly, the operating system will start up whichever jobs she then wants; if she enters it wrongly (normally she gets three chances), the system will refuse to let her connect to the database. There is a file called the *system log*, which records details of any user logging on to any terminal. This will help the operations manager to discover whether someone has attempted to use Suzy's terminal without permission.

Yet another task for the operating system is to check each of these code numbers (called an *access code*). Also stored in a large matrix, kept permanently in the central processor, is a list of the access codes for all the people involved in the system across the city, together with the resources to which they have access. For example, Suzy can call up onto her screen the record of any council house or flat which someone wants repaired, and this allows her to alter certain fields in that record.

8.17

Describe the measures used by the designers of the housing system to prevent unauthorised access to files. (*T*)

8.18

What information do you think would be recorded in the system log? (*D*)

However, Suzy can only call up records of rate payments for the properties in the area served by her office; she is not allowed to call up rate records for houses in other areas of the city. Also, she cannot alter *any* of these records. Suzy can tell Mary Taylor whether her payments are up-to-date, from the record she can display on her screen. She can accept payment too, but she must send the cash or cheques to the City Treasurer's office, as these are the only people who can alter payment records in the computer.

8.19

a Why do you think clerks in the local offices are not allowed to alter payment records in the database?

b Explain how the computer system can tell whether someone sitting at a terminal is allowed to alter payment records or not. (*D*)

This system means that some people have far more power to alter the database than others; the ability to alter parts of the database is given only to the people whose job requires it. There is a file in the computer centre which contains all the access codes and passwords; naturally access to this must be limited to a *very* small group of people.

8.20

Some people (called *hackers*) have managed to link their home computers to large mainframe systems like the Council's. What could happen if the information in the access codes file was obtained by hackers? (*D*)

The computer system and its operation

We have looked at some of the reasons why a city council has a large computer system with terminals around the city. We have seen people using it, but we also need to know more detail about the functions and operations of a large mainframe computer with complex communication links.

We have seen that the immediate access memory in the CPU of the mainframe contains the operating system itself, several programs, data for the terminals currently using these programs, and a list of access codes. If you think of the size of the memory in microcomputers, most of which only ever run one program at a time, you might think that the immediate access store must be huge. In fact, the operating system manages with much less, by using a clever trick called *virtual memory*.

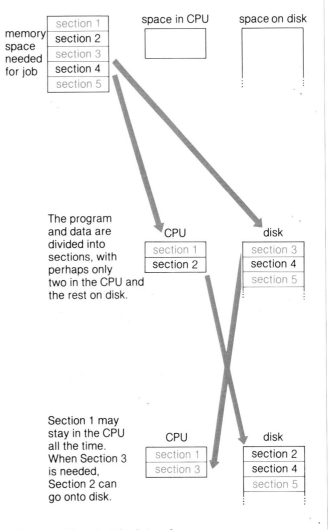

Fig. 8.10   The principle of virtual memory.

This works by using part of a disk drive (possibly as much as 50 megabytes) as an extension of the immediate access store. Some memory locations will be in IAS, others will be on the disk. Programmers write their programs on the assumption that the memory is as big as they need. The operating system is written in such a way that, if it finds itself trying to read data from locations which are on the *disk*, it simply copies a section of IAS to the disk and copies the section containing the data it wants from the disk into IAS. Programmers need not be aware that this is happening; the system does it all for them.

The system itself took many man-years of work to develop, test, and improve so that this copying of data is kept to a minimum. You may have seen similar tricks at work on a micro: several popular word-processor programs may appear to access the disk drive for no obvious reason in the middle of editing a document. This is because they use temporary disk files, later deleted, which they treat as virtual memory.

8.21

What is the advantage of virtual memory, compared with having a larger (and faster) immediate access memory? *(D)*

How does the computer find things so quickly?

When Mary Taylor asks Suzy to call up the details

Alan Brian Carol David Rebecca Richard Soraya Tom Zafar

To find DAVID: look half way along list

DAVID is before REBECCA in the alphabet, so examine the first half of the list and repeat the process:

Alan   Brian   Carol   David

DAVID is after CAROL in the alphabet, so examine the second half of the list and repeat the process:

Carol   David

The Half-way item is David, so the item is found.

This algorithm can be written formally as:

```
first: = 1
last: = 9 (or however many items in list)
found: = false
REPEAT UNTIL first = last OR found = true
   pointer: = (first + last)/2
   IF item_at_pointer = search_item THEN found: = true
   IF item_at_pointer < search_item THEN
      first: = pointer + 1 ELSE last: = pointer_1
```

Fig. 8.11   The binary search method of finding an item in an alphabetical list.

of her flat, from a computer miles away, we have seen that it responds immediately — 90 per cent of her queries are answered within half a second. Yet you may have seen information retrieval programs running on a micro which take much longer than this to search a small database of a few hundred records. The secret is in two parts — direct access and indexing.

A disk is a **direct** (or **random**) **access** device, meaning that the **heads** which read data can move anywhere on the disk, unlike a tape which has to be searched from beginning to end (usually called a **serial** or **sequential** search). In addition, on the disk is an index, which is a file containing just one or two words (called keywords) or numbers about each record, together with information about where the actual details of that record are.

Because the index is small compared with the main file, it can be searched quickly, particularly if the index is stored in a sensible order. Once a program is given a particular house to find, it can look it up quickly in the index, and tell the disk control circuits where to move the heads to find the data required.

Each property in the city has a *unique property reference number* which is used as the main key in the index, both for the housing and rates databases. If Mary can give Suzy this number, the computer can find her record almost instantly.

The idea of a book index.... can be used to index a disk file

File dump   8.12
Floppy disk   1.5
Gigabyte   12.6

Short list of keys arranged so that you can search quickly tells you which chapter and which page to look at for more details

Track 97
Sector 1
contains Suzy's full name, address, rent details, etc.

Track 21
Sector 4
contains David's full name, address, rent details, etc

A full-size 14-inch disk pack usually contains 10 or 12 disk surfaces, each with 200 tracks of 200 sectors.

Fig. 8.12

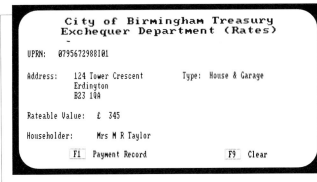

```
      City of Birmingham Treasury
      Exchequer Department (Rates)

UPRN:   0795672988101

Address:    124 Tower Crescent      Type:  House & Garage
            Erdington
            B23 1QA

Rateable Value:   £  345

Householder:    Mrs M R Taylor

      F1  Payment Record          F9   Clear
```

Fig. 8.13

Because few people can remember their number, there are other indexes which use the address as a key. This can be much more complicated for the computer — if Mary happens to live in one of the twelve High Streets or the fourteen Station Roads in the city, the computer will display a list of all of them and ask which one is wanted.

8.22

a Explain what is meant by a field of a record.

b What is special about a key field?

c List the fields of a record in the telephone directory.

d Which would be the best field to use as the key?

e Describe the procedure for finding the phone number of a person called John Smith, who lives in Station Road, Birmingham.

f Explain why the records are not listed in order of phone number.   (D)

Who looks after all this data?

All this information is a security problem. Firstly, there must be frequent backups of all the databases, copying the disks onto magnetic tapes.

8.23

What does backup mean? Why is it necessary?   (T)

There are several ways of making security backup copies of a file or a database. In the case of serial files, (those which are always stored and used in the same order), backups are produced naturally during processing, and we shall look at this method later. With a large database such as the Council's, backup is even more important — a disk failure could ruin work which took months to set up. Security in this case consists of regular file dumps onto magnetic tape; when a copy has been made, a new transaction file is started. All changes are recorded in this file, even though the database has already been updated. Of course, it is no use making three magnetic tape copies of an important file if all three are simply put in the same cupboard. If all three perished in a fire,

the Council would still have lost all its valuable data. The Confederation of British Industry has estimated that 90% of all British companies would be forced out of business within two years if they lost all the information in their computers!

8.24

Describe as many precautions you can think of which could be used to prevent valuable data being lost, either by machine failure, mistakes by operators, theft or other disasters.   (D)

The housing database contains details of all the houses owned by the Council. It also contains details of the rent paid by all tenants, dating back either to when they moved in or to 1983, when the database first came on-line. People occasionally leave their houses, and there is no need to keep their records on-line any longer. The records are kept on disk for two years after they leave, in case of enquiries, but then their records are *archived* onto *microfiche*. *Computer Output to Microfilm* (*COM*) uses special photographic methods to produce very small images of what would be printed on a page.

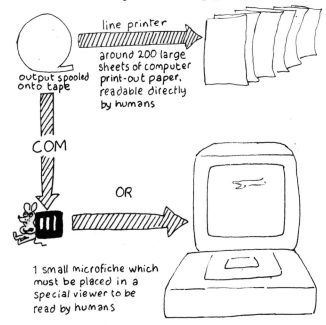

Fig. 8.14   *Archiving for long-term storage.*

8.25

a Explain what a microfiche is.

b Where else do you find microfiche being used?

c Why do you think the housing department's old records are printed onto microfiche instead of paper?   (T)

115

Archiving is another management task, in addition to making sure that new records are created for new tenants. These management or **housekeeping** tasks (copying disks to tape, reorganising indexes, sorting files, merging two tape files into one, archiving) are done by systems software called **utility programs**. These do not directly do anything for the users of the system (Suzy and her colleagues), but they help to keep the operation of the computer as efficient as possible.

Other utility programs perform tasks such as finding how much space is left on a disk, testing the memory of the computer, and testing the communication links to the branch offices. Some of these programs can be run at night, when the computer is not quite so busy, but others require the whole system to be shut down. This must happen occasionally for maintenance purposes.

8.26

Name some of the utility programs concerned with housekeeping on a microcomputer system that you use, and describe how they help the person who manages the system. *(D)*

What does the computer do at night?

We have seen that the terminals work for ten hours a day, and naturally the operating system in the mainframe works on timesharing for the same time. It is not idle the rest of the time, though — the Council cannot afford to let a multimillion-pound asset do nothing.

Fig. 8.15

Many people come in to Suzy's office, and the others dotted round the city, to pay their rates. Many other people never call personally to pay their rates. People who pay their rates in monthly instalments usually instruct their banks to pay a *standing order*, automatically paying the same amount on the same day each month. The housing department regularly receives a magnetic tape from a bank's computer system, which contains details of all the standing orders payable to the housing department. The council's computer reads this tape from beginning to end, crediting its own accounts with payments from tenants. This type of job is not done by the usual operating system; instead it is run by batch processing, and not time-shared with the queries from offices.

Other jobs which can be run as batch jobs include the city's **payroll**, which uses data concerning the hours that people have worked to calculate the pay due and produce printed payslips (for the employees) and magnetic tapes (for the banks' computers). The batch processing system also produces all kinds of printed reports for the housing managers, such as the number of repairs done, who is in arrears with their rent, and so on.

Files which are only used in batch processing mode are often stored on tape, and any transaction files must have their records sorted into the same order as the master file. Security procedures are then a little different; a common method is the **grandfather-father-son system**, which can also be used with disk files.

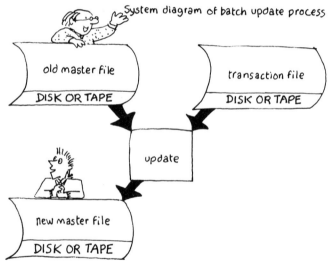

Fig. 8.16 *A system diagram of a batch update process.*

When a file is being updated, the old master file is called the *father* and the new one is the *son*. The next time the file is updated, a third file is produced; this is now the son, the previous file is the father, and the original one is the *grandfather*. These are called **generations** of files. If the master file is lost for any reason, its father, or even grandfather, can be used to restore the data. To save typing in all the transaction data again, copies of transaction files are also kept. To avoid having too many copies of out-of-date files, the tape containing the old grandfather file is usually re-used for the new son file.

8.27

The housing department's enquiry system, on which Suzy works, runs in real time.

a What is the difference between a real-time system and a batch processing system?

b Why does the housing enquiry system have to be a real-time system?

c Why does the processing of standing orders not have to be done as a real-time job? *(D)*

8.28

Draw a systems flowchart for the payroll system. (*Advice:* use Fig. 8.16 as a basis and extend it to include the extra outputs mentioned above.)

8.29

What advantage is there to the Council in doing all its batch processing at night? *(D)*

8.30

The housing department will carry a large amount of stock for repair work. Describe how the computer system could help to make stock control more efficient and save the ratepayers' money. *(R)*

How was the system designed?

The City Council made use of systems analysts in designing their system. Because of the system's size, the tasks of designing, programming, testing, debugging, documenting, implementing, operating and maintaining must each be very much a team effort.

8.31

Explain the meaning of each of the following terms in relation to a computerised system:

a design,

b program,

c test,

d debug,

e document,

f implement,

g operate,

h maintain. *(T)*

The first responsibility of the systems analysts is to familiarise themselves with the existing system, and carry out a feasibility study. Their aim will be to find which parts of the system can be computerised at a reasonable cost. In a large organisation, such as the City Council, there may well be some departments dealing with information which should *not*

be put on a computer accessed by several hundred people: for example, some of the Social Services Department's child care files may be excluded. The analysts must bear in mind that the benefits of the system must outweigh the cost of introducing it, given that this may take many man-years of work.

For those parts which the systems analysts think can be computerised, they can proceed to the design stage. The key to this part of the job is to divide the system up into *modules*. Each module should be small enough for a small team to program and test.

The analysts must devise the right organisation for the data files, and their indexes, so that the computer can provide all the facilities the council wants. During the design stage, the analysts must frequently consult with the eventual users of the system (Suzy and her colleagues, and their bosses in the city). The fact that this involves so many people can lead to the design stage taking several months or even years, but it is worth the effort.

Go straight to the top?

Most computer programming these days is done using the *top-down* method. This means that the system designer starts with an overall view of the system, breaking it down into smaller self-contained units. Each unit is itself broken up further, until the units are small enough to be programmed easily as a single *subroutine*, and be tested independently.

Many of these smallest units may be used frequently by the programmers, either several times in one program or in several different programs. The chief programmer will therefore build up a *library of subroutines*. In a structured programming language, each subroutine will be either a *function*, which calculates a value, or a *procedure*, which performs a specific task. Each subroutine must be documented to show what data needs to be passed into it, what data it returns to the main program (if any), and what process it carries out.

When all the units are complete, they are then linked together to form a complete program (or, more often, a *suite* of several related programs). An example of the principle, showing the construction of a small program for making a database of names and addresses, is shown in Fig. 8.18 (page 118).

8.32

What do you think are the advantages of trying to write programs using top-down methods? *(D)*

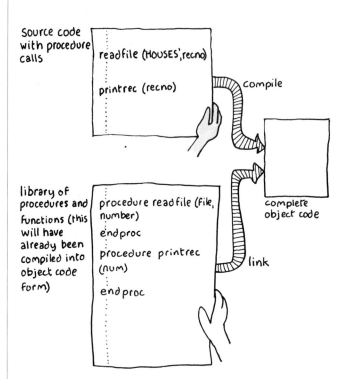

Library subprograms are linked into the compiled version of the main source code to give the complete object code. The parameter values passed from the main program are matched up —

in this example, **file** takes the value 'HOUSES'
               number takes the value of **recno**
               num also takes the value of **recno**

Fig. 8.17   Building a program from modules.

Testing, too, must be very thorough. The computer will keep records about hundreds of thousands of people, and sums of money running to hundreds of millions of pounds. It cannot start real work until every part has been thoroughly tested, not only in normal use, but also in exceptional conditions. The team must be sure that the database will not suddenly 'crash' when asked to handle two hundred queries at once, or when two clerks at opposite ends of the city try to look up the same data simultaneously.

A database crashed when the London Stock Exchange changed to an all-electronic system for dealing in shares, late in 1986. The system was designed and programmed in a hurry, and tested by trying to deal with a hundred transactions every second. On the first morning, to the Stock Exchange's embarrassment, every dealer wanted to try it out, and when it reached a rate of two hundred transactions a second the system crashed in a blaze of publicity!

It is extremely important for the programmers and systems analysts to document their work thoroughly. With a large team, they must each know what the others are doing. They hope that their system will still be running in several years' time. If any of them leaves, the people who take over must be able to carry on the never-ending task of improving the system.

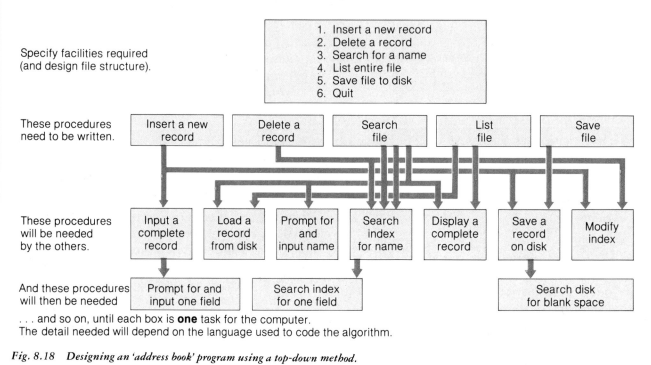

. . . and so on, until each box is **one** task for the computer.
The detail needed will depend on the language used to code the algorithm.

Fig. 8.18   Designing an 'address book' program using a top-down method.

If you were the chief officer of a large organisation, and you had installed a new computer system, describe what you would expect to be done before you allowed the system to go live. (*T*)

Even when the programs have been thoroughly tested, they cannot work unless they have data to process! As we have seen, this is often the longest job of all, taking several months to transfer millions of words onto the new system. The *changeover* to the new system must also be carefully thought out, and this is where the early consultations with users can bear fruit. People who are to use the system must be introduced to it gradually, and carefully trained so that they can see how their work contributes to the system as a whole. The alternative is often for staff to be in *fear* of the computer system. It has been estimated that of the £5 billion spent on new computer systems each year, £800 million is wasted through poorly thought-out changeovers.

How can the system be improved?

When a system of great size and complexity finally works, its development does not stop. In fact the City Council's housing system has evolved over the years. The housing database became operational in 1976, and rents were fully computerised by 1983.

During this time the mainframe CPU has been replaced with more up-to-date machinery, but the data files have been kept; it was a requirement of the programs for the newer machine that they had to keep the old data files. The new computer had to be *upwardly compatible* with the old.

Why do you think the city council insisted that their new computer should be able to work with their old data files? (*D*)

There is, though, one thing the system will *not* do. Suzy can extract data from whichever database she chooses, but she will only get the information she asks for. The databases are quite independent of each other. Some people may make enquiries about repairs to their flats, and the computer will not, for example, show that they are entitled to grants from the council towards their rates, because this is stored in a different database.

The next development is likely to be an integrated, 'client-centred' system. The intention is that a master database will be created indexed on people, not on properties, and that an enquiry by a particular individual could reveal all the information held on that person, regardless of which department was concerned. A system of this kind will be even more complex than the present one, and so its

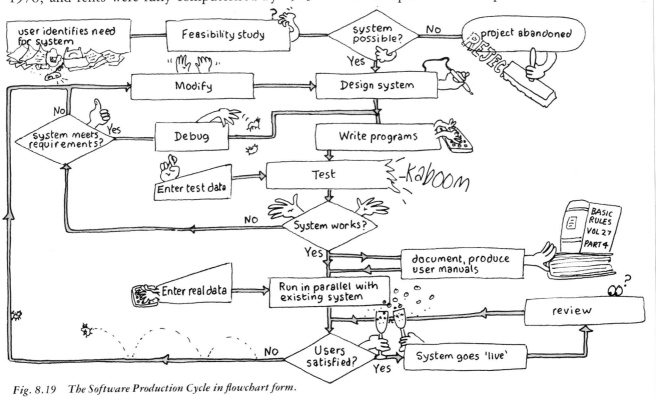

Fig. 8.19   The Software Production Cycle in flowchart form.

designers have to consider all the factors mentioned above. These days, however, there is another important factor for them to bear in mind: *privacy* of information.

In the United States there is a law called the Freedom of Information Act. This does not mean that information can be freely passed around; in fact, it prohibits an organisation from storing information about people without their knowledge. Most European countries have similar laws, and put pressure on Britain, where the **Data Protection Act** was passed in 1984. Its provisions are summarised in Fig. 8.20: its purpose is to ensure that information collected in one computer system is not transferred to another and used for a totally different purpose, and to ensure that data held about people is accurate.

The Act regulates the use of automatically processed personal data. Personal data consists of information about a living individual, including expressions of opinion.

Data users are organisations or individuals who collect and process personal data by automatic means.

Computer Bureau an organisation or an individual who processes personal data for data users, or allows data users to process data on the bureau's equipment.

Data Subject is the person whose information is stored automatically — you or me, in fact everybody.

Both data users and computer bureaus must register.

Rights of individuals (data subjects)

Data users must:
Collect and process personal data fairly and lawfully.
Only hold personal data for specified, lawful, registered purposes.
Only use personal data for registered purposes.
Only disclose personal data to registered recipients.
Ensure that the personal data that they hold is relevant to the purpose for which they are registered holders.
Ensure that the personal data is accurate and up to date.
Not hold personal data longer than necessary.
Ensure that appropriate security is used to safeguard the personal data they hold.

A data subject may:
Seek compensation from a data user if any damage or distress is caused by the loss, destruction or unauthorised disclosure of data.
Seek compensation from a data user if any damage or distress is caused by inaccurate data.
Apply to the courts or the Data Protection Registrar for the rectification or erasure of inaccurate data.
Obtain access to the data to which he or she is the subject.

Duties of the Data Protection Registrar

The Registrar must:
Set up a register of data users and computer bureaus that handle personal data, and make this register publicly available.
Supply information about the Act and its operation.
Promote the observance of the data protection principles.
Encourage the development of codes of practice to assist data users to stay within the principles of the Act.
Deal with complaints about data users breaking the principles of the Act, and deal with complaints about the Act.

Fig. 8.20 The Data Protection Act 1984: a brief outline.

Note There are exemptions to all sections of this Act.

8.35

There are various companies who would find the personal information stored on the City's housing database very valuable.

a Give one type of company who would value lists of people on the housing database.

b Which types of householder would such companies wish to have lists of?

c Explain why it is easier to obtain such lists from a computerised database than from manual files.

d What would be the disadvantage to the householders if the council decided to distribute the lists? (D)

Other developments which the City Council may introduce include **distributed processing**. This resembles the system used by the chocolate company in Chapter 7. When the housing system was first designed, microcomputers were in their infancy and very rare. Today they are very powerful, and much of the processing could be carried out in branch offices, saving the power of the mainframe for other jobs which may become necessary.

8.36

What would be the advantage of using microcomputers in branch offices instead of dumb terminals? (D)

A large system, then, can take many years and millions of pounds to develop. However, it does enable the council to provide a service to the public in their own communities, instead of forcing people to deal with offices many miles away. It is a tribute to the skill of its team of systems analysts, programmers, operators and clerks that the system currently copes with over a million transactions every week, fifty two weeks a year.

End-of-chapter questions

8.37

What is meant by:

a database,

b timesharing,

c virtual memory,

d generations of a file,

e top-down program design,

f housekeeping?

8.38

Explain the difference between:

a multiaccess and multiprogramming,

b direct and serial access,

c backup and archive.

8.39

Backup copies of files must be kept for security on both batch and real-time systems. Explain the difference in methods of backing up files between the two types of system.

8.40

The City Treasurer's Department, which is in charge of the computer installation described in this chapter, employs people in the following jobs:

a operations manager,

b computer operator,

c data preparation clerk,

d maintenance programmer.

For each one, write a brief description of the work that they would be expected to do in the computer department.

8.41

Explain why data is often archived, rather than keeping it on-line permanently.

8.42

Suppose a large organisation (such as a credit card company) had a database containing the names, addresses and annual earnings of several thousand people. Suppose also that they were able to sell these files to a mail-order company.

a In what ways could this company use this information to the disadvantage of the people mentioned in it?

b If any of this information were inaccurate, what possible injustices could occur?

c Does the Data Protection Act prevent the sale of this information? Explain your answer by reference to Fig. 8.20.

8.43

Many other large organisations can use time-sharing systems. For example, British Airways has a computer system which deals with reserving seats on their planes. This system, the CPU of which is at Heathrow Airport in London, needs terminals in many different countries: there is one as far away as Los Angeles.

What difference does the long distance make to the computer system, compared with the system described for the City Council's housing department? (*Advice:* consider the time differences, methods of communication, language problems.)

8.44

In certain parts of the country, local doctors (GP's) have computer terminals in their surgeries. These terminals are linked to a mainframe computer belonging to the Regional Health Authority. GP's and their secretaries both use the terminals for input and output of information.

A large database holds certain personal information and important medical details about each patient. Local hospitals also have access to this patient database.

a Explain what is meant by a database.

b What non-medical details do you think will be stored about each patient?

c Who would be able to see a patient's details in the GP's surgery?

d Who would be able to see a patient's details in the hospital?

e Who would be able to update non-medical details?

f Who would be able to update medical details?

g Explain why doctors do not allow patients medical records to be seen, except by the staff treating them.

h How would unauthorised access to the patient database be prevented?

i Medical records are exempt from part of the Data Protection Act. Explain which part does not apply, giving a reason.

j Describe the advantages to patients of the access to their records through a computer system in both surgeries and hospitals.

k Explain the fears that patients might have concerning the storage of their medical records on a computer system, and suggest how their minds could be put at ease.

8.45

A large company which manufactures ceramic mugs uses a computer system to control its orders and production. There are ten different styles of mug, each made by pouring a china clay mixture into a mould of the shape required. Any style can have one of six different colours of glaze. In addition, three of the styles must have a design applied by means of a 'transfer' which is attached before the mug is 'fired' in the kiln. Each style of mug must be fired for a different amount of time, and precise control of kiln temperature and firing time is essential to maintain high quality.

The company uses the computer to process the orders from customers and to order the correct amount of clay, glaze, transfers and boxes to manufacture the mugs requested. The computer also calculates the wages of the employees and produces delivery notes and invoices for the goods despatched.

a What type of computer would be best suited to this company?

b What type of operating system would this computer use?

c Draw a configuration diagram of the computer system, showing all the peripherals and their links with the CPU.

d Explain how the following jobs could be scheduled to run simultaneously:

— a payroll run

— calculating production figures from orders

— producing orders for suppliers

e A lot of printing is required by the three jobs above. If there is only one fast printer, explain how the operating system would ensure that the printouts are kept separate without holding up the processing.

f Draw a system diagram for the process of calculating the production figures and printing orders for suppliers.

g Describe briefly how the company might control the production process using computers.

hard cash or plastic money? 9

In this chapter we are going to examine the introduction and use of computers in building societies. We shall see how the growing use of computers has increased the effectiveness of the societies, enabling them both to improve, and to expand, the services offered to members. We shall also examine the effects and implications of computer use in other large financial institutions.

Fig. 9.1 Automatic teller machine.

Building societies

The early building societies were formed in the eighteenth century by groups of craftsmen who wanted to live in reasonable houses. The craftsmen felt the only way that they could do this was to build their own houses. The craftsmen each paid part of their weekly wages into a fund, and this fund was used to buy land and materials for building houses. The houses were built in the craftsmen's spare time and, as each house was completed, they held a ballot to decide who should have the house. Even after one of the group had moved into his house, he continued to pay into the fund and work in his spare time, until all the group's members were housed. When all the members of the society were housed, it stopped operating.

9.1

The system of self-help described above worked well for the craftsmen who set up the early societies. Why do you think other working people were not able to use the same system?   (*D*)

How do building societies operate today?

Today's permanent building societies grew out of this principle of self help. Building societies no longer actually build houses. They exist today to help people buy their own homes. Mainly they borrow money in the short term, from investors who belong to the society, and give loans over much longer periods. These loans had until recently to be used for buying or improving a house, and are called *mortgages*. The building society has a claim on the borrower's house, however, and if the loan is not repaid, the house must be sold.

Interest is paid to members who leave money in the building society, and interest is charged by the building society on loans. There is a difference in these two rates of interest. The difference between rates of interest pays the running costs of the society.

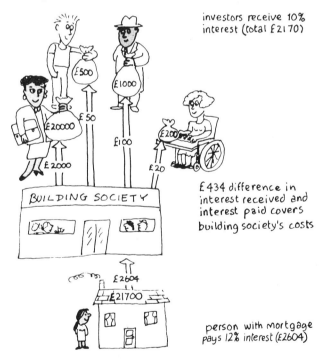

Fig. 9.2 Why rates of interest are different.

One person in six of the population of the United Kingdom is a member of a building society, either as an investor or a borrower, or both, and there are some 200 societies. Some of the societies are very small, with only one office; whilst the largest (the Halifax Building Society) has over 700 offices and 2000 agencies throughout the United Kingdom, with assets of over £20 billion at present.

9.2

a Which of these make up the assets of a building society:

— the value of the houses mortgaged,
— the money invested by the members,
— the money loaned to borrowers?

b How does the society know how much its assets are? (R)

9.3

a Explain briefly the meaning of interest.

b How is simple interest calculated? (R)

9.4

a Explain in your own words what a mortgage is.

b What is the difference between interest on mortgages and interest on investment in Fig. 9.2?

c What is the sum of money in used for ? (T)

The larger building societies needed to deal with some 300 000 customer transactions (deposits and withdrawals) a day. It was in order to deal with this large volume of work efficiently that computers were first introduced in the late 1960s. Prior to then, interest had to be calculated manually. Transactions were written by hand into various record books, called *ledgers*.

9.5

What advantages do you think would be gained by computerisation of building society accounts? (T)

How were accounts updated using manual methods?

Carole Watson has a mortgage with the Moseley Building Society, a small society with one office and no computer. Each month Carole must pay the building society an agreed amount of money. This amount will eventually pay off her loan and all interest due on it. Carole has instructed her bank to make these regular monthly payments through a standing order direct to the building society. Both the building society and Carole find this method of payment convenient.

Every six months, the building society must calculate the interest due on Carole's loan, and send her a statement, detailing all transactions since the last statement.

The Moseley Building Society, even though small, has a large number of members with mortgages, and most pay off their mortgage in the same way as Carole. However, the building society must check all its mortgage accounts manually each month, to make sure they have received payment.

MOSELEY BUILDING SOCIETY
175 High Street, Moseley
Birmingham B25 5SJ

Ms Angela Grant　　　　　　　31st January 1987
555 Swanshurst Lane
Moseley　　　　　　　　　　　MORTGAGE
Birmingham　　　　　　　　　　5784932
B13 2OB

DATE and PARTICULARS	DEBITS	CREDITS	BALANCE
21 Jul 1986 Advance	28 000,00		
7 Aug 1986 Cheque		260,74	
5 Sep 1986		224,59	
3 Oct 1986		224,59	
5 Nov 1986		224,59	
5 Dec 1986		224,59	
4 Jan 1986		224,59	
31 Jan 1986 interest	1 355,09		27 971,40

Fig. 9.3　A statement for a mortgage account.

9.6

A standing order authorises your bank or building society to pay a fixed amount of money to someone regularly (each month or each year). The funds are then transferred from your account to the person you owe money, without you having to fill in forms each time.

a Name three types of bills that could be paid by standing order.

b What are the advantages to the customer of paying bills by standing order?

c What are the advantages to the building society or bank of a person paying his or her bills by standing order?

d What advantages are there to the person receiving the money if he is paid by standing order? (D)

Fig. 9.4　Two pages from a manually updated passbook.

Name and address ALAN BROWN 163 WESTFIELD ROAD.			Roll no 123547		
DATE	CASHIER	DETAILS	WITHDRAWALS	RECEIPTS	BALANCE
14 Oct 86	CS	BROUGHT FORWARD			455.00
14 Oct 86	CS	cheque		50	505.00
20 Nov 86	FE	Cash		100	605.00
15 Nov 86	FE	cheque	200		405.00
31 Jan 87	CS	Interest		22.23	427.23

The Society cannot lend money to people unless others invest money in it. One of these is Mr Brown, who has a savings account with the Moseley Building Society. Mr Brown wishes to pay in £50 to his account, so he hands the cashier his passbook and the cash. The passbook is kept by Mr Brown, and is used to record all transactions on his account. Sally, the cashier, then carries out the following actions:

1. Sally checks the passbook against the building society's records to see if there are any entries in the records not included in Mr Brown's passbook, such as interest. If there are, Sally writes these into the passbook.

2. She next checks the £50 Mr Brown has given her, and writes out a paying-in slip, which she asks Mr Brown to sign.

3. Sally then writes the amount deposited into the Passbook (see Fig. 9.4) and her tillbook, and then completes the balance column in both books.

4. Finally she returns the passbook to Mr Brown.

Fig. 9.5

9.7
What do you think is the purpose of the tillbook? (D)

9.8
Explain in your own words what is meant by the *balance* of an account.
(*Advice:* look at Fig 9.4.) (T)

9.9
The passbook can be considered as a file, and each entry as a record.

a List the fields which make up the file structure.

b Describe the procedure for updating this file when a deposit is made. (F)

Later in the day, when Sally has no customers to serve, she enters the amount paid in by Mr Brown into the ledgers which the society uses to keep its records. There is a member records ledger, which records the details of each member's account, and a daily transaction ledger, so that the branch manager knows about all the deposits and withdrawals at the branch each day.

This procedure is carried out by Sally every time anyone wants to pay into or withdraw money from a savings account. If the Moseley Building Society had more than one branch, summaries of all the transactions occurring at the branches would have to be sent to the head office. This would have to be done manually and would take a considerable amount of time.

9.10
There are some transactions which Sally might find when she compares Mr Brown's passbook with the building society's records which are not at present included in the passbook. What types could these be? (T)

9.11
Sally will need to use the paying-in slip to update the member records ledger. Consider this as a file and list the fields that you think would be included. (D)

The two examples above show that a computerised record system would be useful, even for a small building society. However, for a large building society with many branches, the benefits would be considerable.

How did the building societies start to use computers?

The larger building societies started to computerise in the late 1960s and early 1970s. Mainframe computers were installed in the head offices of the societies, first to handle savings accounts and then mortgage accounts. Networks of *teletypewriter terminals* were introduced, allowing each branch direct access to the central computers. This meant that the societies could hold their records centrally and give access to their branches. Much of the

Fig. 9.6   A teletypewriter.

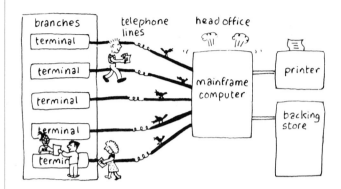

Fig. 9.7 *A network system.*

updating could then be done more or less automatically. However, there was still the problem of entering the transactions, by hand, into the passbook of a savings account. There was also a new problem: the cashier had to queue for access to the terminal, so that she could obtain a printout of any transactions to be entered into the passbook since it was last updated.

When a deposit or a withdrawal was made over the counter, a form had to be filled in by the cashier and signed by the member. At the end of the day, all the forms were posted to the computer centre as a batch. The data was input using a key-to-disk system and the files updated by batch processing methods.

9.12
What were the major problems during the early stages of computerisation? (*T*)

9.13
Explain briefly the procedure that would be used for paying in £25 into a savings account, using the above system. (*T*)

9.14
What were the advantages and disadvantages of using a teletypewriter, compared with a VDU, in the above system? (*D*)

Fig. 9.8 *A counter-top terminal.*

The answer to the problems above was further automation of the procedures involved. Counter-top terminals were introduced in the early 1980s by many of the larger building societies. These devices meant that most transactions could be dealt with over the counter: the cashier does not have to leave her position to deal with a customer. It became possible to make a withdrawal in 30 seconds and a deposit in 20 seconds.

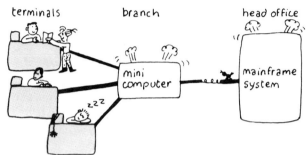

Fig. 9.9 *Each branch has its own network linked via a minicomputer to the mainframe at head office.*

The counter-top terminals are normally on-line to a minicomputer at the branch, which is in turn on-line to the mainframe computer at the building society's head office. To enable a passbook to be updated with the latest possible information, the system used is a real-time system. It is very different from the industrial control system at the paper mill described in Chapter 7, but has a similar need for immediate processing of input data.

9.15
a Explain in your own words what is meant by real-time processing.

b Why is a real-time system used to update passbooks? (*T*)

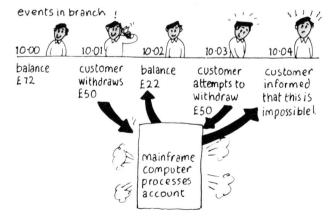

Fig. 9.10 *Real time updating of an account.*

9.16

In Chapter 7, some of the devices were operated off-line.

a Which devices were these?

b Describe the difference between on-line and off-line working, using the counter-top terminals and devices you have listed in (a) as examples.   (*T*)

What are the procedures for savings account transactions?

The Moseley Building Society has now installed counter-top terminals. Mr Brown wishes to pay in £500 to his savings account. He hands both his passbook and the £500 to Sally, the cashier. Sally places the passbook in the slot in the counter-top terminal and types in Mr Brown's account number, which is recorded on his passbook. The book is then automatically updated with any transactions. Sally then types in the code for a cash credit and the amount of the credit. The computer's files are updated and the information is entered into the book.

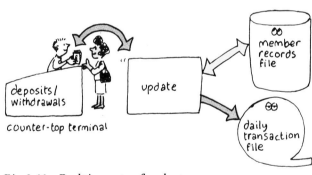

Fig. 9.11   Real time system flowchart.

On another day Mr Brown wishes to withdraw £150 from his account. He hands Sally the passbook, and tells her he would like to withdraw £150. Sally places a withdrawal slip in the slot on her terminal and enters Mr Brown's account number and the amount to be withdrawn. This is printed onto the withdrawal slip, which Mr Brown must then sign. The signature on the book and that on the slip are then compared. The signature of the passbook is invisible to the naked eye and only becomes readable when it is reflected by ultra-violet light. Sally next places the passbook in the terminal, where it is updated with any transactions not previously entered, together with the amount of the withdrawal. Sally then hands Mr Brown his £150, together with his passbook.

An extra advantage of the above system is that members are able to carry out savings account transactions at *any* branch of the society to which they belong. In the past, unless special arrangements were made, members could only use their *own* branch to pay in and draw out money.

9.17

What advantages has the introduction of counter-top terminals given to the members?   (*T*)

9.18

Using ordinary sentences or a structured algorithm, describe what the computer system is doing while a withdrawal is being made. (*Advice:* consider checks that will be needed, as well as updating.)   (*D*)

9.19

Why do the building societies have the signature in the passbook only visible under ultra-violet light? (*D*)

Branch	MOSELEY 531			Roll Number	3/58764 23	
Name and address	Mr P. SMITH 59 ORCHARD ROW MOSELEY			Paid up shares		

DATE	CASHIER	OFFICE	DETAILS	WITHDRAWALS	RECEIPTS	BALANCE
22 Jul 85	MB	531	BROUGHT FORWARD			657.24
22 Jul 85	MB	531	REPAID	150.00		507.24
31 Jul 85		531	INTEREST		25.67	532.91
1 Aug 85		531	BANK CREDIT		50.00	582.92
1 SEP 85		531	BANK CREDIT		50.00	632.92
3 SEP 85	KL	531	REPAID	32.92		600.00

Fig. 9.12   Two pages from a passbook that has been updated using a counter-top terminal.

With a savings account it is possible to have money credited to the account without visiting a branch of your building society. Mr Brown, for instance, has a standing order with his bank to transfer £100 per month to his building society savings account. He also arranges with the building society to make monthly payments of £25 to an insurance company, and £30 a month to the electricity board.

9.20

a How could information about the regular payments be transferred from the bank to the building society?

b Could the same system be used to make payments from the building society to other organisations? (D)

9.21

If a fault occurred in the central computer system, the master file of member records could be corrupted. Explain how a *correct* version of the file could be recreated, stating which other types of file will be needed to do this. (T)

Building societies now offer many different accounts, aimed at people with a variety of investment needs. On the right is a typical advertisement.

9.22

Twenty years ago, there was very little choice of building society account. Do you think that computers have affected the range of services that a building society can offer? Explain your answer. (D)

9.23

Microelectronics could be used to help someone to decide which is the best account in which to invest their money, based on their age, amount to invest, and notice required for withdrawal. Either

a draw a logic circuit,

or,

b write an algorithm,

which will input the variables listed above and output the best account.

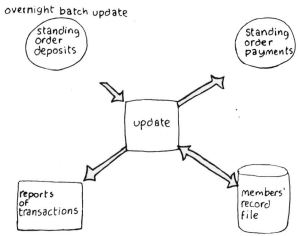

Fig. 9.13 Batch updating is done overnight.

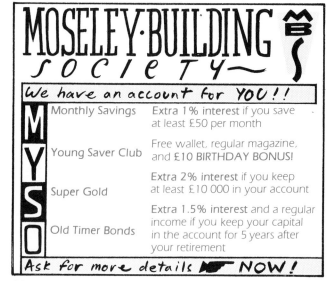

Fig. 9.14

Other effects of computerisation

We have looked at the changes in the way Building Societies handle people's savings, now that they use computers for much of the work. We shall also see how the computers can be used to extend and improve other Building Society services, and how the people who use them are affected.

Today, most societies use their computer to process mortgage applications. This has meant that a prospective house buyer will leave the society's office knowing whether he or she can borrow the money for the house required. In the past this was not the case. Obviously any society has limited funds to lend, and each month a particular branch was allowed to lend an amount specified by head office. This meant that at the end of a particular month, one branch might have had funds left, whilst others had a waiting list of prospective buyers waiting for funds to be released the next month. Computerisation has ended this uneven system.

9.24

The building society would carry out some checks on the borrower and on the house before definitely giving a mortgage.

a   What would they check?

b   What role would computers play in this process?   (R)

Fig. 9.15   *Two possible methods of calculating the balance on a mortgage each year.*

Managing a mortgage account is relatively easy when the system is computerised. Once the account is opened, the house buyer arranges to make the regular agreed monthly payments to the building society. This is normally done by the buyer placing a standing order with his bank, to transfer the required amount each month to the society. This amount is credited to the mortgage account. Every January and July, the building society instructs the computer to calculate the interest due and print out a statement of account, which is then posted to the house buyer. This printing is done at head office using high-speed printers (see Chapter 13).

Fig. 9.16   *Microfiche and reader.*

During the period of time that the building society holds the mortgage on a house (that is, until the loan is fully repaid), they keep the *deeds* of the house. The deeds are paper documents, which include copies of contracts that were exchanged each time the house was sold, plans of the house and grounds, details of the builder, etc. Obviously some of these packages will be very bulky if they relate to a house that may be 100 or more years old. The problem of storing a million or so of these packages is great. The deeds of a house are legal documents which cannot be processed onto microfilm or stored electronically.

Fig. 9.18   *the Conserve-a-trieve system.*

How are deeds stored?

The Halifax Building Society introduced a system called Conserv-a-trieve. This is a fully automated system of document storage and retrieval. The system is situated in a large vault cut into rock. Banks of storage racks each 30 feet high are arranged facing each other. They hold 40 000 containers, each container holding perhaps 50 sets of deeds. 27 electronically controlled columns move between the

Fig. 9.17   *Typical page of the deeds for a house.*

racks, removing and replacing containers as required. Terminal operators in the Deeds Administration Department type in the **roll number**, a unique number used to identify the mortgage account of the requested deeds and the computer then takes over.

9.25

What type of input device do you think the terminal operators in the Deeds Administration Department use? (*D*)

9.26

When information is stored on computer file each record is given a key field.

a What is a key field?

b What would be the key field used to locate a set of deeds? (*T*)

The computer identifies the appropriate moving column, and commands the Conserv-a-trieve system to locate the container in which the deeds required are stored. The column takes the container and places it on the conveyor belt which then takes the container to a workstation, where an operator reads the roll number from his VDU and selects the appropriate set of deeds. The container is then returned automatically to its original place. This system of searching for deeds means that they can be located in five minutes, whereas manually the system would be extremely time consuming.

9.27

How do you think smaller building societies would deal with the problem of deeds storage? (*D*)

What new services have computers brought?

Fig. 9.19   An ATM card.

Fig. 9.20   An ATM.

The introduction of **Automated Teller Machines** (**ATM**s) is a further advance that building societies have made that would have been impossible before they started using computers. These machines allow the members to access their accounts without going through a cashier and even when the branch office is closed.

A member who requests access to Automated Teller Machines is issued with a plastic card which can be slotted into the machine. Magnetic strips on these cards carry the identity of the customer's account. Each member is given a **Personal Identification Number** (**PIN**) by the computer which is known only to the customer and the computer. The PIN and the card are sent to the customer in separate envelopes. When used correctly with the magnetic striped card, the PIN identifies the member and allows them access to a number of services.

1 If the member's balance is adequate, money can be withdrawn from the account
2 Cash (only notes) or cheques may be paid in
3 The member can enquire what the balance is
4 A list of recent transactions (a statement) can be requested
5 Bills can be payed
6 Funds can be transferred between accounts

Fig. 9.21   ATM services.

Fig. 9.22   Using an ATM.

The automated teller machines are normally available for use between 6 a.m. and midnight and are on-line to the building society's computer. This allows immediate updating of the account as soon as a transaction has taken place: real-time processing again. When a member wants to make a transaction, they feed the plastic card into the slot, making sure that they put it in the correct way round. A message on the screen then tells the member to type in their PIN. If they do this correctly, they may then request one of the services available, such as a cash withdrawal. If the member does not type the PIN correctly they get two more attempts, and they are then told to contact their branch if they still do not remember the number correctly. When the member has finished using the machine the card is returned. Some building societies have grouped together to produce a system that allows ATM cards to be used not only in machines owned by the issuing society, but also machines owned by other societies.

The computer system at headquarters must have its member record files constantly on line in order to handle real-time transactions. The disk storage needed will be like the hard disk drive used by VIP Video in Chapter 1 — only much larger and faster, with several disk surfaces accessed simultaneously (see Chapter 13). This is a *fixed disk drive* — in contrast to an *exchangeable disk drive* which uses disk packs that can be changed like floppies — but again, they are larger and with several surfaces stacked together.

Fig. 9.23   Fixed and exchangeable disk drives.

9.28

Explain what a PIN is and how it is used to gain access to a building society account.   (*T*)

9.29

Write an algorithm to explain to someone the use of an ATM.   (*R*)

9.30

a   In what ways have ATMs helped the building societies?

b   What problems might they create?   (*D*)

How is cash being replaced by plastic money?

The Anglia Building Society has taken the use of its 'AngliaCard', one stage further than use in Automated Teller Machines. Together with ICL (International Computers Ltd) the Anglia have set up an *eftpos* scheme in Northampton. The acronym eftpos is made up from two abbreviations:

—   *eft* (electronic funds transfer) which is a system of transferring money from one organisation to another using computers, with neither cash nor forms changing hands,

—   *pos* (point-of-sale) which refers to a terminal used by shops and supermarkets as both a till and a computer input device, often used in conjunction with a bar code reader.

Fig. 9.24   An EFTPOS terminal.

In Northampton there are (at the time of writing) over 100 shops with 200 'Paypoint' eftpos terminals installed. The terminals are on-line to a real-time system, with communications via British Telecom lines.

Mr and Mrs Cole live in Northampton and have an 'AngliaCard'. When they chose a new three-piece suite at a furniture shop that had a PayPoint terminal, they were able to hand their AngliaCard to Jane Curtis, the sales assistant.

A single transaction of up to £10 000 can be dealt with, provided that there is sufficient money in the account to cover the bill.

Fig. 9.26 Using a paypoint.

9.31

What advantages has the use of this eftpos system to:

a Mr and Mrs Cole,

b the owners of the furniture shop,

c Jane Curtis? (*D*)

9.32

At no time does the furniture shop have access to details of the Cole's account. Why is this very important? (*D*)

9.33

Mr and Mrs Cole both have cards for the system and they go shopping separately. Suppose they both try to access the computer at exactly the same time. How will the computer will handle this? (*D*)

9.34

Imagine that someone watches over Mrs Cole's shoulder as she types in her PIN, and then steals her handbag containing her card. What security measures could prevent the card being used illegally?

How else do Building Societies use their computers?

A computer system of the kind used by building societies has very high installation and running costs. We have seen some uses which affect the customer directly; there are other less obvious but equally effective applications.

Using a computer system, it became possible for Head Office to have full details of the accounts and transactions at every branch. This allows Head Office to analyse how a branch is performing, and

to have up-to-date figures on lending and investment so that it can control lending.

The computer of a large building society will also be used for a personnel management system. This allows the Personnel Department to have easy access to information on all staff for assessment purposes, and to analyse factors such as absences and overtime.

9.35

In Chapter 2, Mr Adams' computer was used for word processing. Many building society branches use their minicomputers for this purpose as well as the financial records. What advantages will they gain from being linked to a central mainframe computer at Head Office?

9.36

Any large organisation, whether it sells goods or not, needs a stock control system to keep records of stationery, light bulbs and other items needed for its offices.

a Describe the benefits of using the computer to keep these records.

b What procedures would be carried out if the managing director suggested computerising the stock control system?

9.37

What other tasks do you think the building society's computer might perform? For each one, suggest whether it would be a batch or a real-time process. (*Advice:* look back to previous chapters.)

9.38

a Which of the building society computer's tasks would require files to be registered under the Data Protection Act?

b Explain what effect this would have on customers and staff.

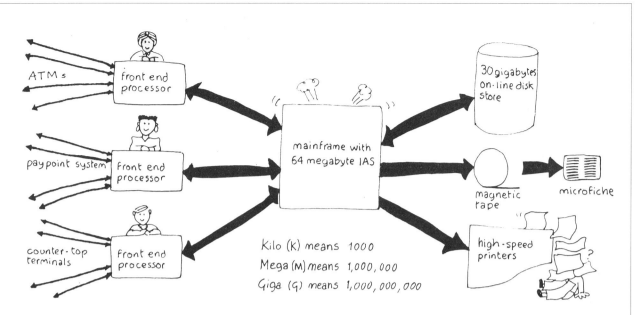

Fig. 9.27 *Typical hardware at a Building Society's Computer Centre.*

How are all these services provided?

The configuration that gives the facilities at present is shown above.

With the rapid expansion of electronic financial services, this is likely to change frequently to provide more on-line storage, faster processing, and more communication links.

When several links are needed between two places that are some distance apart, it is cheaper to use a *multiplexor* than to have several sets of phone lines. Multiplexing combines signals from several sources into one telephone line, in such a way that the signals can be separated again at the receiving end of the line.

9.39

a Explain what is meant by 64 megabytes of immediate access store.

b Explain what is meant by 30 gigabytes of backing store.

c How many times larger is this storage than on the computer systems that you use at home, in school or college?

Building societies employ quite large teams of analysts and programmers so that they can continue to develop their systems — increasing both efficiency and customer services. The computer is run 24 hours a day by staff operating on 8-hour shifts. This means that the operations manager cannot supervise the running of the computer the whole time; each team of operators is therefore headed by a *shift leader*.

This round-the-clock working would also allow them to handle transactions from all round the world if they started international branches. With satellite communications, transactions with the USA, for example, can be processed within 30 seconds.

9.40

a List five of the tasks that the operators at the computer centre would be required to carry out.

b Describe the differences in the work of the day shift (0700 to 1500) and the night shift (2300 to 0700).   (*D*)

9.41

Although the Anglia computer is run 24 hours a day, the branch service, the ATMs and the eftpos system are not available around the clock. What jobs will be done on the computer when these other systems are not in use?   (*T*)

9.42

In the last chapter we saw that the computer system had to be shut down occasionally. Would this also be the case with a computer system belonging to a building society? Explain your answer.   (*T*)

9.43

It is possible that the computer system might break down completely.

a Describe what effects this would have on staff and customers.

b Suggest what precautions the building society might take to reduce the problems caused by a breakdown.   (*T*)

What other developments are leading us towards a 'cashless society'?

The most common method of paying workers in this country is still cash, and nearly half the working population are still paid weekly in this way. This is very high compared to other developed countries: the USA has only 1 per cent, and in Canada and West Germany only 5 per cent are paid in cash.

9.44

a Give two disadvantages for the employer of paying workers in cash. (D)

b What are the advantages and disadvantages for the employee in being paid in cash? (D)

There are two other methods of paying workers that are commonly used in this country: payment by cheque and payment direct to the employee's bank account. The latter is normally achieved by electronically transferring funds from the employer's account to the worker's account.

9.45

a What are the advantages for the employer of paying his workers by transferring funds directly to the worker's account?

b What are the disadvantages for the worker in being paid by either cheque or by transfer to his or her account? (D)

How you can spend money that you haven't got!

It has never been easier to spend money. Although cash is still a common way of buying goods, there are disadvantages, especially when it comes to large purchases. Another common method of payment is by using a cheque, accompanied by a banker's card to prove the identity of the holder. This method requires money to be in the bank, but banks and now building societies are prepared to lend money for a wide range of purposes, as long as you have a high enough regular income.

There are other widely used methods of paying for purchases:

- Payment cards such as American Express and Diners Club. With these you are meant to pay the full amount you owe the card company each month.

- Credit cards, such as Barclaycard, Access and those issued by many chains of shops for use in their various branches. With a credit card you are given a credit limit and you can spend up to that amount. If you want to spend over a certain amount at one shop, they have to check that this amount would not exceed your credit limit. Each month you are sent a statement saying how much you must pay back. The amount paid back does not have to be the full amount, though it must be at least a set percentage of how much is owed on the card.

9.46

What are the advantages of using a credit card to purchase an item, compared with:

a cash,

b cheque? (D)

9.47

Credit cards were not widely used before the advent of powerful real-time computer systems.

a Do you think computers have been responsible for so much extra credit being available?

b Is the ease of buying goods on credit a benefit to society?

Explain your answers.

9.48

Describe the type of computer installation which would be needed by a credit card company, the structure of the files required, and some of the processing carried out.

It has been said that we are heading towards a cashless society — one where very little or no cash is used. In this section we have looked very briefly at some of the factors that are leading us in this direction at the time of writing. Changes are occurring very quickly, and it is only the understandable caution of people who deal with money which is holding back much more advanced uses of the technology.

9.49

Describe two methods which could be used to transfer the payments by standing order from the bank account to the building society account.

9.50

Do you think that cash, in the form of

a coins,

b notes,

will have disappeared by the year 2000? Give reasons for your answer. (D)

End-of-chapter Questions

9.51

Many employees prefer to pay their workers monthly, directly to bank accounts.

a What other two methods of paying employees are commonly used?

b What are the advantages to the employer of paying directly to bank accounts?

c What advantages are there for the employees of this method of payment?

d What objections might there be to this change?

9.52

a What are the four most common ways of paying for goods or services in Britain?

b Give three reasons why cash will be used for some time to come.

c What are the advantages of using credit cards to purchase goods?

d What are the advantages of paying regular bills by standing order or direct debit?

e Give three examples of services which could be paid for using direct debit.

9.53

The use of stolen credit cards and ATM cards is a problem for the companies as well as the customers.

a Explain how an ATM system makes it difficult for a criminal to obtain cash using a stolen card.

b Suggest how a credit card company could use their computer system to detect when stolen cards are being used to buy goods.

9.54

The building societies use remote terminals connected to a computer operating in real time.

a Explain what is meant by: i) remote terminals ii) real time operation

b List three other situations in which a real time system is used and explain briefly why real time operation is needed.

9.55

It is possible to purchase certain goods and services by placing credit cards in special machines linked to the credit company's computer.

Give *two* organisations which offer this method of payment, and suggest advantages they and their customers have gained.

9.56

The 1986 Building Societies Act allows building societies to carry out some of the work which previously had to be carried out by other firms, such as unsecured loans, operating cheque accounts and credit cards, building houses, selling houses, surveys, conveyancing, and selling insurance.

a How could the Anglia Building Society use its mainframe computer to help sell houses?

b Would the mainframe computer give them advantages over Mr Adams' system (Ch. 2)?

c For one of the other new activities listed, describe briefly the possible advantages of using a mainframe computer with terminals in every branch.

9.57

The leading banks have ATMs in many of their branches which are on-line to their central computer.

a Explain what is meant by on-line.

b What information would a customer be able to obtain from an ATM?

c How would the bank ensure that no unauthorised person could obtain this information?

Because of the wide variety of transactions which must be processed in batch mode, customer account files are only updated overnight. Withdrawals at ATMs are recorded on a daily transaction file.

d What is meant by a transaction file?

e What fields would be needed in the ATM transaction file?

f What is meant by batch processing?

g Describe briefly, with the aid of a system flowchart, the procedure for updating the main customer account file.

h Can the bank's ATMs be described as operating in real-time? Explain your answer.

The bank must take every precaution to ensure the integrity and security of their data.

i Describe what processing will be carried out using the data input by a customer withdrawing cash at an ATM.

j What events could result in data being lost or corrupted?

k Describe briefly any precautions that the bank could take to ensure that any data which is lost or corrupted can be quickly restored to the master file.

Project Briefs 3

1 A biscuit manufacturer wants to work out the cost of producing different types of biscuit, using the same small range of ingredients but different quantities for each recipe.

Level 1 Design and implement a system which will calculate the cost per biscuit of each recipe, with the user able to update the cost per kg of each ingredient.

Level 2 Extend the system to take into account the cost of energy, as the baking time varies for each recipe.

2 The amount for which you should insure your house for is the cost of rebuilding it rather than what it would cost to buy it now. This cost depends on where it is and how old it is, as well as its size. In one part of the country, for example, the amount for modern houses is £3.20 per square foot of total floor area.

Level 1 Produce a system that will allow the owner of a modern house to input the dimensions of each of the rooms and will output the amount for which s/he should insure the house.

Level 2 Extend the system so that the owner can input the age of the house. Costs are 30 per cent more if it was built before 1945.

Level 3 Extend the system further to allow owners in other parts of the country to find the rebuilding costs. The cost mentioned (£3.20 per square foot) is for Area 1 (Scotland and the South East); Area 2 (Wales and Northern England) is 5 per cent less; Area 3 (everywhere else) is 10 per cent less.

3 Market researchers require a system which will help them to carry out surveys which require standard questions and to analyse the results.

Level 1 Design and implement a system which allows the user to specify three similar products and the computer will print out questionnaires referring to these three products.

Example questionnaire item
On average, how many times a week do you buy:

A Mars,
B Marathon,
C Wispa?

After interviewing people, the user will be able to type in the answers from each questionnaire, and the computer will print out how many people gave particular answers to each question.

Level 1 alternative Produce an electronic questionnaire system, where people being interviewed type their answers into the computer directly for analysis.

Level 2 Extend the system to produce relevant graphs and charts to illustrate the research findings.

Section D

Computers are useful to both large and small companies; we have seen, too, that they have brought major benefits to organisations which serve the community. In this section, we shall look first at uses by individuals, rather than organisations, in homes, schools, and libraries. We shall then look at the use of computers by central government organisations to help provide the services and carry out the policies of the government.

personal computer: work horse or white elephant?

Many homes in Britain now own a microcomputer, and we shall look at how these are used for leisure and administration. Computers are also used in education, of course, for children of nursery age right through to colleges and universities.

Britain has pioneered the most widespread and effective use of computers to aid learning. We shall examine the methods of use and consider some of the effects.

Fig. 10.1

Computers in your home

Fig. 10.2   An Amstrad computer.

10.1

For each of the uses shown in Fig 10.1, explain how the microcomputer is being used to help someone in the home. Indicate in your description what you think are the input data, the output data, and the process being carried out.   (D)

10.2

These are the members of a family who are thinking of buying a microcomputer for the home:

— Darren, aged 4, who goes to nursery school each morning;
— Tony, aged 11, who has just started secondary school and spends most of his spare time on sports;
— Julie, aged 14, who has just started her GCSE courses, sees a lot of her friends and likes listening to music;
— Richard, aged 19, who is unemployed but works part-time clearing an old canal on a community scheme, and plays the guitar in an amateur group;
— Mother, who works part time in a school canteen and looks after Darren;
— Father, who works as a van driver and keeps racing pigeons as a hobby;
— Grandfather, who is a retired steelworker, looks after the large garden and does any repairs in the home.

a   What do you think is the most common use of microcomputers in homes?

b   Which member of the family described above is likely to use a computer most at home? Place the other members of the family in order of likely use of the computer.

c   For each member of the family, describe briefly one possible use of the computer.

d   Describe the hardware and software that you would recommend them to buy.

e   A business must justify the purchase of a computer by reducing the cost of running the business, or by increasing the amount of trade. Do you think that the family described could justify their purchase in a similar way?   (D)

Many homes now have a microcomputer, though few families use them for as many purposes as they could. There are packages available to allow the home micro to act as a small business computer, offering quite cheaply word processors, spreadsheets, information retrieval utilities and accounting systems. These same packages can be used by individuals at home to keep a check on their home finances, write letters to their friends or keep membership records for a voluntary society.

10.3

A small decorating business employs five painters, and the owner visits customers and sends them estimates for the work they need. He will also order materials such as paint and wallpaper.

For the tasks listed below, suggest what kind of small business package would be used for each:

a calculating the wages,

b ordering the materials,

c sending estimates to potential customers,

d working out the payments for VAT and income tax,

e checking for bills that have not been paid,

f planning whether it is worth employing another painter. (*F*)

10.4

Write down five possible uses for small business packages in the home, and for each application state which of the following would be the most suitable:

a word processor,

b spreadsheet,

c information retrieval,

d accounts. (*D*)

How can the computer entertain us?

Computer games are purchased in large numbers; most involve the shooting down of invaders or following a route made dangerous by obstacles and falling objects. Adventure games are also popular, and these require a lot of planning and logical thought to achieve the purpose of the game, rather than just good hand/eye coordination.

Fig. 10.3   Adventure games.

10.5

Which type of game do you prefer — the exciting chase of weird objects around the screen, the carefully thought out search for missing treasure, or a competition against a friend? Analyse the reasons for your choice. (*F*)

10.6

If you do not have a computer of your own, many games are available as dedicated devices and electronic toys.

a Explain what is meant by a *dedicated* device.

b What are the advantages and disadvantages of a dedicated device, compared with software for a home computer? (*D*)

10.7

Some computer games are just electronic versions of card games or board games.

a Write down some examples of this type of game.

b Choose one such game, and explain why the computer version is better for the players — or why it is *not*! (*R*)

Fig. 10.4   A synthesiser.

The use of sound effects and music seems to make games more interesting. Explosions as the invader is destroyed or a victory tune when the game is won help add to the excitement, and the new sounds have everywhere become more and more noticeable in pubs, clubs and amusement arcades.

Microprocessors that are dedicated to sound production can be incorporated into *synthesisers*, devices which produce music and sounds electronically.

Fig. 10.5 *A computer and synthesizers being used by a pop group.*

alien A   alien B

Fig. 10.6 *Alien A and Alien B.*

Synthesisers can imitate the sounds of many different instruments, and they can also produce sounds that no traditional instrument can make.

The synthesiser can be interfaced to a computer system, so that musicians can enter individual tracks of their compositions to be stored in memory. These can then be recalled, mixed and output at any time, so that the music produced by such a system can always be exactly the same.

10.8

Some musicians think that 'real music' can only be produced on traditional instruments, and that using computers to produce music, to process sounds, and to store them, is 'cheating'. Do you agree? Give reasons for your answer. (D)

How are moving graphics produced?

The computer games that prove the most popular use exciting graphics.

Most of them also allow the character to move in a fairly realistic way. This movement is often jerky, and the reason for this is that the movement is achieved by plotting the object on the screen, then blanking it out. A second changed object is then plotted, this object blanked out and the first object replotted a little further along the screen. If the plotting process is fast enough, however, our eyes cannot convey information to our brains in time to notice the change take place, and the movement then looks smooth — just like moving films.

To change this process into a computer program requires algorithms to be designed carefully. Suppose that we wanted to make the aliens move down a screen, we can use two procedures.

ALIENA   plots the first shape
ALIENB   plots the second shape

To produce a program which makes the alien appear to move:

Stage 1: Write out plan

Use two shapes, plot first shape, then second, move down screen and plot first shape again. Keep doing this until the bottom of the screen is reached.

Stage 2: Expand the plan into individual actions. This can be done in further stages, though in this case it is relatively straightforward.

Start at the top of the screen
Repeat the following steps down to the bottom of the screen:
    plot alien A
    blank out shape
    plot alien B in same place
    blank out shape
    change coordinates to next place down

Stage 3: Change this to a formal algorithm using procedures and simple commands. Comments can be added to explain to someone else what is happening with each instruction:

```
up : = 20            :up is variable which counts
                      how far up the screen
                      the alien is plotted,
                      20 is the top of the screen
Repeat until up = 0  :up is 0 at bottom
   aliena             :plots first shape
   plot spaces        :removes first shape
   alienb             :plots second shape
   plot spaces        :removes second shape
   up : = up-1        :next plot position
```

Fig. 10.7 *Algorithm for moving aliens.*

Very often choices have to be made, so conditions are included:

IF laser-position = alien-position THEN zap ELSE aliena

| condition | action if condition true | action if condition false |

Fig. 10.8 Making a decision.

To control the movement of the character the player of the game has to give it instructions such as left, right, or jump. The keyboard can be used, or alternative input devices, such as a joystick or a mouse can be used.

Fig. 10.9

These devices can send signals directly to the program, and usually the signal's value is proportional to the distance the input device has moved.

10.9

a What type of signals have a value which is proportional to the quantity being represented? (*Advice:* look back to the weighing scale in Chapter 4.)

b What type of device will be needed to adapt this signal for computer processing?   (*T*)

10.10

The program could be extended to allow a laser ray to be sent up the screen. If the laser and alien A are at the same position on the screen, then the alien should vanish. The aim of the game is to protect the alien from laser rays.

a Write the algorithm in Fig 10.7, but include the condition (Fig 10.8) to test for collision.

b Extend the program again to allow for an input from a joystick, the value of which will be either left or right. The joystick input should be tested before the alien moves down the screen, and will move the alien in the direction of the joystick movement. Use a new variable **across** which is 25 at the start. If

there is an input the alien will be plotted at a new x position.   (*F*)

10.11

Suppose that you·are asked by a computer games author to list all the features of the perfect computer game, such as the colours used, amount of text, and method of input. In Chapter 13 you will find a list of the features generally required of good software.

a Describe your ideal game.

b The publisher should make sure that the software has certain other features, besides being a good game, before selling it. State at least three such features, and explain why the publisher will require them.   (*R*)

How does the computer store characters?

Many microcomputers allow the user to make up their own graphic characters. They do this by redefining characters already in the computer memory. Every computer has a set of characters available, called its character set.

10.12

a List all the characters that will be needed for ordinary text.

b How many are there?   (*F*)
(*Advice:* upper case (capitals) and lower case letters are different characters)

Each character has a code, normally the ***American Standard Code for Information Interchange***, or ***ASCII*** code.

In this system, the code for A is 65 in decimal, or 01000001 in binary. The letters continue in sequence: B is 66, and so on. There are 128 ASCII codes, but most home micros have 256 different characters available, so there are a lot that can be specially defined.

10.13

Using the ASCII code for the letters of the alphabet:

a Write out the decimal and binary codes for the letters A to E.

b If the code for a is 97, and the lower case letters also continue in sequence, write out the codes for a to e.

c Write an algorithm that will allow *any* letter which is input to be output as the corresponding capital letter, ie. **A** is output **A** and **a** is also output A, and so on.   (*R*)

How can we get these characters displayed on the screen?

Each character is made up of a number of dots (called *pixels*), chosen from a position on a grid. This may be an 8 by 8 grid, for instance:

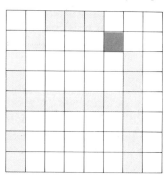

Fig. 10.10   A character built with pixels.

The quality of the image on the screen will depend on how many of these pixels can be fitted across and up the screen. A typical screen size would be 640 by 250. A large number of small pixels will allow fine lines and a detailed image: **high resolution**. A small number of large pixels will give heavy stepped lines and indistinct images: **low resolution**.

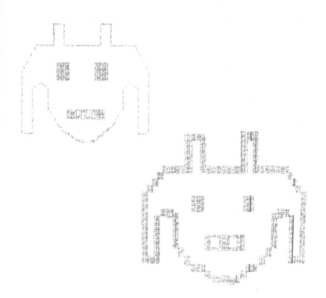

Fig. 10.11   High and low resolution.

To obtain detailed images it is best to use as many pixels as possible, but the problem is that all the data used to describe these pixels has to be stored in memory. Fast processors are also needed to plot graphics rapidly. Unfortunately microcomputers have a limited memory and slow processors, and on these machines relatively large pixels are used.

Storage must also be increased if more colours are needed, and so with limited memory, microcomputer designers and software producers must decide on the facilities that the users are going to want most.

10.14

In a certain computer system, each pixel needs 4 bits of storage, and the screen uses 1024×1000 pixels. How large (in Kbytes) must the graphic memory be?   (R)

10.15

Of the three attributes of computer graphics

— high resolution,

— large range of colours,

— fast plotting,

a designer must choose two. For each of the following uses, state which two would be chosen:

a   drawing bar charts and pie charts for business demonstrations,

b   word processing,

c   arcade-style games.   (T)

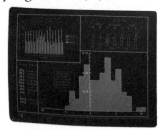

Fig. 10.12   Statistical display.

Fig. 10.13   Graphic display.

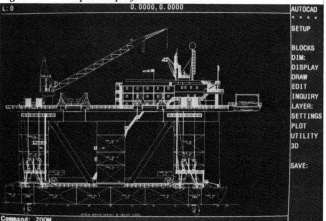

The information needed to display graphics on the screen must often come from photographs and printed diagrams or maps. To do this, a **digitiser** is used.

One type of digitiser is called a **graphics tablet**. This enables a designer to trace out the shape required with a pointer. As the pointer moves over a flat surface, electrical signals are produced which can be converted into coordinates indicating where the pointer is on the surface. This is similar to using a mouse, but with more precise control.

Fig. 10.14 A digitiser transferring an image to a screen.

A digitiser is a device that converts an image to be input into a series of coordinates — numbers that the computer can store and then use to reconstruct the image on the screen. Different digitising devices can input different types of image, including video.

Once the numbers are in the computer's memory, they can be processed using software written for the purpose, so that the image on the screen changes. In this way, pictures can be enlarged, reduced, stretched, rotated, 'cut-and-pasted', and have the colours manipulated to achieve some remarkable effects.

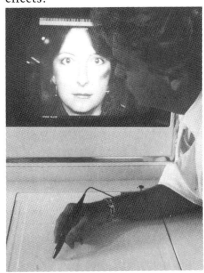

Fig. 10.15
A digitized picture being edited.

The finished picture can be output to a printer, either colour or black and white. These normally work by transferring each pixel from the screen to the printer: this is called a **screen dump**.

Simple dumps of screen images may not be good enough for some purposes, since they reproduce the jagged lines of a low resolution screen. An alternative device, such as a graph plotter (see Fig 6.5 on page 74), will plot on the paper allowing movement in all directions.

10.16

a Draw a simple, small outline picture on squared paper, and label each corner of the design with its coordinates. [Choose a suitable point at the bottom left of the picture to be (0, 0)]

b Multiply every coordinate number by 2, and plot the points you obtain on another piece of squared paper.

c Describe the change to the picture.

d What would have been the effect if you had only multiplied the first coordinate of each pair?

e Using x and y as variable names for the two coordinates in each pair, write an algorithm for a process which makes an image tall and thin.   (R)

The process of producing graphics on a mainframe system is now very sophisticated. Special graphic languages, such as *Tella-Graf*, are available and are close to English language compared with general-purpose high-level languages.

Fig. 10.16 Graphical output.

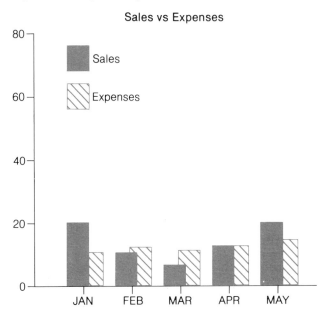

For example, the picture in Fig. 10.16 on page 143 could be produced using this program:

```
GENERATE MONTHLY BAR CHART
TITLE SALE AND EXPENSES
SEQUENCE DATA
SALES 20 10 5 12 20
EXPENSES 10 12 10 12 14
END OF DATA
LEGEND BOX 30 60 60 100 % PLOT
V AXIS MAXIMUM VALUE IS 80
GO
```

The computer will accept these commands and the plotter will produce the required image.

Can we get moving?

One of the most exciting advances in computer graphics is the production of animated films and cartoons. These films are made by photographing many images, each one slightly different from the previous one. Legs and arms will appear to move as the different images are displayed at 20–30 frames a second. A lot of the movement is very similar, so a computer program can readily reproduce these standard movements.

The animation process has many other applications besides producing entertaining films. It can be used to simulate motion to help in the design of products, for instance. The CAD system we met in Chapter 6 could use animation to show how a car body would behave in a simulated crash, hence helping in body design and also in the design of efficient seat belts.

Industrial marketing is a very competitive field, and wide use is made of animation to attempt to give an exciting image of the product. Software is now available for powerful computers which makes the smooth animation of coloured shapes easy to program. Artists can produce fast, smooth graphic sequences, using languages similar to Tellagraf rather than learn difficult assembly codes.

10.17

a Make a list of products that have been marketed using animation.

b Explain why the number of animated sequences on television, in films, and in pop videos has increased greatly during the last few years. (R)

10.18

Write down five possible applications of animation, and suggest the advantages of using animation in each case. (R)

Learning from our mistakes

We have seen that the availability of cheap micros with colour graphics and sound has been very attractive for home entertainment. The fact that computers are *interactive* makes them valuable in helping people to learn, as well as making education more enjoyable. We shall look at industrial training first, and then compare the way computers are used in schools. Staff being trained by companies used to be given lectures and group instruction. The trainers used films, blackboards and slides to make their presentations interesting and easier for the trainees to follow.

Fig. 10.17   Staff training.

It has been found, however, that better results are usually obtained if employees are given tasks, and problems to solve, in a simulation of the job that they will eventually do. They will make mistakes and learn from them, gaining a much better understanding of the way to do the job and an appreciation of the importance of this job to the company. Computer simulations using graphics and animation are often the best way of carrying out this training, prior to trying the real thing. This is especially true concerning safety at work, where the staff have to be prepared for accidents that they hope will never happen.

Fig. 10.18   People working with a computer simulation.

10.19

Airline pilots are trained using flight simulators, which are available for all the major aircraft. Explain the advantages of using simulation for this purpose. (*T*)

As well as simulations, many of the packages used in this process are based on ***programmed learning***. The computer presents some information, and asks the student a question about it. If the answer is correct, then the student progresses to the next piece of work. If the answer is wrong, the student is given the information again. In simple programs, the questions are *multichoice*, for example:

In which order should the nuts be tightened on a wheel:

    A clockwise,
    B anticlockwise,
    C diagonally opposite ones first?

10.20

Explain why it is easier to program the computer to provide multichoice questions, rather than questions where the student has to type in a sentence for the answer. (*D*)

This is only a very simple use of the computer's power, however, and authors of this ***Computer Based Training (CBT)*** material try to program the computer to recognise the mistakes that the student is making, and give more help than the original information provided.

CBT allows training to be completed in a much shorter time, but in order to be effective, the software needed by the computer must be very sophisticated. The software is the major cost in CBT.

As with the complex graphics programs described above, special programming languages (***authoring languages***, such as Microtext) have been developed. These languages are often called ***fourth generation languages*** — they are more like English than standard high-level (third generation) languages, and can be used by people with much less expertise than is needed for conventional programming.

Program generators for data processing applications are also being used increasingly to speed up the production of correct programs. The programmer defines the input, the data structures and the output required, and the fourth-generation language produces the program.

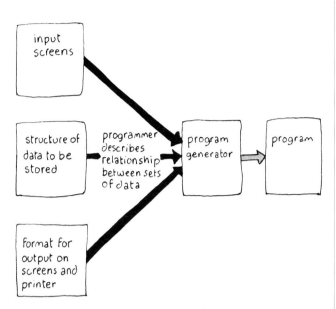

Fig. 10.19 Using a program generator.

10.21

Write an algorithm for a simple programmed learning sequence which presents a student with ten pieces of information in turn, asking a multichoice question before moving on to the next piece of information, and going back to give the information again unless the student gets the right answer.

10.22

Programmed learning is popular with employees, as they can work at their own pace.

a   What do you think are the disadvantages of this method of learning?

b   Explain why these methods are rarely used with children in schools. (*D*)

Can we automate education?

As well as industrial training, the computer is having an impact in schools. Every school in the UK has at least one microcomputer, and the same is true in countries such as France and the USA.

In previous chapters we have seen how many businesses use computers to cut down on paper-work. A school also has a great deal of routine information, normally kept on bits of paper or in card-indexes, such as names and addresses of pupils, class lists, and so on. All of this could be kept in a microcomputer system, using a VDU to extract information from it and a keyboard for input.

10.23

There will be a great deal of information in your school office which could usefully be stored using a microcomputer system. List as many items as you can which you think a computer could help store. (D)

10.24

Suggest what equipment you think the school would use for its office computer system. (D)

It is now quite common for a school to keep its class lists in a computer file, particularly when pupils are taught in several different option groups. Some schools keep their timetable, in coded form, on a disk. This makes it far easier for the Deputy Head, who works out the timetable, as a program can be written to do all the routine cross-checking, making sure that no teacher has two classes at once, a classroom does not get double-booked, and that no class is left untaught!

10.25

The Head Teacher of a school receives a phone call containing an urgent message for Gary, who is in the fourth year.

a If the school has a manual record-keeping system, how would the Head know where to find Gary?

b If the school office had a computer database on all the pupils, as described in this section, how would the Head find Gary? (D)

However, the computer is affecting schools in other ways more directly concerned with education. One use is for testing children's knowledge. As we have seen, the microcomputer can cope easily with tests of the multiple-choice type. It can mark the pupil's answers, because there are only a limited number of decisions to be made; the child would normally only reply A, B, C or D to any question, and this can only be right or wrong — there are no intermediate answers.

10.26

A computer program contains a list of a hundred questions, four answers for each, followed in each case by the letter A B C or D, indicating which answer is correct. The computer has to give a child a test, consisting of ten questions chosen at random from the list, displaying the four answers for each, collecting the child's response and counting the child's score.

Design an algorithm for this program. (R)

10.27

The computerised testing program could be linked to the class record-keeping package, so that at the end of the course the computer could work out a GCSE grade. Do you think this would be a satisfactory method of assessment? Explain your answer.

In many classrooms children use information retrieval packages in order to store and classify information they have collected. The same packages allow them to search the information they have collected in a systematic way, to find out any patterns there may be in their data. These packages are a smaller and less powerful edition of the database management systems used in large mainframe computers.

10.28

Give some examples of databases which children in a school could make use of in their lessons. You could, for example, choose subjects from history, geography, science, or any other lesson. (R)

One advantage of using a computer in this way is that it can be used to link several different subjects together. For example, a class could create a database about the industries in their locality. A chemistry class could use this to find out what chemicals were used in each factory, a geography class could investigate where the raw materials came from and the trade routes used to get them there, an economics class could examine the profitability of each plant, a history class could investigate the development of local industry over the last 200 years, and a mathematics class could use the data for applied statistics work.

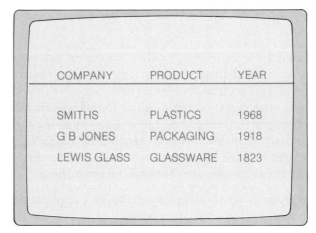

COMPANY	PRODUCT	YEAR
SMITHS	PLASTICS	1968
G B JONES	PACKAGING	1918
LEWIS GLASS	GLASSWARE	1823

Fig. 10.20 The class database.

This is just one form of ***computer assisted learning (CAL)***. There are also programs available for school microcomputers which enable children to use their imagination. Some of these are *simulations*, in which children are asked to put themselves in a different situation, and the computer works out what might happen in that situation and asks the children to make decisions about what to do. One example is a program (called Suburban Fox) in which you pretend to be a fox living in a city suburb, and make decisions on where to find food, how to avoid being run over, and how to survive other hazards.

The point of these programs is to develop the child's decision-making skills and understanding of situations that they cannot experience directly. They are often dressed up as adventure games to make them more interesting, and most of them make much use of colourful graphics displays.

Fig. 10.21 Educational software.

10.29

Do you think programs like Suburban Fox make children learn more effectively than the testing programs described earlier? Give reasons for your answer. (D)

Another type of computer program, designed to help children learn, is aimed at *investigative learning*. This is rather different from the industrial training programs we met earlier. In industry, the computer may often ask the trainee a question which has a right and a wrong answer. In school, teachers are more concerned to encourage the children to ask the questions, and use the computer to explore the consequences. One very popular example of this process is *LOGO*. This is a form of programming language which allows children to start with simple ideas and gradually expand them. In its commonest form, this program accepts commands like 'forward

10' and 'right 90', which cause the computer to move a shape which leaves a trail on the screen or moves a line-drawing device called a 'turtle' around the floor. The child is able to use these to build up procedures for more complex shapes; Fig. 10.22 shows how such a shape may be made more and more complex.

Stage 1: a side

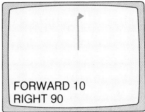

FORWARD 10
RIGHT 90

Stage 2: a square

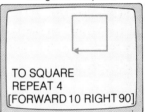

TO SQUARE
REPEAT 4
[FORWARD 10 RIGHT 90]

Stage 3: a pattern which can go on for ever

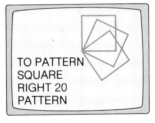

TO PATTERN
SQUARE
RIGHT 20
PATTERN

Fig. 10.22 A LOGO style language.

LOGO is not confined to graphics; in fact, it is a general purpose high-level language, and can even be used to create and interrogate databases.

One disadvantage of using computers in these ways in schools is that, at present, the number of computers in most schools is limited. Pupils cannot gain access to a computer as easily as trainees in industry. Because of the success of simulation and investigation programs in making children think and talk about problems, and the decreasing cost and increasing power of microcomputers, there is likely to be continued expansion in the use of computers in education over the next few years. Pupils will be able to have more control over what they learn in the classroom, and the computer can help the teacher in giving them advice, information, and interesting problems.

And after school . . . ?

Schools are not the only place where learning takes place, however. For most people, the public library is the place where both children and adults go first to find out information they need. People can borrow most of the books, and use others for reference.

All public libraries have a system for keeping track of who has borrowed what books; in the past this involved a card for every borrower and a card for each book, but today many libraries make use of a computerised database system for this purpose.

10.30

Explain how a card system might enable a library to find out, at any time, which books were out on loan, and who has them. (F)

10.31

Computerised libraries often make use of bar codes for data capture: each book has a bar code inside or on the cover, and each user has a bar code on his or her card.

a Explain what the librarian would do when a borrower takes out a book, and what data will be recorded by the computer system.

b What happens when the book is returned?

c What will be the advantages of the system, compared with a card system, for the borrowers, the library staff, and the ratepayers?

d What disadvantages would the computerised system have?

e A big city might have several branch libraries, all accessing the book database stored in a central mainframe computer. Explain, with the aid of diagrams, how the data about books issued and returned would be input to the computer. (R)

A city library, with several branches connected to a central mainframe computer, is able to save money by keeping all the records of the books it owns, and who has borrowed them, in one place. But the existence of a communications network between the branches and the computer has side effects which are very useful to the community.

People wanting to find out about something, such as children doing school projects, or students doing research, often have to search through a library's catalogue to find books about the subject in which they are interested. If all the records are in one computer, a search of the catalogue, using a keyboard and VDU, would reveal any books the library possessed, not just those in the branch the person happened to be in. Thus any library user is able to make use of a much wider collection of books than

is kept in one branch; if he or she finds out about a book which might be of use to them, the same communications network can be used to send a message, via electronic mail, to another branch, reserving the book, in far less time than the post would take. If several libraries in different cities were linked in this way, it would be possible for library users to obtain information from books which could be anywhere in the country.

10.32

Suppose a library offered users the ability to search its catalogue, held in a central computer, from any branch. What peripherals would you expect to find in the branch for this purpose? Give reasons for your choices. (F)

The library's communications network could be used for another purpose, too. Traditionally, libraries have contained a reference section, where people could refer to information, such as railway time-tables, voter's lists, brochures of forthcoming theatre productions, and so on.

Such information does not have to be kept in written form, for it is constantly changing. In many modern libraries, the computer communications network can also be used to display information sent from remote computer databases; this avoids the need to keep expensive reference books which have to be replaced every month or two.

Electronic information services are now becoming more widely available through libraries, and we shall look at these in detail in Chapter 11.

10.33

Give some more examples of information you would expect to find in a library's reference section, either of local or national importance. Choose one of these and explain how a computer system could help people to access the information. (R)

10.34

In chapters 7 and 8 you saw configuration diagrams which showed the hardware used by two different mainframe computer systems. Using the information in this chapter, construct a similar diagram showing the hardware used by the library system. (*Advice:* include the central computer, two or three branches each containing the hardware needed for issuing books and searching for information, and the necessary communications hardware.) (R)

End-of-chapter Questions

10.35

a How many pixels are there on the micro-computer system which you use?

b Why is a high-resolution system needed for CAD?

10.36

The ASCII codes for the upper case letters are from 65 to 90. The word HELLO is a password that is checked by a program that totals all the ASCII codes. If the total is correct then entry to the system is allowed.

a Write out the codes for the word HELLO.

b What is the total of the codes for these letters?

c Do you think that this is a good way of testing passwords for access to a computer system? Explain your answer.

10.37

On a microcomputer the number of pixels that can be used to display graphic images is limited.

a Explain why small computers cannot display as many pixels as a powerful mainframe computer.

b If each pixel is represented by 3 bits that recorded its colour, how many different colours could be used?

c If one extra bit were to be used for colour, how many colours could then be displayed?

d With four bits per pixel and a screen size of 1000 × 600 pixels, how large would the graphic memory be?

10.38

Chapter 7 described a large manufacturing company. Suppose that they are thinking of buying a graphics package from a software house to run on their mainframe computer at head office. It would be accessed from high resolution terminals in several offices around the building.

a Suggest how this company could make use of computer graphics in their business.

b What facilities do you think they would look for in the package they purchase?

c State, with reasons, what other hardware they would need to take advantage of these facilities.

10.39

The ASCII code for the ESCAPE key is 27, and that for the RETURN key is 13. A procedure is required that will check all input letters and if RETURN is pressed then input is complete. If ESCAPE is pressed then the input is started again from the beginning.

10.40

Microcomputers can be used in secondary schools to help with pupils' learning about various subjects, using simulations, information retrieval, graphics, and so on. They can also be used to keep records of pupils' achievements in school, including examination results.

a Choose one type of software package, and explain how it could be used in Careers lessons.

b A local authority keeps records on a mainframe system of all people between the ages of 16 and 18 who are college students, on YTS schemes, or looking for work. Explain how the schools' pupil records could be used in this system.

Using special television sets, or microcomputers, it is now possible for the general public to have access to large amounts of information stored on remote computers. In this chapter we will examine some aspects of the use of computers in providing information and communication services, by examining videotex and interactive video systems.

Videotex services

Fig. 11.1

Videotex is the name given to systems which allow text to be transmitted and then displayed on screens. There are two main types of videotex systems: *viewdata* and *teletext*. *Viewdata* systems usually operate over a telephone network, and are two-way systems, capable of both receiving and sending messages. The **Prestel** system operated by British Telecom is one example of viewdata. *Teletext* is broadcast along with normal television pictures and is a 'receive-only' service. Ceefax (operated by the BBC) and Oracle (operated by ITV) are examples of teletext systems.

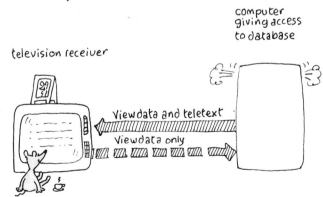

Fig. 11.2   *Videotext systems: Viewdata and Teletext.*

What is teletext?

Teletext transforms your television into an information store very much like a newspaper or a magazine, allowing you to read the latest news, sports results, weather reports, etc, and to select from a lot more information at any time the television company is transmitting, even if only the test card is on the screen.

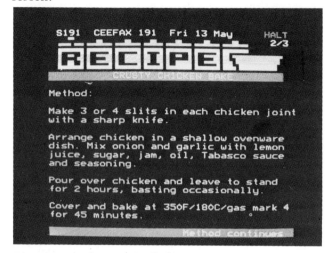

Fig. 11.3   *A teletext screen display.*

11.1

What advantages and disadvantages has a teletext system compared with a newspaper for finding out the latest news?   (D)

The television companies in Britain transmit their pictures onto our TV screens using a 625-line display. The signal being transmitted controls the intensity of beams which light up spots of three different colours on the screen. The beams cover the 625 lines so quickly that your eye cannot see them being formed.

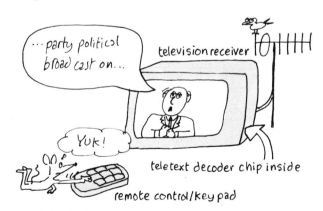

Fig. 11.4   *A teletext system.*

Not all of these lines are used by the normal television picture, however. Teletext in the UK makes use of this fact by using four of these unused lines for sending coded information. Everybody with a television set receives this information in the same way as they receive such programs as 'News at Ten'. However, only people with special teletext sets can access the information being transmitted. A teletext set is fitted with a special decoder that translates the information and then displays it across the whole screen when requested.

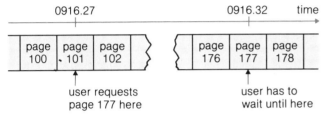

Fig. 11.5 *Why you wait for teletext.*

The viewer uses a special keypad to change from normal TV mode to teletext and then selects the page he wishes to see.

BBC1 and BBC2 both carry Ceefax whilst ITV and Channel 4 both carry Oracle, so there are actually four 'magazines'. Each magazine has about 100 *pages* of information. The pages are transmitted rapidly in sequence, repeating from the beginning again as soon as the end is reached. When a viewer selects a page, it does not take long for the transmission cycle to reach this page and for the decoder to display it.

Fig. 11.6 *A teletext keypad.*

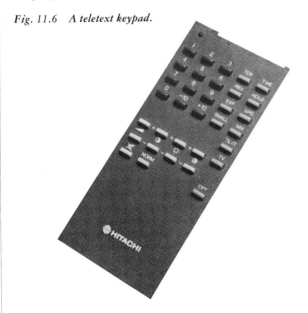

Some pages may contain more than one *frame*, or screen full of information. These frames automatically cycle, with each frame remaining on the screen for about 30 seconds.

The contents of the magazines vary, but generally include news, entertainment guides, travel and business information, weather, consumer advice, competitions and even jokes. Many of the pages, such as the news and sports pages, are continuously updated during the day, thus giving a very up-to-date service.

11.2
Explain the difference between a frame and a page when applied to a teletext system.   (*T*)

11.3
Some of the types of information on Oracle and Ceefax are listed above.

a Find a page containing information which does not fall into any of the categories listed.

b What information would you like to see on Ceefax or Oracle that is not already available?

c Why do you think the information that you would like to see is not available?   (*R*)

How do you access Ceefax or Oracle?

Provided that the station broadcasting the magazine you wish to access is on the air and you have the appropriate hardware, access is simple compared with most large computer systems. Normally a hand-held controller is used, consisting of a numeric keypad and various other function keys.

Fig. 11.7 *Choosing a page.*

Firstly, you select the station carrying the magazine you wish to access. Next, you switch to text mode by pressing the appropriate button. Normally you then call up the main index by pressing the appropriate 3 keys (100 for BBC1 or ITV, 200 for BBC2 and 400 for Channel 4). From here you may then select either the topic that interests you or possibly the full alphabetic index. You need to press just three digits on the keypad and wait until the information is displayed. The page displayed may contain more options, and you will need to narrow down your choice further and key another page number to obtain precisely what you want.

Fig. 11.8 *The main menu on Ceefax.*

One major innovation brought about by the introduction of teletext systems was the provision of sub-titles over television programmes for the three million people in the UK who have hearing problems. This sub-titling service is limited but gradually increasing.

Fig. 11.9 *Sub-titles for the deaf on teletext.*

Teletext systems are free to the user other than the cost of the special television receiver and the normal TV licence fee. However, the amount and types of information that can be transmitted are limited.

11.4

A teletext keypad (see Fig. 11.6) can usually be used for purposes other than selecting pages of text for viewing.

a   What can the viewer use the numbered keys for?

b   What other function keys are normally on the pad?   (R)

11.5

a   What is the difference in price between a standard TV and a similar type of model that can receive teletext?

b   Explain why a teletext set is more expensive. (R)

11.6

Write an algorithm explaining how to find as much information as possible on 'Spanish holidays'.   (R)

11.7

a   What are the advantages and disadvantages of the alphabetic index, compared with menu pages?

b   Explain why you think The TV Times gives a printed alphabetic index to Oracle each week.   (R)

What are the limitations of a teletext system?

The teletext screen display is limited to a 40 column, 24-line display. This means a maximum of 40 characters can be displayed on any one line, and that only 24 lines of text can be displayed at a time. Only 8 colours — black, red, green, blue, yellow, cyan, magenta and white, are used. Graphics are very limited on the British system due to the way in which the characters that make up a picture are transmitted, so pictures are made from blocks. The Telidon teletext system used in the USA and Canada allows lines and curves to be drawn.

11.8

Teletext codes can change two other features of any character, as well as colour. What are these?   (R)

Teletext information is transmitted serially — over and over again, and this causes problems relating to both the time taken to access a particular page and the amount of information that can be transmitted over a teletext system. The more information that is transmitted, the longer the page you require will take to appear, even though the transmission speed is very high, approaching seven million bits per second, which gives just over 4 pages of information every second.

There are several ways in which access time is reduced. The first method is to use more of the lines that are not used to carry the television picture. If we double the number of lines we can either halve the access time or double the amount of information available. The second technique depends on the information. If pages of information are designed to contain blank rows (a row containing no information) then it is not essential to transmit them.

Finally, pages that are accessed most frequently, such as the index pages, can be transmitted in more than one position in the cycle, thus reducing access time to these more frequently required pages.

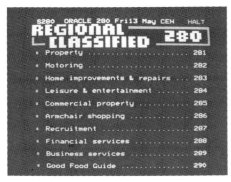

Fig. 11.10 A typical teletext screen display showing blank lines.

11.9

a Choose some pages to access on a teletext system and time how long it takes for them to appear. Calculate the average.

b Make a list of the frames that you would repeat on a teletext system to reduce access time. (*F*)

What is viewdata?

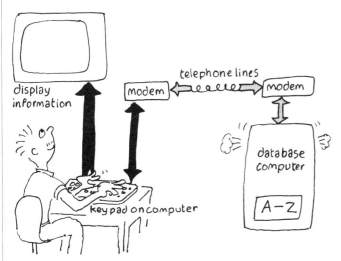

Fig. 11.11 A Viewdata system.

Viewdata is an interactive information technique which uses cable links (usually the telephone network). A viewdata system allows the user with a suitable terminal and a modem to interrogate a remote computer and also to send messages to it.

11.10

a Explain what is meant by *interactive* use of a computer.

b Explain what is meant by interrogating a computer system. (*T*)

In the UK the viewdata system available to the public is Prestel, run by British Telecom. Prestel links a number of computers around the country, and once a user has paid a fixed subscription, access to the system costs the same as a local telephone call. Unlike teletext, you have to pay for *access* to Prestel during the working day. You must also pay extra (a *frame charge*) for access to some of the pages, such as up-to-date Stock Exchange information.

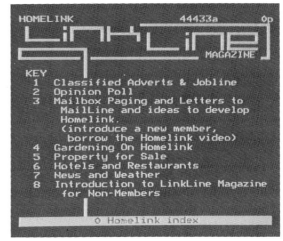

Fig. 11.12 A typical menu page on Prestel.

The information on Prestel is provided by over 500 organisations, known as Information Providers, or IP's. There are at present 330 000 pages of information which can be accessed by anyone with a Prestel set. A page holds about 90 words in a 40 column, 24 line format, and all the pages form a vast database stored on a large number of fixed magnetic disks which are constantly on-line. There are a number of linked computers around the country carrying out the same job, and the popular pages are stored on each system. Normally, a Prestel user will automatically be connected to a local computer. If she wants some specialised information, or if the local system is closed down, then she will automatically be connected to another computer.

As well as collecting requests from users, retrieving the pages from disk, and sending them down the appropriate phone line, the central computer also has to keep records of costs, and send bills regularly to customers for their subscriptions, access charges and frame charges.

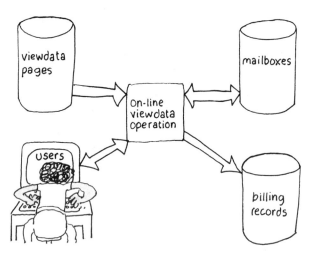

Fig. 11.13   Operations at a Viewdata central computer.

Prestel can be used to obtain very similar information to that provided by the teletext services. In addition, as the system is interactive, you can do such things as order shopping, request holiday brochures, play games, send messages to other users of the system, and even access other computer systems.

11.11

Assuming that the phone call and computer access both last for one minute, find the cost of accessing a 'free' page of Prestel

a   during the morning

b   during the evening.   (R)

11.12

Many of the pages on Prestel have frame charges.

a   List some types of information which carry a frame charge.

b   Choose one of the types of information you have listed, and explain why certain users of Prestel are prepared to pay for access to the information.   (R)

11.13

a   Make a list of some major IP's on Prestel.

b   Choose one of these IP's, and suggest what benefits they gain by using Prestel compared with broadcasting (TV and Radio) or printed media, such as newspapers.   (R)

11.14

Fig. 11.13 shows a system diagram for the on-line operation of a viewdata system. Draw a system diagram for the batch processing operation which produces bills, using the 'Billing records' file.

How do you access a viewdata system?

You must first connect your viewdata terminal or microcomputer to the central computer, and this can be done in a number of ways. For example, if the link is through the telephone network, it is possible on some terminals to press just one key and the viewdata terminal automatically dials the appropriate code and connects to the computer.

Fig. 11.14   A numeric Viewdata keypad and terminal.

Fig. 11.15   An alphanumeric Viewdata keypad.

Once you are linked to the computer, you can access the pages of information by typing the page number required. Page numbers are often contained in printed directories published by the viewdata operator or the information providers. Alternatively you can search the information indexes (menus) by keying in the numbers as prompted. Access to a page appears to be virtually instantaneous, but each page takes time to build up — about 8 seconds if the page contains no blank lines and the full line length is used. Computer data is transmitted at 1200 bits per second (*baud*) and user data is sent to the computer at 75 baud.

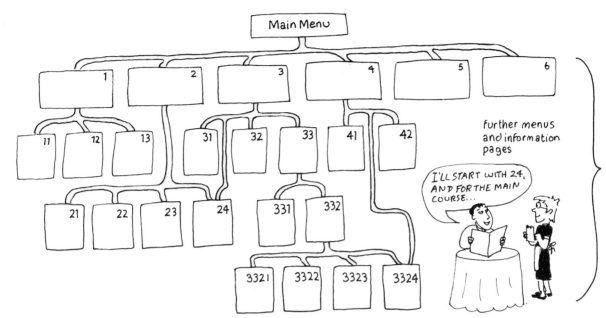

Fig. 11.16   Tree-structure menus. There will often be more than one route to a page of information.

11.15

The transmission rate of Prestel is far slower than teletext systems. However, access to pages is faster and the amount of information stored is much greater.

a   Explain why a user of Prestel does not have to wait as long for the required page as a user of Ceefax.

b   Explain why the Prestel database can be so much larger than the Ceefax database.   *(D)*

Tree structures are normally used to organise the information stored in viewdata systems. You are offered a menu of routes on a page, and you move on to another page by pressing a single digit. You continue to make choices from menu pages until you locate the required information.

11.16

Local viewdata systems are available for most micro-computers. These software packages allow users to create and store pages of their own design, and specify the routes from each menu page. The pages can then be accessed by other users of the computer, or by other network terminals.

a   Describe how such a system could be used by Mr Adams, the Estate Agent in Chapter 2.

b   What advantages does the viewdata system have compared with databases having the usual structure of records and fields?

c   What disadvantages would there be for Mr Adams, if he changed his House file to a local viewdata system?

d   What advantages and disadvantages would the local system have, compared with a link to a full viewdata system on a remote computer?   *(D)*

You may not always have to look through pages and pages of menus or thumb through a directory if you know what sort of information you are looking for. If, for instance, you are thinking of buying a car, and wish to find reports on different makes, then you can use a *keyword search* facility. Instead of typing in a page number, such as *423567, you could type in *CAR.

11.17

Describe the advantages of a keyword search facility compared with: *a* a directory, *b* tree-structured menus.   *(D)*

The transmission of data via a telephone line can often lead to data being corrupted. The fact that viewdata communication is two-way enables errors to be eliminated. When a sequence of codes has been transmitted, a futher code (called a *check-sum*) is calculated from the total of the codes making up the page and sent to the receiving system. The check-sum calculation is then repeated for the sequence of codes *received*, and if the answer is different from the check-sum *sent*, then the receiving system requests the computer to transmit the page again. This procedure checks the *integrity* of the data transmitted.

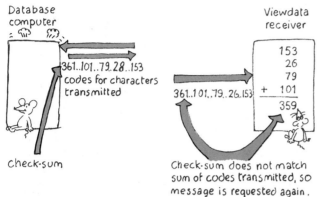

Fig. 11.17 *A check sum is used to check the integrity of the transmitted data.*

How are pages created?

At the Prestel headquarters, several operators devote their time to creating new pages and updating existing ones. There is another piece of software, not available to the user, called an *editor*. A page designer takes the IP's requirements, and plots out on squared paper the precise position and colour of letters and shapes chosen to show the information clearly and attractively.

Fig. 11.18 *An operator using a Prestel editor.*

Using the normal keyboard, together with combinations of function keys, the operator builds up the letters and blocks of teletext graphic characters to produce the complete frame. This is not the end of the job, however; the number of the page which will be displayed next must be typed in. If the page has options for the user to choose from, then the operator must list all the options and the page to be displayed next for each one: this is called *routeing*.

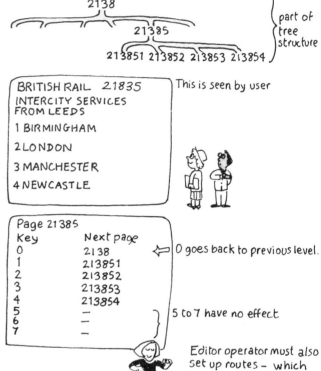

Fig. 11.19 *Routeing Prestel pages.*

What viewdata services are available?

We have already discussed briefly the information retrieval aspect of viewdata systems. There are other information services that are available in the UK through the use of large, remote computer systems. Many of these are specific to business users, but there are some important ones designed for education and home users.

Prestel 'Gateway' allows the user to access, via the viewdata system, a remote computer that is not really part of the viewdata system. This has advantages compared to giving the user direct access, by saving some of the costs of both hardware and telecommunications charges.

'Home banking', for instance, is one of many Gateway applications currently available on Prestel. A bank customer becomes a Prestel user and logs into Prestel in the usual manner. He can then access a particular page which links him to the bank's computer. The customer must then enter a code to proceed any further. Once this security check is passed, the customer can obtain details of his account, transfer funds from one account to another, and pay bills.

11.18

a Suggest some of the benefits to building society investors if their society's computer system was available through a Prestel terminal.

b Describe briefly one use of Gateway other than those given above. (*R*)

11.19

Many users of Prestel are businesses which have private pages on the system, not accessible outside the company. What advantage do they gain from using Prestel, compared with their own computer system? (*D*)

What is Electronic Mail?

The major feature of a viewdata system that distinguishes it from a teletext system is the interactive facility, which allows the user to send information *back* to the information provider or to another user of the system.

We have already referred to *electronic mail*. This is a technique for sending messages, addressed to particular people. The receiver can read the message immediately if he is connected on-line, or the message will be stored until the receiver logs on.

A simple form of electronic mail is the use of a response frame. Using a response frame the user can order books, magazines or groceries, book holidays, flights, hotel accommodation or theatre tickets; all by simply keying answers to questions displayed on the screen by the information provider. The order is then received by the information provider next time he accesses the system.

The user-to-user message service available on Prestel is called Prestel Mailbox. This facility allows one user to type in a message to another user; the message is addressed by typing in the user number of the person to whom the message is to go. The r. time the person to whom the message is sent logs into the system, the message will be displayed on the screen automatically.

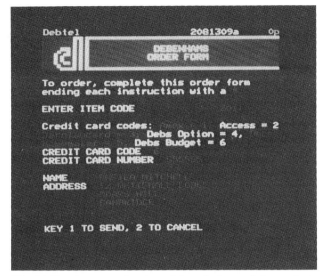

Fig. 11.20   A response frame used for ordering goods (or services).

There are other systems for electronic mail available which are not restricted to viewdata format, and these have more facilities for handling the messages.

Telecom Gold is a British Telecom service that is part of a world-wide electronic mail network. When a person registers, they are given a *mailbox identity code*, which is like a phone number or address. Messages can be sent to this address from anywhere in the world and normally arrive in under three minutes. Messages are not limited in length and copies can be sent to a number of different addresses. One of the many facilities is the ability of the system to notify the sender when the message has been read by the person to whom it was sent.

The Times Network for Schools (TTNS) is based on Telecom Gold and is dedicated to education. TTNS is an electronic mail system with a central database built up from educational and outside resources. Schools usage is subsidised by sponsors from commercial companies. The system is designed so that pupils can enter competitions, send and receive software, find out about local and national events of interest, and send messages to other schools as well as carry out research for projects.

11.20

Electronic mail is a new medium for communication.

a List other methods of communication which carry messages between people over long distances.

b Choose one of the methods you have listed in (a), and describe the advantages and disadvantages of electronic mail for business users. (*D*)

11.21

a Describe how a viewdata system with response frames could be used to order groceries and other goods which can be delivered to your home.

b Which sections of the community could benefit most from this electronic shopping service?

c Do you think that electronic shopping will lead to the disappearance of supermarkets, or of the corner shop? Give reasons for your opinion.

Telesoftware is a term used to describe the storage and transmission of computer programs. Most microcomputers can be equipped to *download* data from remote computers, so that they can receive and store programs via telesoftware. A downloading package generally consists of a modem, communications software and a wire to connect the modem and the micro. In most cases the software and documentation received are stored to disk (or tape) for later use. The documentation is transmitted as a text file (ASCII characters only) which the user can then print from his own micro.

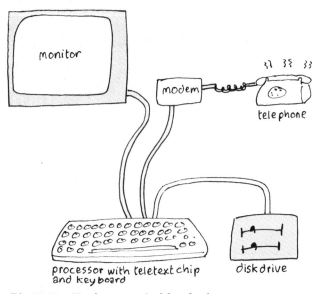

Fig. 11.21   Hardware required for telesoftware.

11.22

What are the advantages and disadvantages of obtaining software and documentation via telesoftware, compared with purchase from a dealer?   (*D*)

11.23

Software is expensive to produce, and commercial publishers have to charge enough to make a profit. Explain how a software house which sells through telesoftware obtains payment from customers. (*R*)

11.24

The error checking procedures are important for many of the uses of viewdata and electronic mail.

a Explain how errors can be eliminated from frames received.

b Give two uses of viewdata which rely on the data received being absolutely accurate.   (*T*)

11.25

There are many other specialised viewdata services available including:

a MEGLINK, which is a system run by the Midlands Examining Group to accept GCSE entries direct from schools;

b Blaise-Line, which carries details of books held by the British Library;

c Pergamon Infoline, which covers areas such as patents, materials technology, standards, trademarks, health and safety;

d Hostess, which contains a database detailing which computers have databases on particular topics.

Choose one of these services, or any other that you know of, and explain how it is used by the customers and how they benefit from the service. (*R*)

Optical storage

We have examined some ways in which access to information has been increased or made easier by the growth of videotex systems. As yet there is no widely available system that gives the public access to high resolution pictures, because the amount of data is just too great. We shall now look at methods of storing data that enable ordinary microcomputers to retrieve video pictures ('stills' or moving films) and vast amounts of data in text format.

Interactive video (IV) attempts to solve the problem on a smaller scale. IV is a system of linking a microcomputer to a video player so that the user can control access to the video using a software package. It uses an optical system of storage (a laser beam is shone onto the disc and detects tiny marks on the surface) rather than magnetic storage.

Many current interactive video systems are based on videotape, but these are frustrating to use as the time taken to access a particular frame (picture) can be great. Videodiscs could overcome this problem,

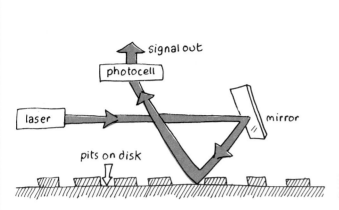

Fig. 11.22   *Reading an optical disc.*

Fig. 11.23   *An interactive video system.*

but at present they suffer from the cost of producing a videodisc and the fact that the information stored on the disc cannot be changed.

11.26

Normal magnetic storage media for computers have the same disadvantages as video systems: tape is slow in finding the information required, and disk systems (hard and floppy) are more expensive for the same amount of storage. There is a big difference in use between a magnetic disk and a videodisc, however, and this has led to magnetic disks becoming a very popular storage medium.

a   Explain briefly why a system using tape is slow to find a particular item of data.

b   How does a magnetic disk system overcome this problem?

c   What is the advantage of magnetic disks over videodiscs that has made them so popular?   (D)

How has interactive video been used?

We have seen in Chapter 10 how the combination of moving pictures and computer control can be harnessed to create training material. Other uses are now being sought for this type of technology which will be of benefit to community interests and learning.

The BBC Domesday Project set out to construct a database on life in Britain in the 1980s. The results of the Project are to be found on two videodisks which provide the first major example of interactive video in use on a wide scale. The two disks are known as 'The Community Disc' and 'The National Disc.'

The Community Disc carries all the national survey information which is linked to 24 000 Ordnance Survey maps (at four different scales), street maps,

aerial and satellite photos which cover the whole of Britain. In total The Community Disc contains 15 000 screen pages of text, 20 000 photographs, 500 satellite and 900 aerial photographs together with text for every 30 × 40 km 'block' of the UK.

Fig. 11.24   *The National Disc.*

Fig. 11.25   *The Community Disc.*

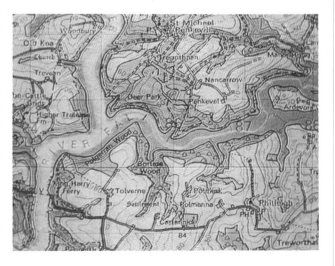

11.27

a Explain briefly some of the ways information was collected for the community disc.

b Describe how the use of the computer makes the retrieval of selected information easier. (*R*)

The National Disc contains, for example:

- articles and essays,

- photographs from private and public collections (22 000 photos),

- public records, such as Parliamentary proceedings and the latest census data,

- 60 minutes of film (with sound),

- massive amounts of data divided into four sections:
    culture (eg English Tourist Board statistics, TV trends and leisure surveys),
    the economy (eg economic data, family expenditure survey, transport),
    the environment (eg energy resources, pollution, wild life),
    society (eg attitudes to all aspects of life, crime survey, social trends).

This is a massive amount of information, and the BBC estimates that it would take seven years to explore the two videodiscs if you were to dedicate 40 hours a week to the task. If it were just to store text, a disc could hold the equivalent of the Encyclopaedia Britannica, and still have 30 000 pages to spare!

How are the discs accessed?

The discs can be interrogated by using the microcomputer's keyboard and/or a mouse. You can retrieve information from The Community Disc by typing in either one of a quarter of a million place names, or a grid reference, or one of 7000 keywords, or by using the mouse to point to places on the maps. At any particular spot, you can choose to see a more detailed map or a set of three still photographs representing the area with brief descriptions — provided someone has put the information onto the disc in the first place.

11.28

a What is meant by a keyword?

b What words would you expect to find used as keywords on a community database such as the Domesday Project?

c What types of word would you expect never to be included in a keyword list? (*T*)

You can also carry out a 'surrogate walk' around various places — a small town, or different types of typical house. Thousands of still photos taken in all directions from different positions are stored on the disk, and as you use the mouse to specify which direction to go in, the computer retrieves the correct picture from the disk and displays it on the screen. This process is so quick that you can move around in 'real time' and feel that you are actually visiting the place. The idea of a walk is used again in the Domesday Gallery — a set of exhibitions on topics such as Royal Heritage, Arts and Craft, Society, Daily Life, and Sport. This also uses thousands of still photos, and they are organised for access using the same sort of tree-structured menu system as is used in viewdata. The user selects options by pointing to pictures on the screen.

11.29

Explain how the idea of a surrogate walk could be used in training members of the emergency services, such as firemen. (*D*)

11.30

What are the advantages of interactive video in education and training, compared with:

a normal video cassette recorders,

b microcomputers with software for text and computer graphics? (*D*)

End-of-chapter Questions

11.31

Ceefax and Oracle are both examples of teletext systems.

a Who broadcasts Ceefax and Oracle?

b What hardware does a user require to access a teletext system?

c Explain how you find a particular item of information stored on a teletext system if you do not know its page number but know it is on Ceefax.

d What limits the amount of information that can be stored on a teletext system?

11.32

Ceefax and Oracle provide general consumer information, such as the typical price of different vegetables. Explain why it is not possible to order your fruit and vegetables through teletext systems.

11.33

Viewdata systems like Prestel are similar in some ways to teletext systems.

a What additional equipment is required for a viewdata system compared with a teletext system?

b How does the user access a viewdata system?

c What three running charges does the user have to pay with Prestel?

d Give two advantages that Prestel has when compared with a teletext system.

11.34

Prestel has a facility called Gateway.

a Explain briefly what is meant by Gateway.

b What possible advantages does the use of Gateway offer to a business compared with installing its own private viewdata system?

c Discuss briefly the problem of security of information posed by Gateway usage.

11.35

Interactive video is only one application of optical disks.

a What are the advantages of using optical disks as a form of computer backing store?

b What are the disadvantages of using optical disks as a form of computer backing store?

c Explain briefly some of the uses that could be made of the Domesday project discs.

d List briefly some other applications that you feel are appropriate for interactive video.

11.36

The use of viewdata systems to connect home computers to other computers by telephone lines could well change our lives greatly, both in work patterns and in the way we spend our non-working lives. Give five examples of how life might change and for each example explain briefly an advantage and a disadvantage of this change.

11.37

The Yellow Pages information gives the phone numbers of a large number of companies in a telephone subscriber's local area. The businesses are classified under headings such as 'Video Libraries', 'Estate Agents', and 'Central Heating Services — Domestic'. British Telecom, who publish the information, have decided to offer a viewdata service.

a What advantages will this give consumers in homes and businesses, compared with the book that they have now?

b Explain the advantages for the user of viewdata format, rather than a record-structured file.

c Describe how a user would find the phone numbers of local video libraries, using the viewdata system.

d Could the same system be used for finding the phone numbers of private subscribers? Explain your answer.

will we need an umbrella tomorrow?

Most of the chapters so far have dealt with data processing applications. In these jobs, the computer does a lot of work, but most of it is concerned with very simple arithmetic. The rest of the computer's work in these applications is concerned with storing information, moving it from place to place or sorting it, and retrieving it.

However, the computer was born as a high-powered calculating machine, as you will see in Chapter 14, and there are still applications which make use of its enormous power to carry out complex calculations. In this chapter we will look briefly at a few tasks which make use of this power.

Weather forecasting

The accuracy of the weather forecast has, of course, a more important purpose than simply telling us whether to carry an umbrella or not. Farmers need to know what the weather will do during harvesting operations; managers of North Sea oil rigs need to know whether they can operate in safety or need to shut down; airline pilots need to know whether the wind will help or hinder their journey, which determines how much fuel they must take on board.

12.1

Write down any other people who you think will need to know the weather in advance. (F)

The essential facts for weather forecasters are wind direction and speed, and air pressure. Wind is no more than movement of air; so if you know what a mass of air is doing and where it is going, you know what the weather will be like when it gets there. The complication is that the air masses are not very obliging; air currents keep colliding with each other and forcing each other up and down or round and round (these form the *fronts* you see on the charts).

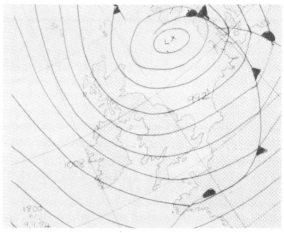

Fig. 12.1   An isobar chart.

The Meteorological Office in fact uses a computer database which treats the British Isles (and most of Europe as well) as a grid of squares. At each corner of every square in this grid, the computer stores the wind speed and direction, temperature, humidity (amount of moisture in the air) and pressure. This set of data is collected at 15 different altitudes, for the weather is very different above the clouds.

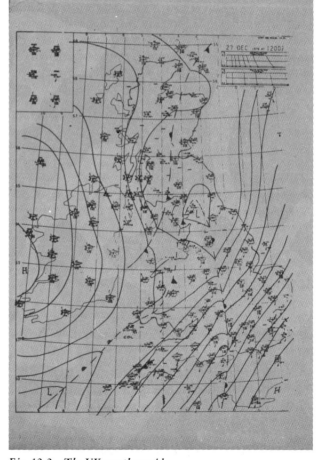

Fig. 12.2   The UK weather grid.

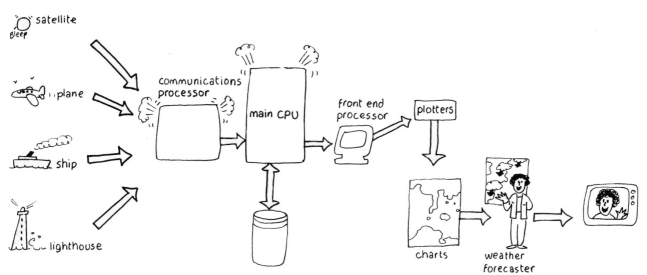

Fig. 12.3   Producing the weather forecast.

12.2

Suppose the map covers an area 2000 km square and is made up of squares measuring 20 km by 20 km. Data stored at each point on the grid consists of four numbers: wind speed, wind direction, temperature, humidity. Each value is recorded at 15 different altitudes. In addition the ground level data at each point includes pressure.

a   How many points make up this grid?   (A 'point' being a corner of one of the grid squares.)

b   How many numbers are stored in the database for each point of the grid?

c   How many numbers make up the database?

d   If each number takes four bytes of data to store, how big is this database (in megabytes)?   (*F*)

Although this is a lot of data, it only gives a snapshot of the weather at a particular moment. As we shall see shortly, it is only a small part of the data handled by the computer.

Where does all this data come from?

All this data is constantly being collected from a number of different sources. Some data arrives automatically from satellites. Other data comes from weather balloons, which are programmed to broadcast their measurements of wind speed, and so on, at certain times each day. Reports are also sent in by lighthouse keepers, coastguards, pilots, and many other people, who keep an eye on the weather in their locality and inform the Meteorological Office. Because this is such a large amount of data, a separate communications processor is used to sort it all out and pass it to the CPU of the main computer.

12.3

Explain what is meant by a communications processor.   (*T*)

The main processor at the Meteorological Office is in fact one of the world's most powerful computers — a Control Data Cyber 205, one of the *supercomputers* you will meet in Chapter 14. Its main job is to take all this weather data and work out where the various air masses will be in a few minutes' time. The program which does this is based on the principle of looking for similar patterns in the past, and assuming that similar events will happen this time. The results, which are in exactly the same format as the data input, are stored on disk.

When it has done this, the computer then takes its predictions as a new starting point, and repeats the whole exercise; this is repeated enough times to cover the expected weather for the next two or three days.

Unlike most of the large systems you have met so far, the Cyber runs somewhat faster than real time — if it merely kept pace with the weather it would not be much use! In fact, the Cyber manages to run through a day and a half of 'weather' in six minutes.

As well as storing its results on disk, the processor also sends them to another computer, which in turn sends them to a graph plotter which produces the charts which you see on television and in newspapers. These show isobars (lines of equal pressure, as on Fig. 12.1), and sometimes also isotherms (lines of equal temperature). This computer, rather smaller than the main one, is known as a ***front-end processor***.

Explain why the graphs are not produced directly by the main processor.   (F)

The computers do not actually *produce* the weather forecast, however. The staff of the Meteorological Office do this, by looking at the charts and deciding from experience what kind of pattern is emerging. The computer is merely a powerful aid which enables them to concentrate on the pattern of weather without having to do thousands of tedious calculations.

When the meteorologists have produced a forecast, the communications processors come into use again. This time, their job is to send the forecast details to pilots, ships' captains, and the thousands of people who depend on accurate forecasts for their livelihoods — not forgetting the television stations, who pass on the forecaster's work to the rest of us.

Fig. 12.4   *A television weather forecaster.*

Virtually every technique you have met in the previous chapters is involved in weather forecasting: powerful processors, front-end processors, automatic data entry from analogue sensors, communications systems, graphics displays. Without all these, our knowledge of the weather would be much less reliable.

A small step for man — a giant leap for computers

Almost certainly the most ambitious scientific project ever undertaken was the Apollo project launched by President John F Kennedy in 1962. The object was to send a man to the Moon within the decade. It succeeded when Neil Armstrong and

Fig. 12.5   *The Apollo lunar lander.*

his crew landed on July 20th 1969. Without the extensive use of computers the project could not even have been considered, and it is an indirect result of this project that we have microcomputers today.

The Apollo spacecraft itself only carried three men, but getting it to the moon and back needed thousands more. The design and manufacture of the rockets which launched it was a large project in itself. It required powerful computers to estimate its performance, carry out complicated calculations of the size, shape, strength and weight of critical components, and so on. The spacecraft itself had to be designed, packing an incredible number of machines and instruments into a tiny space.

Fig. 12.6   *Spacecraft interior.*

The biggest use of computers came during the mission itself, in tracking and monitoring the spacecraft's performance. Altogether this needed more than a hundred different computers, all linked together through a complex communications network, and each responsible for a specific task.

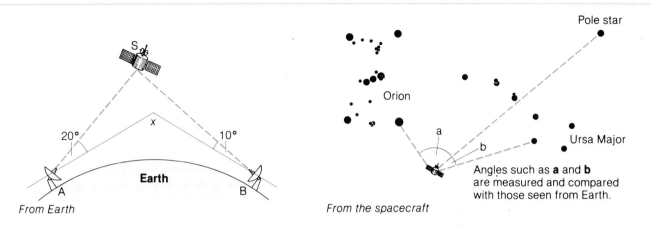

From Earth

Earth

20°   x   10°

A   B

From Earth

Pole star

Orion

a

b

Ursa Major

Angles such as **a** and **b**
are measured and compared
with those seen from Earth.

From the spacecraft

At ground station A, radio signal from spacecraft is 20° above horizon.

At ground station B, radio signal from spacecraft is 10° above horizon.

Distance AB is known, so angle **x** can be worked out from the latitudes of the ground stations,
and distances AS and BS can be worked out by trigonometry.

Fig. 12.7   How to find a spacecraft.

You may know how much mathematics is involved in working out the lengths of lines in two dimensions, using trigonometry. In three dimensions the problem is much more difficult. On the spacecraft, the problem of working out its position consisted of measuring the angles between various stars, then using 3-D trigonometry to work out its distance and direction from the Earth and Moon.

These results would have been useless by conventional calculation — the spacecraft was moving at thousands of miles an hour, so by the time the astronauts knew where they were, they would no longer be there! Using powerful mainframe computers though, the spacecraft could work out its position quickly enough to correct it if necessary by firing its control rockets.

Of course, the programs doing these calculations had to work in real time (see chapter 7).

12.5

Explain why the spacecraft's computers have to work in real time.   (*T*)

12.6

During the Apollo 13 mission, an accident robbed the Apollo 13 astronauts of all their on-board computing power. What actions do you think were needed to get them back to earth safely?   (*D*)

During each flight, the spacecraft was tracked by several ground stations in different parts of the world. Computers were used extensively as part of this tracking. For reasons of speed, all information sent by the spacecraft's instruments was coded by computers on the spacecraft. Computers on the ground then had to receive a continuous stream of information, decode it all, and send it to Mission Control's computers. These computers analysed the craft's performance and decided what actions it needed to take. The instructions then had to be sent back by the reverse procedure, to work the control systems thousands of miles away in space.

All this was even more complex in the case of the Soviet spacecraft which landed on the moon during the 1960's. As these spacecraft did not have any men on board, the entire mission was controlled from Earth, using television cameras to see what was going on.

Obviously it was vital to keep the weight of the lunar module in which the American astronauts travelled as small as possible, so that it could leave the ground more easily. On the other hand, safety required that there had to be three of every type of computer on board the spacecraft. If one, or even two of them went wrong during the flight, there would be another to take over. The Space Shuttle, a much more complex machine, has five computers, plus two in reserve, and at least three of them must agree before any action is taken. On one mission, the flight was aborted less than a minute before lift-off, because one of the computers was not synchronised with the others, and the difference was less than a microsecond!

For such flights in space the circuits of the computers had to be reduced to a small size and weight, without sacrificing any of their processing power. The microprocessors which we know today are possible because of the research effort on space projects.

12.7

Why do you think the Apollo spacecraft carried three computers all doing the same task? What could have happened if they had only one? (*T*)

The nation's defences

Computers play a vital part in the defence of a modern country. For obvious reasons, most of their work is shrouded in secrecy. We can, though, look at some of the techniques which can help to make a computerised defence system work.

Britain, France, the USA and the USSR, as well as several other countries, maintain sophisticated computerised early warning radar equipment, in order to give national leaders early warning of any attack by another country. These systems must obviously work in real-time, and must work very rapidly, because of the speed of modern aircraft and missiles. Furthermore, they must work twenty-four hours a day, seven days a week, fifty-two weeks a year.

12.8

a Explain why it is so important for the radar system's computers to work continuously.

b Briefly describe methods of ensuring that there is no break in the service given by the computer systems. (*T*)

The computers have two main purposes — to recognise objects which unexpectedly appear on radar screens, and to track them.

How does the radar system recognise an object?

The first of these tasks involves pattern recognition. *Radar* works by sending out radio signals and detecting those that are reflected by large objects, such as aeroplanes and ships. The signal received is transferred to a monitor screen marked with a scale,

so that the operator can tell what direction the signal is coming from.

If a radar screen picks up a signal which does not correspond to any scheduled plane, the computer has to decide what the object is. This it can do by digitising the radar image, using the same principle as we used in Chapter 10 to build up a graphic image. It then has to compare the resulting set of numbers with other sets stored in its memory. These other sets of numbers are the digital representation of other objects which might appear, such as fragments of rockets at the end of their lives, small private aircraft, and foreign military aircraft. All these objects are classified in the file as 'friendly' or 'unfriendly'. If the radar's computer finds that the object is probably unfriendly, then it must give a warning to the operators and start tracking it.

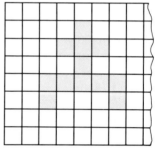

becomes(1 for black, 0 for white)

0	0	0	0	0	0	0	0		0
0	0	0	0	1	0	0	0	which	8
0	0	0	1	1	1	0	0	is binary	28
0	0	0	0	1	0	0	0	for	8
0	0	1	1	1	1	1	0	(see	62
0	0	1	0	0	0	1	0	Chapter	34
0	0	0	0	0	0	0	0	5)	0
0	0	0	0	0	0	0	0		0

so this picture could be coded as (0,8,28,8,62,34,0,0)

Fig. 12.8   How a picture is changed to a set of numbers.

In fact the software which does the comparison is much more complex than it sounds, because it is extremely unlikely that two pictures obtained in this way will match exactly: the program has to decide what the strange object is *most likely* to be; and it must do so very rapidly. The real pictures are much more detailed than those shown in Fig 12.9, and there are many more of them. This pattern-matching process is one of the largest areas of research into **artificial intelligence**, in which computer scientists are trying to make computers able to carry out more and more of the work of the human brain — and to do so more reliably.

How does a computer recognise an object?

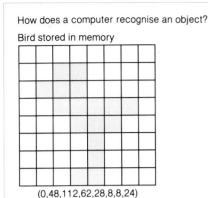

Bird stored in memory

(0,48,112,62,28,8,8,24)

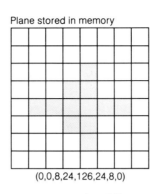

Plane stored in memory

(0,0,8,24,126,24,8,0)

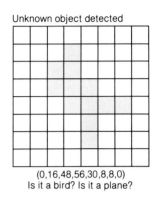

Unknown object detected

(0,16,48,56,30,8,8,0)
Is it a bird? Is it a plane?

The unknown object matches the first on 3 lines and the second on 3 lines —
the computer has to decide which of the objects is the best match.

Fig. 12.9 *How does a computer recognize an object?*

12.9

It is possible, of course, for the radar's computer to make a mistake, just as humans can. Describe what could happen if:

a   an unfriendly object most closely matches a friendly object,

b   if an object which is in fact harmless resembles an unfriendly object stored in the database.   (D)

How does the radar keep on the track?

If the radar computer decides that an object is in fact hostile, it enters the second phase of its job: tracking.

To see how this works, think about this simple example. Suppose a car passes you on a road; you have no way of knowing instantly how fast it is going. If, a second later, you see it is thirty metres away, you can tell its average speed during that second was thirty metres per second. If another second goes by and you see it thirty metres further on still, you can tell it is neither speeding up nor slowing down. You can therefore deduce that in another minute it will probably be 1800 metres away.

If you can see that the car is going round a corner at the same time, it is somewhat harder to predict where it will be, but it can be done. If it covers thirty metres one second and thirty-two the next, the mathematics becomes a bit harder, but it is still possible. For a rocket, the target being tracked is moving at thousands of miles an hour, in three dimensions, so a lot of calculation will be involved in working out where it will land.

This is why so much money is spent on defence computers. Even when the computers have done their sums, they must communicate their results instantly to the defending forces — which also rely on computers to steer their missiles to the targets.

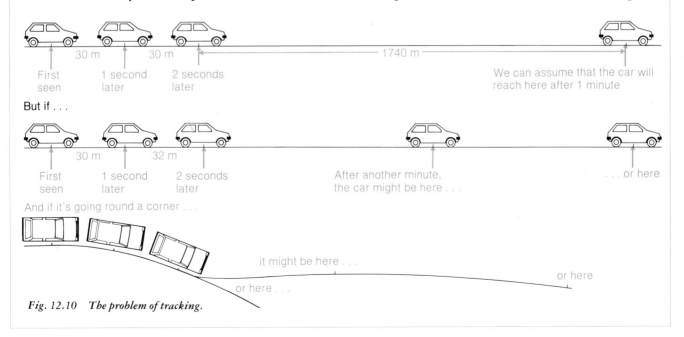

Fig. 12.10 *The problem of tracking.*

The programs which control the defence computers are among the most complex anywhere — some of them contain millions of instructions and took years to write, even using high-level languages such as FORTRAN and ADA. They are tested regularly, by giving them the kind of inputs which would come from a genuine radar alert and seeing how they react, and what messages they pass on. Great care has to be taken to ensure that they only result in *simulated* missile launchings. This could be done by using magnetic tapes containing details of false targets, and excluding the electronic codes which would arm the warheads.

12.10

Suppose that one of the simulation exercises described above is in progress; if one of the computer operators accidentally loads a magnetic tape containing details of real targets, what could be the result? *(D)*

12.11

The computers which control an intercontinental ballistic missile (ICBM) run real-time programs involving complex trigonometry in order to navigate them to their targets. Explain why it would be difficult to test these programs thoroughly. *(D)*

Economic affairs

We have seen how computers are used in defence, to help ensure that we survive armed attacks. We have come to expect more than just survival! Central government is also expected to plan the nation's future prosperity.

12.12

Whereas *local* councils and authorities have day-to-day control over matters such as education, housing, and emergency services, *central* government deals with defence, tax, benefits, the law, and international trade, as well as defence. Choose one central government function and describe briefly how you think computers could be used effectively in your chosen application. *(R)*

You may have played a game on a microcomputer in which you imagine you are the ruler of a small island. The computer asks you to make decisions about spending money on your people, on planting crops, on education, on industry, and so on. After a few years, the computer usually announces that your subjects have revolted and overthrown you, or some even worse fate has befallen you, and the game ends.

These can be great fun, but in reality they are just simple versions of computer programs which really do carry out an important task in the running of a country, or a large business, or a large plant, such as a power station or oil refinery. This is called *modelling*, as we saw briefly in Chapter 7.

What is a computer model?

Consider a small, imaginary country called Ruritania. The Government of Ruritania, like any other government, has to provide many services for its citizens — schools, roads, hospitals, defence, pensions, and so on. To pay for it they levy taxes, which are paid by individuals and by companies. In Ruritania there are dozens of different kinds of tax. People pay tax on their wages, companies pay tax on their profits, tax has to be paid on goods entering the country, tax can be reduced for companies investing in new factories, and so on.

12.13

Write down as many ways as you know by which the UK government raises money. *(R)*

If the government wants to raise more money, they can alter these taxes. Unfortunately the effects are not always predictable. For example, the government may decide to raise another 100 million Ruritanian pounds by increasing company tax. This might have the desired effect, or it might force a few companies to close down, meaning the government has to find another R£150 million for unemployment pay.

The effects of changes like this can take a year or two to happen. Unfortunately, the government needs to plan further ahead than that, because a new project, such as a hospital, can take several years, and the money has to be guaranteed or the project might have to be cancelled halfway through.

The Ruritanian Government has got round this by using a computer model. This is a large program, which *simulates* the behaviour of the economy. The input to this program includes data such as the rate of income tax, the population, average wages, the rate at which prices are going up (or down!), the size of recent wage increases, the size of projects to be financed, and the age to which people are living.

Once this data has been input, the program goes through some very complex calculations. These are designed to represent the way the economy behaves, how much money the government is likely to receive, and how much it will probably need to pay out. For example, if wages increase by one percent more than average prices, there is more money to spend on imported goods, so one part of the program will calculate how much extra import tax the government is likely to receive as a result. Another part will calculate how much pension payments will need to increase if old people live longer as a result of medical improvements.

12.14

There are many other figures which the government needs to know, in order to plan public services, but cannot predict exactly. Suggest some examples. (D)

In theory, the government can work all this out for itself, since all the relevant equations are known. In practice, this is much too slow with manual methods, because of the sheer amount of calculation involved. Ruritania is a small country, but even so its government has to deal with several dozen forms of tax and several million people. The computer program needs over a hundred variables. (The computer model used by the British Treasury uses over 250 variables.)

A change in any one of these will affect all the others, so working out the best way of achieving a particular result, using trial and error, would take millions of calculations.

12.15

Explain what is meant by a variable. (T)

The Ruritanian government runs this program on a large mainframe computer, similar to those you met in chapters 7, 8 and 9. It does not have a sophisticated communications system, however; all the required data can be entered using a key-to-disk system. The results will include tables showing likely tax revenue for the next few years, likely unemployment figures, exports and imports, and so on. These are all printed on a line printer (described in more detail in Chapter 13).

A program such as this can involve millions of calculations, and yet still only take an hour or so to run. The government can therefore improve its forecasting by running it several times. For example, if they want to cut the rate of income tax, they can run the program several times, each time entering a different rate and keeping every other variable the same. In a few hours they will know whether the country can afford this policy, and if so which tax rate would benefit the country most.

12.16

Describe how an economic model of this kind benefits Ruritania, both the government and the people. (D)

12.17

One set of variables in the model is the ages of the population, since age has an effect on the amount of tax collected and benefits paid out. The model allows the government to try alternative sets of ages, as well as the real ones.

a   Explain how the government obtains data concerning the age of everyone in the country.

b   What do you think the age ranges will be of the people who:

—   pay the most tax?

—   receive the most benefit?

c   Suggest what dangers there could be for the people of Ruritania if an extremist government decided that the country was not collecting enough tax to pay the benefits. (D)

Who else can use a computer model?

We have considered the use of the engineering database for different aspects of car design; a model can be devised to study the aerodynamics of different body shapes, for instance, or the distance moved by the steering column in crashes at different speeds.

There are other situations where models of this kind are extremely useful. One example is a large industrial plant, such as an oil refinery or a plastics factory. We saw in Chapter 6 how computers are used to control the machinery in a paper mill, and the computers in such a plants can also be used in the same way as the Treasury model, for carrying out 'what-if' calculations.

For example, suppose the managers of a plastics factory want to know whether they could improve production by, say, increasing the temperature of a particular process. The scientists running the plant know from experience how the plant behaves in normal use, and this knowledge is incorporated in a complex program. When the programs which control the plant are run, the output is normally used to work the machines themselves.

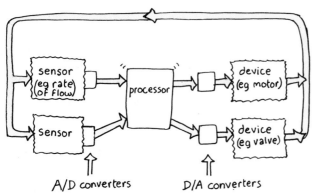

Fig. 12.11 *'Simulation' compared with the 'real thing'.*

Where the working of the plant is modelled on a computer, instead of controlling the actual machinery, the output is stored on disk. The program then uses its knowledge of the plant to work out what would happen next, and this data is sent back to the program (which pretends the data is coming from the plant's sensors).

The program can then tell the managers, within hours, what effect the proposed change would have. They can tell whether or not their changes would be to the company's (or the community's) advantage. More important, they can tell whether the change would produce a dangerous situation, without the risk of actually doing so.

Thus the computer model of the plastics factory enables the management to experiment with different production methods, which would otherwise be too expensive, dangerous, time-consuming, or a combination of all three.

12.18

Describe how a computer model could help the managers of a nuclear power station. (D)

A computer model of this kind naturally has one disadvantage — it is only as good as the people who program it. If they leave out any variables or decisions from their program, the computer will *appear* to predict how the plant behaves, but when the plant is actually run the results may be very different, with potentially disastrous results. This could be caused by something as trivial as rats in a drain at the plastics factory, or as major as a general strike in Ruritania.

12.19

Choose one of the examples given above of a process modelled by a computer, and suggest what problems could be caused by changes in factors which had not been included as variables. (R)

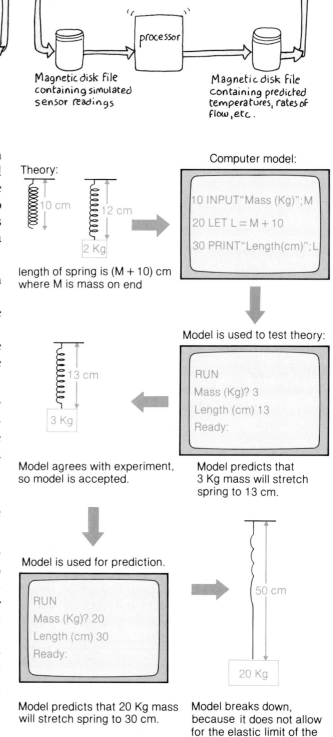

Fig. 12.12 *An example of computer modelling.*

170

End-of-chapter questions

12.20

Describe how the data needed to forecast the weather is collected and input to a computer.

12.21

Explain what is meant by a computer model.

12.22

Computer simulations are often used by Science teachers instead of a real experiment in Chemistry, Physics or Biology.

a Describe one such simulation, and explain why a computer is used.

b Give other reasons for using simulations rather than real experiments.

12.23

In a certain factory, a robot, controlled by a computer, has to pick up one of several objects and decide what it is. Sensors on the robot can follow the outline of the object and thus detect its shape. The computer knows that the object is one of five possibilities, and has in its memory these five shapes plus other details which are needed, such as weight, cost and so on. Describe briefly how it might decide which of these is the correct one.

12.24

Aircraft design requires a great deal of computing power.

a What data would a computer be used to analyse when designing the wings of a new airliner?

b What kind of peripherals would be used to input such data to the computer?

c Apart from printers, what kind of peripherals could be used to output information in a form useful to the designers and engineers?

d What other peripheral devices might be useful to them in producing the design?

12.25

Using a computer model rather than the real process may be of value in planning because:

— it gives quicker results

— it is more convenient

— it is safer.

Briefly describe some situations where a computer model could be valuable, and state which of the above reasons apply.

12.26

A factory produces steel, using coal and iron ore as the ingredients. The factory uses a large quantity of electricity in the process. One of the by-products is sulphur dioxide, which comes out of a tall chimney and can pollute the atmosphere.

a How can the detailed weather forecasts we met earlier in this chapter be helpful to the factory's managers?

b The company wants to increase the efficiency of the plant, without increasing the amount of pollution released to the atmosphere. How do you think a computer model of the process might help them?

c If the company wants to change the amounts of the ingredients used, how would a computer model of the process help the Electricity Board, and how could it help the Factory Inspectors?

Project Briefs 4

1 Police 'Photofit' techniques enable witnesses of crimes to build up faces of suspects from separate parts — hair, ears, eyes, nose, mouth.

Level 1   Design and implement a system which will display a set of numbered face shapes and allow the user to choose one. Onto this shape the witness can then place one of a choice of hairstyles in position, then select ears, eyes, nose and mouth. The final result should then be printed out.

Level 2   Add a database of criminals to the photofit system. This should record their name, which number hairstyle, nose, etc, makes up the face, and other details of their description. Users should be able to interrogate the database and obtain a list of criminals satisfying any particular description.

2 An estate agent wishes to set up a system whereby vendors can pay an extra fee; in return information about their houses will appear on a screen in the window of his office.

Level 1   Design and implement a system in which each house will be displayed for a few seconds, and the last house will be followed by the first one again, so that the sequence cycles.

Level 2   Design and implement a system in which potential purchasers can choose options from menus, and narrow their choice until details of a particular house appear.

3 A tank of water can be heated by burners which have 10 settings, from 0 (off) to 9 (full). As time passes, the rise in temperature each second due to the heat is 0.3 times the burner setting. However, the loss in temperature due to the cold air surrounding the tank is 0.1 times the difference in temperature between the water and the air. A thermometer shows the air temperature.

Level 1   Design and implement a model which simulates a one-minute time period after a user inputs the air temperature and the burner setting. The water temperature each second should be displayed, in a table or a graph.

Level 2   Change the model so that the user inputs a certain temperature. The computer sets the burn rate, and when the water temperature reaches the level set, the burn rate is reduced. When the water temperature drops too far below the level required, the burn rate should rise again. The burn rate each second should be displayed in a table or graph.

Section E

and now it's your turn. 13

The previous chapters have shown real computer systems at work: what they do, how they are designed, what machinery they use and why, and the people involved with them.

One day you may have to design and use a computer system yourself; and you will probably have to use a computer system in practical work. In this chapter, we will try to summarize the choices open to you, the features of different kinds of hardware, what options are available for programming, and the features you should try to design into your system. You can also use this section for reference when working through the other chapters, if you want more detail on a particular device.

Designing a computerised system

The following outline of the process of systems development is designed to show the work of a team of systems analysts and programmers, and at the same time to be helpful to you when you are solving similar problems for your coursework requirements. Whether you are using a programming language with a library of procedures, pre-written software packages, or a combination of hardware modules and control software, the same procedures should be followed.

Stage 1   Feasibility study

Discuss with the management what problem is to be solved, and consider what aspect of the problem can realistically be tackled, considering constraints of time, cost, personnel and equipment. Write a brief description of the aims of the system to be developed.

Stage 2   Investigation

Find out the results that are expected from the system and the data that is available. Consider the format of source data and resulting information to ensure that the computerised system will be accepted by users who have no computer knowledge, and that they will consider it to be better than their current procedures.

Stage 3   Design

Draw out what is to appear on the screen and on the printout, and describe exactly what is required of any other form of output. In the same way, write down the format of any input required, designing forms for data capture if necessary. Write down the structure of any files used by the system. Write down outline algorithms for any processing to be carried out by the system, and produce more detailed algorithms for procedures which are not standard.

Produce sets of data designed to ensure that each process in the system is tested, including typical, unusual and extreme values.

Stage 4   Implementation

Produce either program code, detailed instructions on how to apply pre-written packages, or a hardware configuration which will achieve the desired results. The solution should be built up using separately produced modules, so that errors are easy to find and the system easy to adapt.

Stage 5   Technical documentation

Write notes on the method of solution. The notes should be sufficiently detailed so that someone else who is knowledgeable about the programming language, the package, or the hardware units, will be able to understand what has been done to implement the design and be able to change it if necessary.

Stage 6   Testing and revision

For each set of test data, note any problems that occur when running the system. For each error, identify in which part of the system it lies and make the necessary corrections. Repeat until no more errors are found. (Modules are often implemented and tested independently, and when each is correct, the whole system is tested together.)

Stage 7   User documentation

Write notes on how to use the system to solve the problems for which it was designed, in such a way that they can be followed by people with no more than a basic knowledge of computer use. Make clear what the system is aiming to achieve, and incorporate useful demonstration material, such as diagrams of screen layout, output forms, and hardware connections.

Report on the running of the system, including limitations and problems in use. Suggest how any improvements could be made, and include any further information requested by management at the time of the feasibility study.

Whatever your computer system is for, you will need both *hardware* (the actual machinery) and *software* (the programs which work it); you may also have to make decisions about *communications* if your system needs to communicate with other computers or other information systems. We will first look at what hardware is currently available, and then at how you can set about producing the necessary software.

Systems flowcharts are commonly used to show the flow of information through the system, and the connection between hardware and software.

Summary of hardware

Whether you are designing a small household system using a tiny Sinclair ZX81, or part of the team working on space exploration with the help of a Cray-2 supercomputer, every computer system has the four basic components shown in Fig. 13.1; we will consider each of these separately.

From these lists you can choose the devices which seem most suited to the aims of your system, just as in previous chapters. Computer technology is developing rapidly, however, and some of these devices may become out of date while other new ones are invented.

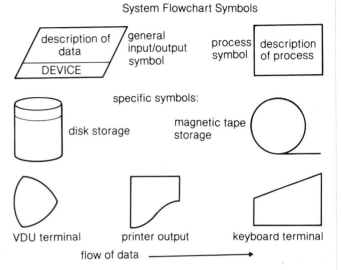

System Flowchart Symbols

Fig. 13.1   System flowchart symbols.

What choice of input devices do we have?

You have met many different ways of getting information into a computer system. Here is a summary of these, together with a few more.

Keyboard   Most common input device for microcomputers, and also used as operator's console for mainframes; keys generate pattern of electrical pulses (representing binary digits) which are sent to CPU; each key generates different pattern. Usually used in conjunction with an output device, often a VDU. See especially Chapters 1, 7.

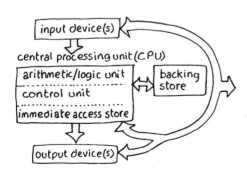

Fig. 13.2   (i) Block diagram of information flow in a computer system.

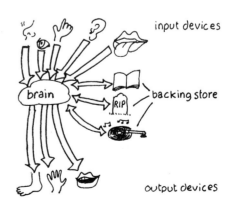

Fig. 13.2   (ii) Block diagram of information flow in humans.

Numeric keypad   Used for fast operation where only digits are needed for input. See Chapters 5, 11.

Concept keyboard   Version of keyboard with un-labelled keys; 'overlays' are placed on top of a key or group of keys to give it a meaning, and the computer software has to give the same meaning to the codes generated by those keys. Popular for educational use, as very young children can use it if the overlays contain pictures, and it gives handicapped users better access to the computer.

Mouse   Small hand-held device which is rolled on a flat surface; interface detects movement and sends coded electrical impulses to CPU. Software usually uses this data to display corresponding position on a VDU. Mouse also has buttons which are pressed when at the desired position; these send different pulses to CPU which software can use to start some action. Now commonly used for business micros, eg for word processors, graphics packages. See Chapter 2.

Joystick   Works on much the same principle as a mouse, except that a lever moved by hand is used to generate the electrical pulses. Popular for games programs on micros; **games paddle** uses a similar principle. See Chapter 10.

Graphics tablet   Essentially same principles as mouse; electrical pulses are generated by the movement of a 'pen' on a flat bed, so that the design drawn can be reproduced (by software) on a screen. See Chapter 10.

Light pen   When moved across a VDU screen it detects the light emitted, when a button is pressed a pulse is sent to the CPU. By synchronising with the timing of the moving electron beam which produces the screen display, the software can detect where on the screen the light pen is; software can then take appropriate action. See Chapter 6.

The drawings on the screen are formed by a beam moving very rapidly across the screen and down in rows. The light pen sends a signal when this beam strikes it, and the computer works out the position of the pen from the time at which the beam strikes it

Fig. 13.3   A light pen.

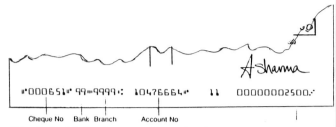

Fig. 13.4   MICR characters (shown in blue).

Cheque No   Bank Branch   Account No

Fig. 13.5   An OCR reader.

Magnetic Ink Character Reader (MICR)   Used in bank clearing system; numbers (cheque number, bank branch, account) are pre-printed on cheques in ink which can be magnetised, each digit with a characteristic pattern, and further figures (such as amount of money) are added before a cheque is 'read'. Numbers are read by a device which senses the magnetic pattern and generates corresponding pattern of electrical pulses, which is passed to CPU.

Optical Character Reader (OCR)   Similar to MICR in principle, but uses reflected light instead of magnetism; OCR devices can read letters printed in certain typefaces, but not handwriting (yet!), as it varies too much.

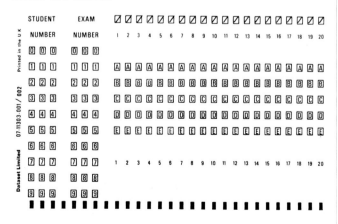

Fig. 13.6   A form for mark sense reading.

Mark sense reader (Optical mark reader) Also uses reflected light, or some versions sense presence of carbon (pencil marks) in particular places on a document; unlike OCR it only detects presence or absence of a mark, generating 1 or 0 respectively, but cannot recognise patterns.

Bar code reader Common in supermarket trade and in some libraries. Sends a beam of light and detects reflections from white/black stripes (on cans, packets, books, etc.) These patterns generate corresponding bit patterns for sending to CPU. See Chapter 6.

POS (Point-of-Sale) terminal Resembles a cash register, but data (price and stock information) is sent to CPU for processing; has a numeric keypad and function keys or a bar code reader. Common in supermarkets. See Chapter 9.

Automated Teller Machine (ATM) Reads magnetic pattern on plastic cards, sends to CPU; used as terminal for banking/building society systems. See Chapter 9.

Key-to-disk Common in mainframe systems; data typed on a keyboard is stored on a disk which is not read into CPU until the input data is complete. Often used with a micro or minicomputer to control it, so that several keyboards can record data simultaneously on one disk, the micro/mini software ensuring that different keyboard operators' data are kept separate. See Chapter 7.

Key-to-tape Similar to key-to-disk, ie off-line input to mainframes, but using a magnetic tape instead of a disk.

Punched card reader Reads data punched as holes on cards; uses light passing through hole, or not, to generate 1 or 0 respectively; obsolete because of work needed in data preparation. However, a small form of punched card, known as a **Kimball Tag**, is still used in the retail clothing industry for stock control, often in conjunction with POS terminals.

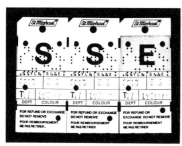

Fig. 13.7 A Kimball tag.

Paper tape reader Similar to punched card reader but uses continuous roll of paper; also obsolete.

Teletypewriter Keyboard often used in conjunction with paper tape punch and modem for sending data to a remote computer; incorporates a print head for printing replies. Very slow and now obsolete. See Chapter 9.

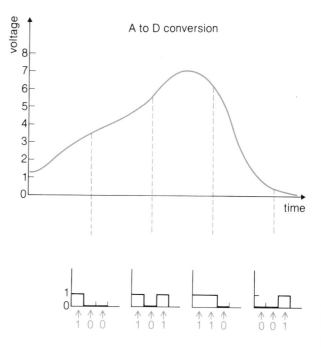

At regular times, the analogue voltage is compared with larger and larger known values until a match is found. This known value is sent as a series of pulses, representing a bit pattern.

Fig. 13.8 Analogue to digital conversion.

Sensor (or detector) Various kinds (eg temperature sensor, humidity sensor, rate-of-flow detector); used for analogue inputs in process control applications. The electrical signal produced has to pass through an **analogue-to-digital converter**, an electronic circuit which changes the signal to a series of pulses (representing a binary number), which the digital computer can then use. See Chapters 4, 6.

Voice recognition device By far the easiest and most natural input medium to use, because it is similar to normal human communication, but those so far marketed are very limited. Picks up sound via a microphone, digitises it and analyses sound pattern received, comparing it with the 'words' it has previously been given to store in its memory. Needs to be 'trained', by specifying the actions to be taken for each word.

What choice of output devices do we have?

Visual Display Unit (VDU) Probably most common output device at present. Converts electrical pulses produced by CPU into characters displayed on a cathode ray tube (like a TV screen), sometimes in colour; gives almost instant output. Almost invariably used in conjunction with a keyboard; VDU is commonly used to mean the *monitor screen* and *keyboard*. See Chapters 1, 7 in particular.

Graphical display unit Similar in appearance to VDU, but can also display drawings; often used with a light pen, to modify the drawings on screen. Expensive, but widely used for computer-aided-design. Available as high-resolution (giving fine detail) or low-resolution (fewer 'pixels', therefore faster output but less detail). See Chapter 6.

Page printer Capable of printing an entire page in one operation. Several types exist; some use small lasers (***laser printers***) to create a pattern of static electricity on paper, to mark the characters, and ink is attracted to this pattern; some fire a fine jet of ink at the paper (***ink-jet printers***). These printers are extremely fast but very expensive, so they are confined to mainframe systems; but development is very rapid, and some cheaper versions are beginning to appear for microcomputers. See Chapter 2.

Line printer Prints a complete line of output onto paper, in one operation. Normally used with mainframe computers. Several types exist: ***barrel printer*** uses letters engraved on a rotating barrel, hammers striking paper (and an inked ribbon) onto the barrel as the appropriate letters pass; ***chain printer*** has the letters engraved on a continuous chain. See Chapter 7.

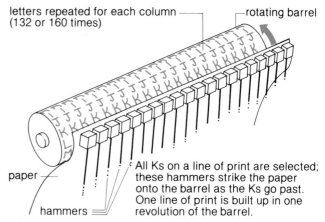

letters repeated for each column (132 or 160 times) — rotating barrel

paper — hammers

All Ks on a line of print are selected; these hammers strike the paper onto the barrel as the Ks go past. One line of print is built up in one revolution of the barrel.

Fig. 13.10 A barrel printer.

Dot-matrix printer Small, cheap printer very common with microcomputers. Prints single character at a time, using a matrix of needles striking a ribbon to form dots on paper; controlling circuits determine which dots form which characters. Ink-jet printers which use the same principle are available. See Chapter 2.

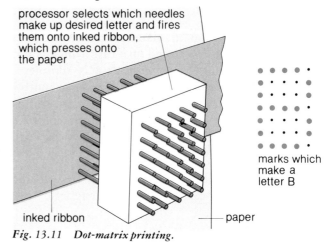

processor selects which needles make up desired letter and fires them onto inked ribbon, which presses onto the paper

inked ribbon — paper

marks which make a letter B

Fig. 13.11 Dot-matrix printing.

photocopier drum

whole page image placed on drum

Rotating mirror.

The controller needs to store information for the whole page. For full-dot image graphics up to 1-2 megabytes of memory are needed. If it is using characters only then it could use as little as 64 Kb.

laser

controller circuit board to turn laser on/off, containing 1 or 2 powerful microprocessors.

A small machine for desk-top publishing applications available at £3-4000. But fast machines could cost £150-250000.

Fig. 13.9 Laser printing and a desk-top publishing system.

Daisy-wheel printer Also single-character printer. Letters are attached to a wheel; controlling circuits revolve this wheel until desired letter is opposite a hammer which then strikes onto paper. Produces typewriter-quality printout. See Chapter 2.

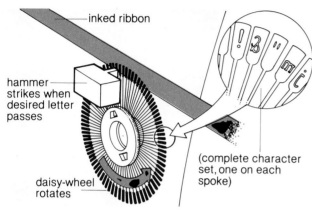

Fig. 13.12 A daisy-wheel printer.

Graph plotter Device which receives data and uses the digital codes to control movement of a pen which draws on paper. Two main types: ***drum plotter***, where pen moves sideways across a drum which also revolves backwards and forwards, and ***flat-bed plotter***, where paper is on a flat bed — two separate circuits control movement in two directions at right angles to give two-dimensional drawing. See Chapter 6.

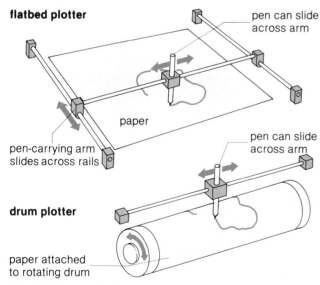

Fig. 13.13 A graph plotter.

POS terminal and *automated teller machine* Both of these devices are output devices as well as input devices; generally display CPU's responses on either a cathode-ray display or a liquid-crystal display. See Chapter 9.

Teletypewriter See input devices. Was also used as operator's console for mainframes, for passing messages from CPU to operator, but now largely superceded by VDU. See Chapter 9.

Card punch Output binary patterns are used to punch coded holes in cards; can later be re-input. Was used as a form of backing store in the early days of computers, but with the advent of magnetic storage became obsolete.

Paper tape punch Similar to card punch, but produces continuous roll of paper tape. Also obsolete, but was used for a long time for controlling machine tools.

Computer output on microfilm (COM) Output is displayed on a cathode ray tube, which is then photographed and the film reduced in size. Several (up to 200) screens are then put together on one card-sized piece of celluloid (microfiche). These can be read by a viewer which enlarges the image back to normal size. Used for archiving, and also for large reference data (library catalogues, garage stock lists, telephone directory enquiries). See Chapter 8.

Activator Group name for any device which receives a computer's output signal (digital), and uses it to perform some action (such as move a robot arm, open a valve, or switch on a boiler), without human intervention. Often incorporates a ***digital-to-analogue converter***, an electronic circuit which converts a series of pulses (binary number) into a voltage corresponding to the number. See Chapter 6.

Voice synthesiser Another device resembling human communication; still under development. Output signals produce patterns of vibration in a metal ribbon or diaphragm, which we hear as sound. Usually has limited vocabulary (the sound patterns need a lot of memory), but improving all the time.

What choice of backing store do we have?

Magnetic disk Circular disk coated with a magnetic substance; an electromagnetic 'read-write' head magnetises a small part in one direction or the other, representing a 1 or a 0. Recorded in concentric tracks, each divided into sectors; heads can be positioned over any track, and any sector found as the disk rotates, giving direct access to any data.

There are several varieties of disk. ***Exchangeable disk packs*** comprise several metal disks (usually 14″ diameter) on one axis, with a read/write head for each surface which moves in and out to locate the track; used in mainframes. **Fixed head disks** are similar in principle, but have a read/write head for every track; they revolve in a sealed container and cannot be removed. **Winchester disks** (often just called **hard disks**, in contrast to floppies, below) are single, smaller disks ($5\frac{1}{4}''$ or $3\frac{1}{2}''$ diameter are most common) with a single head in sealed units, used in micros and minis. **Floppy disks** are plastic, and can be removed from the disk drive; these come in many sizes but $8''$, $5\frac{1}{4}''$ and $3\frac{1}{2}''$ are the most common; used in micros. See Chapters 1, 8.

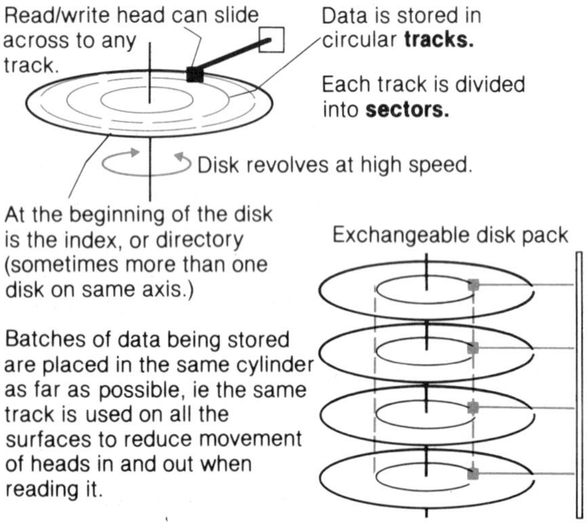

Read/write head can slide across to any track.

Data is stored in circular **tracks.**

Each track is divided into **sectors.**

Disk revolves at high speed.

At the beginning of the disk is the index, or directory (sometimes more than one disk on same axis.)

Batches of data being stored are placed in the same cylinder as far as possible, ie the same track is used on all the surfaces to reduce movement of heads in and out when reading it.

Exchangeable disk pack

Fig. 13.14   Magnetic disk and exchangeable disk pack.

Magnetic tape   Resembles disk in principle of recording data magnetically, except that the magnetic coating is on a long reel of tape, which can therefore only be read or written in one direction; tape may need rewinding or winding on to find a piece of data, so it is a 'serial access' device. Used extensively in mainframe systems; some micros also use smaller tapes (standard cassettes) as a cheap backing store, and **tape streamers** are often used to back-up complete Winchester disks regularly in case of corruption.

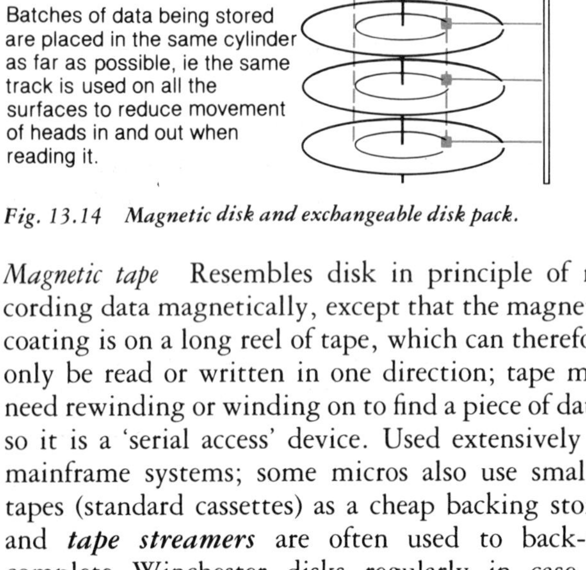

Code stored across tape, and each track read by individual heads. Ninth track used as a parity track.

read head, 1 for each track

0101101

ASCII codes used as on paper tape, but with magnetic spots instead of holes.

Fig. 13.15   Magnetic tape.

Magnetic drum   Large high-speed revolving cylinder, divided into several 'tracks' along its length, with a separate read/write head for each track. Can be extremely fast (no head movement to find data), but now very rare.

Optical disks   CD-ROM is a disk which uses light reflection (a small laser) instead of magnetism, using the same principle as 'hi-fi' compact disks. Can be made to very exact tolerances and therefore hold huge amounts of data; but at present available only as 'read-only' memory. Undergoing rapid development, and systems which allow users to *write* data to the disks will soon be in common use. Closely related is LV-ROM used in interactive video. See Chapter 11.

How is the Central Processing Unit (CPU) organised?

The CPU has three main sections which are linked together:

Arithmetic/Logic Unit (ALU)   This is the part of the the CPU which does all the arithmetic and processing of data. It contains: one or more accumulators and registers for temporary storage of values during calculations; adders; circuits for comparing two binary numbers; and others, depending on the capabilities of the processor.

Control unit   Contains circuits for controlling all the other parts of the central processor. These include decoders (to decide what instruction a particular code will carry out); gates to open or close paths from memory to ALU and vice versa; circuits to send control information to, and receive it from, peripherals; and a clock to synchronise all the various actions of the computer.

Immediate Access Store (IAS)   This is a form of memory used for storing data while it is being processed, and for storing programs while they are being executed. Its size is usually quoted in kilobytes (K) (a kilobyte is about a thousand bytes — in fact 1024). Some modern machines are measured in megabytes (multiples of 2^{20} or 1 048 576 bytes). A byte is usually 8 bits.

Early computers used **core store** for their IAS, which consisted of tiny iron rings magnetised or not to represent 1 or 0, but these have virtually disappeared. Most computers now use **semiconductor memory**, which is a large number of electronic circuits with the property that they can stay in one of two states (on or off), and switch from one to the other when a pulse is sent to them. Thousands of these can be made on one chip. There have been experiments with **bubble memory**, using tiny magnetic bubbles, but these seem to have been abandoned as not commercially viable. Optical memory using light seems to have long-term potential but is still in its infancy.

Immediate access store can be **ROM** (read-only memory) or **RAM** (random access memory). ROM is memory in which data is 'burnt in' during manufacture and cannot be erased; this is often used in micros for a simple operating system which is available immediately on switch-on. Some micros have a complete high-level language interpreter in ROM, avoiding the need to load it from disk. RAM can be both read and written to, and is used for a user's own programs and data. See Chapters 4, 5.

Some machines also use a **PROM** (programmable read-only memory), which normally functions as ROM but can be rewritten with special equipment.

Most present forms of immediate access store are **volatile**, that is, data stored in them is lost when power is switched off — hence a backing store is also necessary.

How do we connect devices together?

To enable any peripheral device to communicate with a computer, or a computer to communicate with another computer, an **interface** is needed. An interface is the hardware (electronic circuit) needed between processors and peripherals, in order to allow for different speeds, voltage levels, etc. Interfaces obviously vary but most contain **buffers**, which are temporary stores used to hold information sent by a fast device whilst a slower device catches up, and **flags**, which are registers used to signal status information, for example when the interface

is ready to receive more data.

Interfacing modern peripherals is simplified nowadays, as the peripherals usually include a microprocessor dedicated to the control of the device and the transfer of data to and from the CPU.

A **protocol** is a set of rules for communication. For example, if one person communicates with another over a telephone a sequence of operations is normally followed. This sequence starts when your phone rings: you lift the handset, and say 'Hello' and possibly your name and number. The caller then gives his name and the conversation begins.

Computers use similar sorts of rules to communicate with each other, but they must be more srictly defined. A protocol for communication between two *electronic* devices must ensure that: one device transmits the same amount of data as the other expects to receive; both devices recognise the same codes (bit patterns) for start and end of transmission; and that the receiving machine uses the same coding system for data as the sending machine (just as it is no use sending a letter in English to someone who can only read French!).

Whenever data is transferred between devices there is a possibility that errors can be introduced. There are various methods of detecting and compensating for these.

• Data is transmitted twice and the two versions compared.

• Parity check — this is a test that is applied to binary data, to check that each character has (for example) an even number of bits (even parity).

• Check sums — when a record is transmitted the numeric values of the codes of each item are added together, to give a check sum which is also transmitted. On receiving the data, the check sum is recalculated and compared with the original. See Chapter 11.

When data is transmitted over long distances it can be sent over standard telephone lines, lines dedicated to data transmission, optical fibres, or as radio or microwave signals.

Speeds of data transmission obviously vary greatly, partly depending on the transmission medium. Transmission rates are measured in bits per second or **baud**; they are typically 1200 baud (or less) for transmission over telephone lines, 9600 baud or greater for transmissions between two micros.

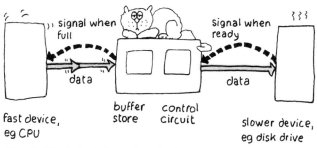

Fig. 13.16   Interfacing using a buffer.

The crudest way of transmitting data from a terminal to a remote computer, over telephone lines, is by the use of an *acoustic coupler*.

Fig. 13.17   An acoustic computer.

This operates using an entirely conventional telephone system. The user dials the telephone number of the computer, and when the tone is received from the computer they place the handset into the acoustic coupler, which is connected to the terminal. The user can then communicate with the computer via the terminal. A major disadvantage of the acoustic coupler is that sounds from other sources can be picked up by the microphone used in the acoustic coupler, which will cause corruption of data.

A more sophisticated system of communication with a remote computer is the use of a **modem** (modulator/demodulator) — a device which converts bits into analogue electrical impulses for transmission over telephone lines, and vice-versa.

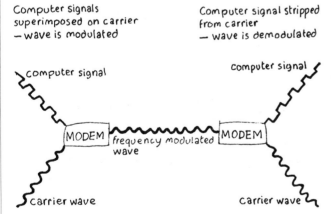

Computer signals superimposed on carrier — wave is modulated

Computer signal stripped from carrier — wave is demodulated

Fig. 13.18   A MODEM system diagram.

When a number of of remote users are connected to a computer the transmissions are normally *multiplexed*: a number of signals from different sources are combined on to one communication medium. This can be done in two ways (see above):

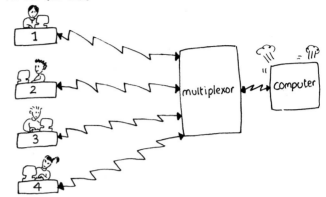

remote terminals

Fig. 13.19   A multiplexor system.

- *Time multiplexing* is when the transmission medium divides its time into separate slots, each time slot carrying information from a different source.

- *Frequency multiplexing* is achieved by operating each of the lines from remote sources on a different frequency; therefore, when the signals are combined onto one medium, they can be transmitted simultaneously.

When the multiplexed signals arrive at the computer they must be unscrambled. With time multiplexing each time slot allocated to a particular source is given an identifier to allow this unscrambling to take place, whereas with frequency multiplexing the source is identified by the frequency of transmission. See Chapter 9.

Summary of software

Software is the name used to describe all computer programs, routines and procedures together with their associated documentation. It can be considered as *applications software* and *systems software*.

Applications software is the name given to a set of programs and associated documentation (a package) used to carry out a particular application (for example stock control). These packages fall into two broad categories:

- packages written by specialist programmers, either employed by the computer manufacturer, or by a 'software house' to meet the needs of many users who wish to perform similar tasks;

- packages written to meet the special needs of a particular user.

Tasks for which applications packages are commonly available include:

— payroll calculations,
— stock control,
— information retrieval,
— word processing,
— resource scheduling — eg for making the most efficient use of a fleet of lorries,
— engineering design,
— financial analysis and planning.

Quite often there are a number of applications packages, produced by different companies, available for a particular computer to carry out the same tasks. See Chapters 1, 2, 3, 7.

Systems software is the software used by the computer itself in order to operate, and can be thought of as being of three types:

— software used to simplify the writing of programs — *language translators*,
— software used to control the operation of the computer system — **operating systems**,
— software used to carry out the routine tasks needed by any computer system — **utilities**.

If you choose to produce software yourself instead of using an existing package, you will come across all of these. See Chapter 7.

Algorithms specify step-by-step procedures to be used to solve a problem. They are built up from sections of linked instructions (*structures* or *constructs*), and we have used the notation shown below in this text.

Fig. 13.20 Algorithm constructs used in this book.

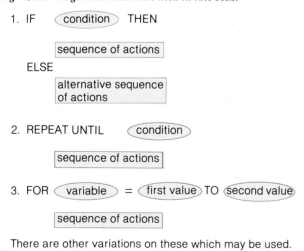

There are other variations on these which may be used.

Why do we need translation programs?

All digital computers work in their own particular language: *machine code*. A machine code program consists of a series of instructions written in binary code.

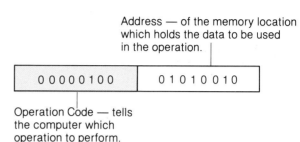

Address — of the memory location which holds the data to be used in the operation.

Operation Code — tells the computer which operation to perform.

Fig. 13.21 A 16-bit machine code instruction word.

In the early days of computing, all programs had to be written in machine code. This was both tedious and time consuming, and gradually programming languages were developed which were easier for humans to understand, but needed translation before the computer could follow the instructions contained in them.

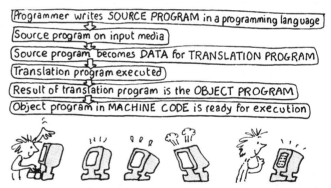

Fig. 13.22 The translation process.

Programming languages can be divided into two groups — *low level* (or assembly) languages and *high level* languages.

Low level languages developed from machine code, containing various features that make them easier for the programmer to use. In general they allow:

● *mnemonics* instead of binary operation codes. A mnemonic is a memory aid (see Fig. 13.23).

● *names* (or *symbolic addresses*) to identify a memory location, instead of having to give an actual memory address in binary.

● *labels* to identify a particular point in a program we wish to jump to.

Binary Operation Code	Mnemonic	Meaning
00000101	LDA	LoaD a number into the Accumulator
00000001	ADD	ADD a number onto the value stored in the accumulator
00000010	SUB	SUBtract a number from the value stored in the accumulator

Examples of Mnemonics.

Fig. 13.23 *Examples of mnemonics.*

A low level language must be translated into machine code before it can be processed. The program used to translate a low level language into machine code is called an assembler — hence the alternative name for low level languages, *assembly languages*. See Chapter 5.

Assembly languages are still used for writing some utilities and applications packages, especially for programs which need to use the special features of a particular computer, and also for testing hardware.

As computer usage grew, it was soon realised that assembly languages could be developed further and made nearer to the language used by programmers. The aim was to produce a language in which instructions could be communicated using commands and symbols much closer to the programmer's ordinary language and mathematical notation — high level languages. See Chapter 7.

Machine code	Assembly language
Very slow to write	Quicker to write
Easy to make mistakes when writing strings of 1s and 0s	Less likely to make mistakes
No need for translation	Easy to translate — one assembly language instruction translated into one machine code instruction
Efficient and economic in use of memory	Efficient and economic in use of memory
Very difficult to locate mistakes	Usually contains debugging aids to assist in finding errors in programs

Fig. 13.24 *Comparison of machine code and assembly language.*

Low level or assembly language	High level languages
Close to machine code accepted by the computer	Close to the language normally used by the programmer: English, mathematical notation
Difficult to learn and slow to write	Easier to learn and quicker to write and more easily read by a non-expert
Requires little to change into machine code, therefore saves computer time, and space in the IAS	Requires complex software to translate it into machine code, which takes both computer time and storage space in the IAS
Machine dependent, ie different assembler for each make/model of computer	A high level language can be run on any computer that has the necessary compiler to translate it into machine code
Used for testing hardware, and writing some utilities and applications software	Used for programming mathematical, scientific and commercial problems — applications software

Fig. 13.25 *Comparison of low and high-level language.*

Assemblers	Compilers
Takes one low level language instruction and translates it into *one* machine code instruction	Takes each high level language instruction and translates it into *several* machine code instructions
An assembler can only be used on the computer for which it was designed	Translation process is more complicated than assembly and therefore takes longer
Assembly is comparatively simple therefore takes little time and space in the IAS	Compiler takes up more storage space than assembler
	Better debugging facilities

Fig. 13.26   Comparison of assemblers and compilers.

High level languages must also be translated into machine code prior to running. This is normally done by a program called a *compiler*, although sometimes an **interpreter** is used.

Should we use an interpreter or a compiler?

Some high level languages are *interpreted* instead of compiled. Whereas compilers (and assemblers) translate the whole *source program* into a machine code *object program* which can then be run, an interpreter deals with one instruction at a time while the program is running, translating and then immediately executing each instruction in turn.

If a compiler is used, the program is only translated once, whereas if an interpreter is used the program must be translated every time the program is to be run. Furthermore, if an instruction is to be executed more than once in a program, it must be translated each time. Execution of interpreted programs is

therefore far slower than of compiled programs.

How do we deal with errors?

Assemblers, compilers and interpreters all have *diagnostic aids* of some sort, that is, a facility that helps in finding certain types of errors. Diagnostic aids in translation programs show up *syntax* (grammatical) errors, and in general do not show up *logic errors* (mistakes by the programmer which cause the program to work, but incorrectly). Diagnostics in compilers are usually better than those supplied with interpreters or assemblers. However, it is often easier to *debug* (correct) an interpreted program than a compiled program. Every time a compilation error or a logic error is located within a compiled program, the source program must be corrected, it must be recompiled and then test run again. This is not so time-consuming with an interpreter, which usually contains an editor as well, for correcting mistakes. See Chapter 6.

Fig. 13.27

Language	Examples	Programming time	Storage required	Translation time
4GL or program generator	PRO-4 The Last One	very short	huge	very long
High level	ALGOL COBOL ADA PASCAL FORTRAN PROLOG	short	large	long
Assembly/ low level	PLAN SIR ZASM MACRO-86	long	small	short
Machine Code		very long	minimum	zero
Note that more fourth-generation languages, in particular, are being introduced at frequent intervals, and that the dividing line between third-and fourth-generation languages is not a sharp one, nor are pre-written packages a completely distinct category.				

The latest method of producing application software is the use of *fourth-generation languages (4GL's)*, *program generators* and *authoring languages*. These all use the same basic idea: instead of analysing how a job is to be done, the programmer merely specifies the kind of results he wants from the computer — such things as what fields a data file should contain and how an output screen should look — and also specifies where the data is to come from. The program generator then carries out the rest of the job automatically. Naturally these languages are specific to a particular type of problem: a real-time control 4GL would be no good for an accounting program. On the other hand, they require much less specialised training, and enable companies to produce software tailored to their own requirements. See Chapter 10.

What kind of operating system should we use?

An *operating system* is a program which controls the operation of a computer system in such a way as to reduce the need for human intervention to a minimum. In general, an operating system provides the following services as a minimum:

- loading and running programs

- controlling the operation of peripherals

- sending messages to and receiving messages from the computer operator concerning such things as loading magnetic tapes, supplying paper to the printer, etc.

- dealing with program errors and interruptions to the running of a program.

A mainframe operating system will, in addition to the above tasks, normally provide accounting and statistical information on the usage of the system.

The design of the operating system depends on the type of processing to be done. See also Chapter 7.

Batch processing This system in its simplest form takes a number of programs and puts them together to form a batch. The batch is then fed into the computer and processed, one after another, without the need for further operator intervention. Crude forms of batch processing are very wasteful of CPU time.

Multiprogramming This method of processing maximises the use of the CPU by making use of the difference in speed of the CPU compared with a slower peripheral device. Two or more programs are processed, apparently at the same time, but actually in bursts, controlled by the operating system. While one program is awaiting data to be input, or printing results, another program is allowed access to the CPU for processing. See Chapter 7.

Multi-access is a system whereby a number of users have apparently simultaneous access to the CPU. The system is used mainly for interactive working on a time-sharing basis. With time-sharing, each user is in turn allowed a small slice of CPU time, but it appears to the user that he is in continuous sole use of the system, due to the high speed at which the CPU operates compared with the terminals used to communicate with it. See Chapter 8.

A multi-access system may be a number of users using one particular package, or a number of programmers each developing their own program.

Real-time processing This means a computer system which is capable of receiving data from an outside source, and which is able to process that data rapidly enough to influence the sources of data (for example process control, building society ATMs, airline booking systems).

Note that some complex systems may require a combination of some of these; for example, an airline booking system, connected to many agents, must be both real-time and multi-access. Obviously the more complex the system, the bigger and more expensive the programs. See Chapters 6 and 9.

There are many tasks performed in running a computer that are common to all installations, no matter what the major use of the system is. The computer supplier will normally supply the systems software to carry out these routine tasks; such programs are in general referred to as *utilities*.

Examples of utilities are:

- a program for making backup copies,

- a program for copying a file from one storage medium to another (eg disk to tape),

- a *sort* program (or a set of them, using various methods).

- a *directory listing* which enables the user to check what is on a disk,

- a program that enables the user to check on size of files and disk space left available for new files,

- an *editor* that allows the user to create or amend files,

- a *merge* program, that allows a user to combine two files into one.

Put them all together and what do we get?

When you design a computer system, having gone through all the stages of systems analysis, programming, data preparation, testing and documentation, you end up with a system which is meant to serve the needs of its *users*, not yourself (although of course you can use it yourself if you wish!) You may not always succeed in every respect, but always try to ensure that your computer system meets these important aims:

Worthwhile The computer system should save time and money, improve the quality of results, and remove tedium from a job; otherwise it is not worth the time and money spent on it.

User friendly It must be easy to use, having language and words familiar to the intended user (not computer jargon); users should not need to read an enormous manual before starting or have a wide knowledge of computers.

Robust The system should not crash when given unexpected or wrong data; the software should detect users' mistakes and display helpful messages to assist them.

Versatile The system should do all that the users need in order to do their jobs.

Flexible The system should be capable of adapting to different circumstances.

Reliable The system should be capable of repeated or extended use without crashing; it should do what it claims to do, without bugs which cause it to fail or produce wrong results.

Transparent The user is interested in the results, not how the system works; its internal workings should not be visible to the user.

Portable The system should be capable of running on different computers without too much alteration; otherwise the user could be locked in to out-of-date machinery when better becomes available.

Easy to maintain It must not leave the user in the lurch when the system goes wrong; the authors of the software, and the hardware manufacturers, must either provide help and support to users when needed, or make arrangements for other firms to do so.

If your computer system has all of these qualities, it will indeed make life easier for the people using it.

yesterday . . . . and tomorrow

The previous chapters of this book have shown some of the many ways in which modern life is being changed by the growth of the computer. Some things we now take for granted would have been quite impossible without computers: space flight, for example. Space flight has brought with it communication satellites which often bring us instant pictures from all over world, so that we seem to know as much about distant countries as we do about the next street; the world in some ways resembles what Marshall McLuhan described as a *global village*. Without computers, however, no-one could do fast enough the arithmetic needed to control the rockets which sent the communications satellites into orbit.

In this chapter we shall look into the future, and give some ideas about how the computer might continue to affect your lives. Understanding what might happen in the future is much simpler if you know how we reached the present day, so first we will look at the origins of the computer.

Although the electronic computer as we know it today is comparatively young, its roots go back a long way. Throughout history, important developments have been the result of people's needs, and the computer industry is no exception. This section will mention some of the important milestones on the road to modern information technology, and explain why they came about.

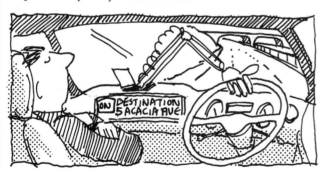

Fig. 14.1 *Driving in the future?*

The development of information handling

From very early times, people have needed to store and process information in their daily lives. About ten thousand years ago, when early man ceased to be

a hunter and became a farmer, he needed to count his animals to make sure they had not gone astray; to keep this information he used piles of stones, or carved notches on a stick. To keep track of the seasons (essential for growing crops), he had to record the passing of the days, the phases of the moon, when the longest day arrived, and so on.

14.1
Why did early farmers need to know when the longest and shortest days of the year happened?.(*R*)

14.2
When would a farmer need to update his records of animals? How could he do it?   (*D*)

We now believe that several ancient stone monuments were used for calculations concerning the seasons, the most famous of which is Stonehenge in Wiltshire, probably built around four thousand years ago. Indications are that this was surprisingly accurate in showing when midsummer and midwinter arrived, and may even have been able to predict eclipses; thus Stonehenge was a distant ancestor of the computers described in Chapter 12.

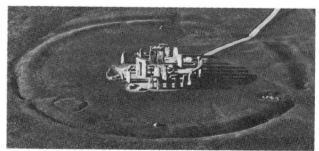

Fig. 14.2 *Stonehenge.*

As men and women became more sociable, and people began making things to sell to others as well as for themselves, they had to invent money. This led to the need to keep track of what they had bought and sold, and how much money they had. Apart from writing down figures, the need also arose to be able to add and subtract sums of money, and merchants who could do this became very important. Remember that our modern figures did not exist, and so arithmetic was extremely difficult.

In China, a device called the *abacus* was developed to help the task. In principle an abacus is like the bead-frames with which many young children still learn how to count. In some parts of the Far East the abacus is still in daily use by traders; in the 1970's in a test comparison a skilled operator was able to work one faster than an American using a computer, at least for straightforward calculations.

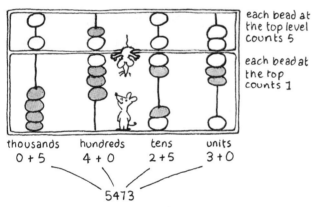

each bead at the top level counts 5

each bead at the top counts 1

thousands	hundreds	tens	units
0 + 5	4 + 0	2 + 5	3 + 0

5473

Fig. 14.3   Calculating using an abacus.

14.3

What arithmetic operations cannot be done with an abacus?   (R)

During the sixteenth and seventeenth centuries, trade became much more international and much more widespread. This brought new problems of navigation: if a ship left London or Bristol it could be days or weeks before it reached India, the East Indies or America, and during that time the ship's crew had only the sea, the sun and the stars to tell them where they were (radio and radar were still several centuries away). New mathematics using the sun and stars had to be discovered for finding the way, and trigonometry was developed for this very purpose. Tables were worked out and printed, with enormous effort, showing star positions, tides, and other essential information.

A Scottish mathematician named *John Napier* also invented logarithms to help with multiplication and division. It took him twenty years to work out

the necessary tables, such was the work involved, though today a mainframe computer could work out the same tables in a few minutes. Napier also invented a system of calculation using some pieces of bone with sequences of numbers engraved on them (called Napier's Bones).

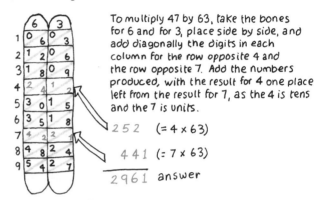

To multiply 47 by 63, take the bones for 6 and for 3, place side by side, and add diagonally the digits in each column for the row opposite 4 and the row opposite 7. Add the numbers produced, with the result for 4 one place left from the result for 7, as the 4 is tens and the 7 is units.

252   (= 4 × 63)

441   (= 7 × 63)

2961   answer

Fig. 14.4   Napier's Bones.

14.4

A sailing ship in the Middle Ages would have carried a sextant (to find the positions of sun and stars) and tables showing the positions of the stars at various times, and the times of the tides. What other invention was necessary to use these tables properly, in order to navigate safely and accurately? (R)

14.5

Logarithms and slide rules were still widely used by engineers and scientists for multiplying and dividing until a few years ago. What has replaced them? (R)

At this time, too, governments became more involved, collecting taxes based on the goods being traded. This involved arithmetic which was beyond the simple abacus: to calculate the duty on twenty bales of wool, for example, needed multiplication. One particular tax inspector in France, Pascal by name, found this particularly irksome, as his arithmetic was none too good.

In 1642, however, his son *Blaise Pascal* had already, even at the young age of 18, found considerable fame as a mathematician, and that summer he invented a remarkable new machine to help his father. By setting levers and turning a handle, he could use it to multiply; by turning the handle backwards, he could divide. Improved versions of this machine were in use in businesses until about ten years ago, and can still be found in some schools.

Fig. 14.5   Pascal's machine.

14.6

The basic method of Pascal's machine was to multiply two numbers by adding one of them repeatedly. How does this resemble the process used by many modern computers to multiply and divide?   (*D*)

How did the growth of industry affect information processing?

The Industrial Revolution brought many new problems to solve. The propulation was growing rapidly throughout Europe, and there were many more men and women to clothe. A Flemish weaver named ***Joseph Jacquard*** thought about how to increase the amount of cloth he could make. Patterned designs needed a lot of repetitive work and concentration by the workers, if enough was to be produced to make the price reasonable. In 1784 he found the answer: automation.

His solution was to code patterns on pieces of card, by punching holes in them. The holes engaged levers which worked parts of the weaving looms; holes in different places would work different levers and so produce a different part of the cloth pattern.

For the first time it was now possible to produce two absolutely identical pieces of cloth, moreover it could be done quickly. This brilliant idea led to

Fig. 14.6   Hand weavers.

mass production, one of the main features of nineteenth-century industry. The idea of punched cards to store information was later borrowed whole-sale by the computer industry, where it is only now going out of use.

Fig. 14.7   A Jacquard loom.

14.7

What computer device uses the same principle as Jacquard's loom?   (*T*)

Meanwhile problems of navigation were growing more acute. The volume of trade in the early nineteenth century had reached such proportions that the astronomical calculations needed to navigate ships could not be done fast enough for the number of ships and the level of safety required. Producing tide tables, star charts and so on, and printing them, was still a hugely complex task.

One brilliant English eccentric and inventor named ***Charles Babbage*** decided that a machine could be built for the job. He managed to build one and named it the ***Difference Engine***, which can still be seen in the Science Museum in London. His true brilliance, however, lay in his realisation that a *general-purpose* calculating machine could be built. Babbage called such a machine the Analytical Engine. The *specific* features of a problem would be given to the machine while it was working; for this purpose he borrowed Jacquard's punched card idea to feed various values into his machine. In other words, the machine would be *programmed*.

Ada, Countess Lovelace, was a good friend of Charles Babbage who did a lot of work in working out suitable 'programs' for his machine. She was responsible for the idea of *branching* — making the machine do one thing if certain conditions were true, or another thing if not. This idea was ahead of its time, but came into its own with the languages developed for computers after World War Two. Today one of the most advanced high-level programming languages, Ada, is named after her.

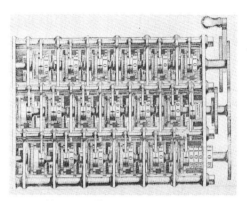

Fig. 14.8 *Babbage's Difference Engine.*

The whole Analytical Engine would have been steam-powered, instead of being turned by hand as Pascal's machine was. Babbage persuaded the British Government to pay for its development, but the engineers of the day simply could not build the parts of the Analytical Engine to the accuracy needed for it to work. After some years the Government withdrew its support, shortly before Babbage died. Babbage's ideas did not die with him, however; they were merely ahead of their time.

14.8

How could Babbage have changed the 'program' of his machine in order to calculate a different formula?   (*D*)

Where is everybody?

During the second half of the nineteenth century, growth reached the United States — indeed population growth there was explosive. The government of the USA, trying desperately to keep track of its population to plan the necessary services, conducted a ten-yearly census, in which they wrote down everything they could think of about everyone they could find. One of their clerks, a young man named **Herman Hollerith**, realised that this was useless. It would, at the current rate of growth, take twelve years to analyse all the information collected, by which time the next census would have made it all out-of-date. Hollerith reduced this to three years. His idea was, again, borrowed from Jacquard's punched cards: he realised that the holes in the cards could be used to store information as well as control machines.

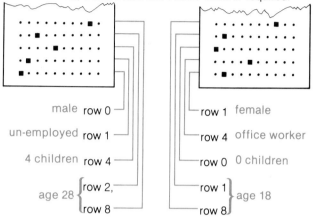

Two punched cards, storing information about people's sex, occupation, number of children, and age. There would be more columns, which could store more detail if required.

Fig. 14.9 *Punched cards.*

A card was produced for every person. If a person was male, a hole was punched at a certain position; when a machine dragged the card across a set of levers, the hole engaged a lever which added one to a mechanical counter. When all the cards had been dealt with, this counter showed the number of males; other counters would, in the same way, show the number of females, children, households, carpenters, Italians, and so on. Hollerith built and tested, successfully, machines which used this idea to analyse the millions of cards which the census office collected.

14.9

What other kinds of information might Hollerith have included on one of his punched cards, as well as the examples mentioned above?   (*F*)

14.10

If any of the data on Hollerith's cards needed correcting or updating, how could this be done? (*D*)

Hollerith was a shrewd man: he patented his machines, left the census office and set up a company to build and sell them to other companies for dealing with their paperwork, and for producing tables of figures (hence they were sometimes called **tabulators**). Today the Hollerith Tabulator Company has grown into **International Business Machines**, the giant of the computer industry and one of the world's largest companies in any sphere.

During the first part of the twentieth century, more and more companies and small businesses, such as shops, turned to machines like Hollerith's for sorting out their paperwork, and variations of

Pascal's machine for their office calculations and book-keeping. The typewriter was also developed at around the time of Hollerith's work, and this simpler device became the one machine which proved indispensible to the office.

All the calculating machines were mechanical; moving gears, wheels and levers did all the work. Most were hand-powered, although the newer models had electric motors to take out the hard work. Engineering skills had improved, so that the machines were fairly reliable, but they wore out, needed a lot of maintenance, and were not much quicker than using pencil and paper.

What led to the birth of the electronic computer?

The Second World War was by far the largest conflict in history, and brought with it many new problems. For all military leaders it has always been essential to know what the enemy was doing, preferably by reading their messages. However, the sheer scale of the war meant that the Allied commanders were deluged with information, all of it naturally in code. (The Germans coded all their messages by a machine, itself a very clever calculating machine called Enigma.) Breaking a code, and then decoding a message, is a complex mathematical problem, but the problem facing the British codebreakers at Bletchley Park, in Buckinghamshire, was decoding hundreds of messages every day, in codes which were changed every day.

This meant that they were faced with thousands of repetitive calculations each day. Much of their work was kept on the secret list for many years, but, forty years on, enough is known to say that the team there could be called the inventors of the electronic computer.

A simple code would involve changing each letter for another, such as

A B C D E F G H I J K L M N O P Q R S T U V W X Y Z
C D A I G Z E V D S W X U P B N Y T J R M H K L Q F

so that the word GENERAL becomes EGPGTCX.
But what if you know that someone is using a code where GENERAL is represented by UILKNTN?
Fig. 14.10   Code.

14.11

Why was it necessary for the Germans to encode all their messages?   (R)

One of this team was a young genius named **Alan Turing**. He had read all about Charles Babbage's machines and was very interested in the theory behind them. He realised that a machine like Babbage's could solve many of the problems of codebreaking, by speeding up the calculations. The difference this time, though, was that instead of cumbersome gears and levers, Turing's team used thermionic valves and relays, which were then being developed in radio, radar and other fields. (Basically, a valve worked like a kind of electric tap, in which one electric current is used to switch another current on or off automatically.)

Worked entirely by electricity and with few moving parts, their machine was far faster than Babbage could ever have dreamed. The machine they built, the first true all-electronic calculating machine, they christened *Colossus*. It was working as early as 1943, and played a vital part in sending information to the Allied leaders during preparations for D-Day and after.

Fig. 14.11   The Colussus computer.

14.12

Because Colossus had few moving parts, what other advantage would it have had, besides speed, compared with mechanical calculators?   (T)

With the end of the war, the team which had invented Colossus was dispersed to other tasks. Many of them continued development work on their new invention; the task of rebuilding Europe after the war was so large that there was plenty of work for the new calculating machines.

The war had created a range of problems which required large numbers of repetitive calculations to be carried out quickly, and Britain, Germany and the USA all made great advances. One of the crucial steps in the evolution of the modern computer came very soon after the war. Babbage's machine could remember numbers it had calculated (in fact, the positions of various gears told it what information it was working on). Colossus and *ENIAC* (the first electronic calculating device with memory to be built in America) could also remember numbers, using the state of various circuits to serve as memory.

John von Neumann realised in 1948 that one of the things a machine could remember, if it were suitably designed, was its own instructions. Once started, it could run automatically at high speed, without waiting for the operator to supply further instructions. In other words, the computer could be *programmed*. The first stored program computer was completed at Manchester University in 1948. Several machines, with names like *EDVAC* and *UNIVAC*, were built using this principle, and enabled researchers in Britain and the USA to concentrate on the principles of their work while their new computers did the routine calculations.

14.13

What would the advantages have been for the users of early stored program computers, compared with previous machines? (*D*)

The first few computers built were amazingly complex machines: only a few specialised scientists and mathematicians knew how to work them. They were huge machines, frequently broke down, and consumed large quantities of electricity. Thus the first generation of computers spent their lives number-crunching their way through highly complex, but repetitive, mathematical problems: helping to test aircraft and rocket design, the design of the atomic bomb and reactors for the peaceful use of nuclear power, and other kinds of scientific research.

How did computing enter the business world?

Early in the 1950's, a prominent businessman, who had heard about the work of the early computer scientists, decided that these fast calculating machines did not have to be confined to advanced work in universities. In an average office, the mathematics involved is seldom more involved than adding, subtracting and percentages, but there is a great deal of it. The businessman decided that a computer could do this work just as well as rocket design, so he decided to buy one for his company headquarters. Finding that no-one could supply one, he had to set up another company to build it; thus was born LEO (which stood for *Lyons Electronic*

Office!), the first computer built specifically for commercial use.

These early computers might have remained rare but for another invention which occurred about the same time. William Shockley, in California, had discovered the *transistor*. This was a small piece of a material, usually silicon or germanium, which could be made to behave just like a thermionic valve, except that it worked on low voltages and was therefore much smaller and safer, used much less power and, most important, could be mass-produced. From the early 1950's, transistors replaced valves as the principal components of computers (and radios, television sets and other electronic equipment).

A transputer.

Transistors.

Fig. 14.12   *A valve.*

14.14

What purpose does a valve, or a transistor, serve in a computer or other electronic device? (*T*)

Computers began to be smaller, faster and more powerful than their ancestors, and each passing year brought new advances. Memories were also improved in reliability and increased in size. The result of this was that programs could be much longer.

```
001100  101101
111001  001100
101010  101111
110011  000110
011100  100010
111001  011001
```

binary code (1940's software)

Fig. 14.13

Advances occurred in software, too. An early development was assembly codes, which we met in Chapter 5; programmers could write their instructions in words, without having to understand the mysteries of binary numbers. The translation into machine code was done by the computer itself. As memories became larger, so the translation programs could be made bigger; the computer did more of the work, the programmers less.

```
LDX   #1
ADD   847
STX   #5
MUL   878
STX   #6
JSB   505
JPR   -13
```

Section of assembler (1950's software)

Fig. 14.14

By the mid-1960's, high level languages, such as FORTRAN, had been developed. These enabled people who had no detailed knowledge of how a computer worked to write programs. Along with them were produced programs called compilers which automatically translated high-level instructions into binary machine code, as described in Chapter 13.

```
      X = 0
      DO 200 I = 5,100,5
      X = X + A (1,1)
      IF (X) 200,11,11
11    DO 300 J = 2,150
300   X = X + A (I,J)
200   CONTINUE
```

Section of Fortran (1960's software)

Fig. 14.15

Many routine tasks could be done automatically, so more people could use computers. More people and companies bought them, realising that their advantages in reducing paperwork outweighed the problem of training people to work them.

As more computers were sold, the companies making them could invest more money and effort in making them more powerful and easier to use. The big computer companies realised that there were large numbers of firms and business people who would buy machines if they were cheap enough and easy to use.

One result of this investment was the integrated circuit, now popularly known as the *silicon chip*. This was a slice of silicon which could be made to behave, not just as a single device, but as a complete circuit, hundreds of components all made in one go. Mass production was now possible. From the mid 1960s, in Britain, Europe and America, the growth of the computer industry became explosive. The number of computers in Britain rose from a handful in 1950, to a few hundred in 1960, to thousands in 1970 and over a million by the end of 1984.

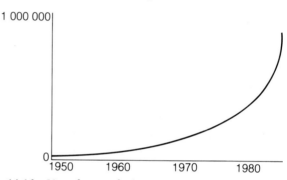

Fig. 14.16   Manufacture of microcomputers.

14.15

a   Why does mass-production make computers cheaper?

b   What effects does it have on the skilled electronics technicians who are needed to make specialised circuits?   (*D*)

14.16

Do you think the trend shown in the graph in Fig. 14.16 will continue? Explain your answer.   (*D*)

How did the use of computers start to reach ordinary people?

In the mid-1970s many large companies employed computers (the kind we now call mainframes) for their routine paperwork, accounting, invoicing and similar tasks. The components from which they were built were getting smaller; put another way, you could get more computing power in the same space. Therefore 'minicomputers' came on the scene: being smaller and cheaper than their larger relatives, they could be afforded by smaller businesses. A whole new industry grew up to provide the software needed, in a form which many more people could understand and use.

Enterprising teachers began to take notice of the change in business and industry. A few schools began to teach their pupils about computers, and to acquire computing facilities of their own, usually by a terminal linked to a large computer somewhere else. Secondary school children were now able to write their own programs, because the software had become much easier to use.

14.17
Why do you think so much effort was put into making software more 'user-friendly'? (D)

14.18
What development in software made it easier for children to write their own computer programs? (R)

The late 1970s saw an even more significant development: the microcomputer. Developments in electronics meant that the whole of the arithmetic/logic unit of a computer (the part that does all the processing) could be made in one integrated circuit (the silicon chip), and mass produced by the thousand. Truly portable computers suddenly came on the market, at a price of only a few hundred pounds. A few enterprising businessmen decided that these microcomputers, at such low prices, opened up all sorts of new markets. There was no reason to restrict sales to businesses.

A potential market of millions existed; efforts were made to bring computers within an average family's reach. Backing store was an ordinary cassette recorder, and specialised output devices were discarded when it was realised that an ordinary television receiver would do.

14.19
Microcomputer makers sold thousands of small, cheap computers to families (particularly children) in the early 1980s.

a What did they think families would use them for?

b What did families actually use them for? (D)

Because the mass computer market had arrived, a number of changes in public attitudes to computers began to take place during the early 1980s. Many small businesses, such as corner shops, small factories, and offices, discovered that the microcomputers their children were playing with could make their business run more smoothly. Many more people became involved in producing software for them; the high-level languages used by programmers were becoming more and more easy to use, but by now another trend was growing.

The computer user could do away with programming altogether, provided that he or she had certain easy-to-use complete packages. A shopkeeper could buy a microcomputer from one firm, an accounts package from another, and a stock control package from another, and have them running successfully in a few days. The most important feature of these packages is a 'user-friendly man-machine interface', which means that anyone should be able to use them with no more than a few hours specialised training. Along with the software have come new input devices, such as *mice* and *joysticks*, to make input of data and commands easier than using the conventional typewriter-style keyboard.

14.20
Mr Adams (Chapter 2) had a word processing package.

a Would you recommend such a package to all small businesses? Explain your answer.

b What other general purpose software packages would you recommend, and why? (D)

14.21
What hardware developments in the last few years have made user-friendly software possible? (R)

14.22
Most microcomputer software in recent years has made use of data typed on a keyboard and displayed on a screen.

a What other peripheral devices are now coming into use, to make software even easier to use?

b What kind of devices would need to be developed in order to make communication with a computer as easy as possible? *(D)*

14.23

Developing a software package takes a long time and involves a lot of thought by highly-paid programmers. The development of a powerful word processing program, for instance, will cost several hundred thousand pounds. How are computer software companies able to sell such packages to small computer users at a price they can afford? *(D)*

Because the price of computers was coming down so sharply, the governments of both Britain and France decided on a bold plan — to equip every school in the country with its own computer. In France, the Government has gone further. For example, all domestic telephone users have been given an adapter to connect their television, via a telephone communication link, to a computerised directory service, among other things; they no longer have telephone directories, since the computer provides a permanent, complete, up-to-date and accessible list of subscribers.

More teachers have started to use the computer, and children are learning *with* the computer, rather than *about* the computer. The computing power in microcomputers, together with the increased use of communications, leads many people to wonder whether children in the future will go to school *at all*. Familiar subjects like Mathematics, Science, Geography could be explored using computers to find information, to try out ideas, to make mistakes and put them right. School may even be a place where children are encouraged to talk to friends, play games and entertain people!

14.24

a Name a service in Britain which connects households to computers.

b The service in (a) above is run commercially, not as a government service, so people only have access to it if they can afford to pay. With such a service in homes, what use can an average household make of it?

c What extra advantages would it have for businesses? *(D)*

14.25

One idea of what the school of the future will be like is given above.

a Describe a typical day in the life of a pupil in such a school.

b What do *you* think school will be like in 20 years' time? *(D)*

There are changes happening, too, in the world of commercial data processing. Software for producing mainframe application programs is developing further from the high-level languages like COBOL. We saw examples of first, second and third generations of language earlier in the chapter; with increasing use of fourth generation languages, programmers are able to produce powerful, correct programs very quickly.

So dramatic is this change, that the procedure for developing systems may well change too. Instead of weeks of analysis and design before any program code is produced, it may well be more efficient to produce simple programs straight after a feasibility study, try them on the users, and then adapt them step-by-step as the design of the system grows.

Where are the Supercomputers?

'Small is Beautiful' is not the only motto of the computer industry in the mid-1980s. Developments in technology have meant that a computer of given power has become much smaller and also cheaper; but another way of exploiting technology is to use the same space (and the same price!) to build a more powerful machine. More powerful software, more versatile operating systems, allowing many people to use the same computer simultaneously, utility programs for automatically carrying out housekeeping tasks such as maintaining backup copies of important files, have all been developed; we saw some uses of these in Chapter 8.

At the other end of the scale from the microcomputer, some extremely powerful computers have been built, called *supercomputers*. These are equipped with the fastest chips in production, so that these machines are capable of carrying out millions of instructions in one second. The *Cray-2*, for

Fig. 14.18 The Cray-2.

instance, weighs several tons, and requires a complex refrigeration system to prevent its chips overheating. Ironically, it uses as much electricity as Eniac did; but then it is a million times faster, doing a long multiplication in one billionth of a second!

There are very few of these machines (the actual number is not known): development costs, and the very specialised nature of the work they perform, means that they are very expensive. One such supercomputer is responsible for analysing data from hundreds of weather stations (see Chapter 12), and computing the weather forecasts. It is believed that others are employed at the Government Communications Headquarters, engaged in the same work as Colossus was, breaking codes; and still more at the Atomic Weapons Research Establishment at Aldermaston.

14.26

Why do you think the existence of some of these supercomputers is kept secret from the public? (D)

In 1984, the United States Government announced the Strategic Defence Initiative (popularly known as 'Star Wars'). The idea behind this was to build defence systems capable of destroying missiles carrying nuclear weapons, before they had a chance to destroy cities. Because these missiles can travel halfway round the world in half an hour, and would fly far out in space, tracking them involves carrying out complex mathematics very rapidly. Since missiles are likely to be launched in large groups, including decoys, the problem is made many times greater. No present-day computer is anything like powerful enough, so a lot of research is now being carried out in order to build even faster and more powerful computers.

14.27

Why would the computers needed to control such

defence systems need to be so fast? (D)

14.28

The most powerful computers are likely to be developed for military use, for controlling missile and defence systems.

a How might this research be likely to benefit ordinary computer users?

b Why may these benefits not, in fact, be passed on? (D)

14.29

The computers controlling missile systems would have to respond very quickly to enemy attacks, and must therefore be programmed to operate largely automatically. What dangers must the software designers guard against? (D)

What is the place of Information Technology in society?

As we have seen, most advances in technology have occurred as a result of society's needs. As the world's population has increased, so have the problems involved in feeding and clothing the human race and satisfying man's desire to improve his standard of living. Obviously, the more people there are, the more new people are born, so the population goes on and on expanding.

By the year 1 AD the number of people in the world had reached a few million; by the beginning of the present century it had reached a thousand million; today it is over four times as many and it is expected, at the present birth rate, to reach six billion before the century ends. This phenomenal growth is the main reason why technology is progressing so rapidly in the computer age: man's ingenuity in overcoming these problems is being stretched to the limit, far more than ever before.

We need to know more and more about the way nature works and how to harness it to our needs, so that more and more information is being discovered, shared around the globe, and used. At present the total of all the information stored in the world's libraries doubles every four years; thus information technology is having to develop in leaps and bounds to keep up. Not only must this knowledge be kept, it must also be *communicated* between people and countries. If people or governments do not understand what others are doing, they become suspicious of each other and conflicts arise.

To show how rapidly progress is being made in the

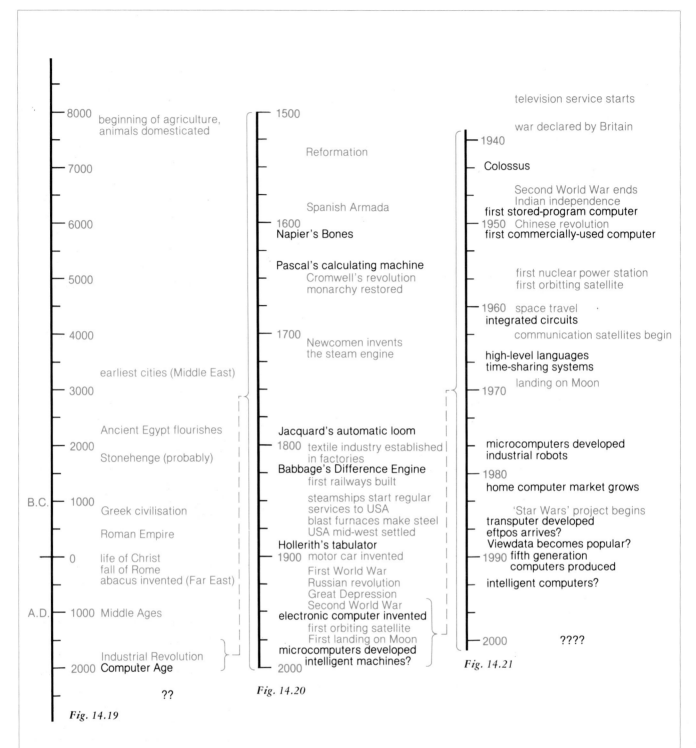

Fig. 14.19

Fig. 14.20

Fig. 14.21

modern age, Fig. 14.19 shows the development of industrial society, and the subsequent growth of the computer age, set against the whole of recorded history; Fig. 14.20 shows the highlights of the later stages (the Industrial Revolution and after), while Fig. 14.21 shows the advances that have been made since the Second World War. This period, a blink of an eye compared with the million years or so of man's existence, has seen more technological advance (and with it an increase in the material standard of living for much of the human race) than the whole of the preceding history.

For most of the million or so years of human existence, men have depended on hunting for their food. It was only about ten thousand years ago that men learned to grow crops, and feed other people as well. At that time most of the population worked in agriculture, and this was still true as recently as 1800, but today, in the USA, only three per cent of the population works in agriculture. This three per cent manages to grow enough to feed the entire population and have enough left to feed several other countries as well. So the process of evolution from hunter to farmer took a very long time (it is still going on in some remote parts of the world).

By contrast, the second great change in life-style, the Industrial Revolution, was much quicker: Thomas Newcomen invented a workable steam engine in 1712, and by the 1860's steam engines powered mills all over Lancashire, Yorkshire and the Midlands, steam locomotive pulled passengers and goods from London to Scotland in hours rather than days, and steamships crossed the Atlantic in days rather than weeks.

The next big change came as a result of the growth of electronics and computers, and is going on all around you. The authors of this book were all born around the time that ENIAC was built — remember that this machine weighed several tons, consumed as much electricity as several houses, and was as big as a house. The machine on which we are writing these words has ten times the computing power, sits on our desks and could be carried in a suitcase — and hundreds of thousands of similar machines exist in ordinary homes.

14.30
Describe briefly the contribution of the following people to the development of automated data processing:

a Blaise Pascal,

b Herman Hollerith,

c Lady Lovelace,

d John von Neumann. (*T*)

14.31
Describe the development of methods for either

a input,

b output,

c storage of information,

over the last 100 years, indicating where you can the *reasons* for, and *effects* of, the changes. (*T*)

The future of information handling . . .?

It is important to understand the speed at which the computer has spread — because it makes prediction of the future very uncertain. Nevertheless, we shall now try to look at where the computer might be taking us in the next few years.

Most computers are *serial* machines: they will carry out one instruction, and only when finished will they go on to the next. They may work at a rate of millions of instructions per second, but they can only do one thing at a time. This is not good enough for some scientists. For example, physicists probing the mysteries of the atomic nucleus have found that they need to do some calculations which would take even a Cray-2 thousands of years. By contrast, although no-one fully understands it, the human brain appears to work in a different way, which is termed *parallel processing*. This means that the brain is actually carrying out many tasks at the same time. Even such a mundane task as crossing the road involves ears and eyes in feeding the brain information from dozens of places, all of which it coordinates and uses to control the muscles.

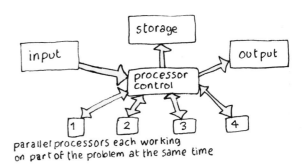

parallel processors each working on part of the problem at the same time

14.32
Think of another activity which apparently involves the brain in several activities at the same time, and list those activities. (*D*)

Computer scientists have now built a few experimental computers which try to do the same thing (this is one of the objects of the so-called fifth-generation project in which Britain, Japan and America are investing). Instead of one processor chip, they have several: a task is broken up into several independent parts, each processor is given its own part to sort out, and all the results are put together as soon as they are available. One British firm, Inmos, has launched a new chip called the Transputer, which is so miniaturised that the whole of a powerful processor, some memory and a control unit all fit onto one chip (see Fig. 14.12).

A number of firms are using several of these linked together to try to produce a parallel processing computer. The most extreme machine so far built along these lines involves 65 536 processors all linked together, all working on different parts of the same problem. It is, however, more likely to be well into the 1990's before such powerful computers go into commercial production in any numbers.

14.33

512 is a more typical number of processors for a parallel processing computer. Why are the figures of 512 and 65 536 chosen? (*Advice:* think of binary numbers. How many are possible with 1 bit, with 2 bits, 3 bits, and so on? There must be one register in the computer which decides which processor to use.)   (*R*)

Can computers replace humans?

As you can imagine, computers of this kind pose a few software problems. For this reason, many computer scientists are also developing new computer languages for writing programs, some of which (such as Prolog and Occam) use a radically different approach from traditional programming. The aim is to create ***artificial intelligence***, by trying to copy human thought processes in solving problems.

```
X is-reported if (X a problem) is-told
X possible-fault-with Y if
    (either Z indirect-part-of Y or Z EQ Y)
    and x indicates (X in Z)
    and x is-reported
```

Fig. 14.23   Section of PROLOG code.

Most languages involve telling the computer *how* to tackle a problem step-by-step, whereas we tend to see a problem by *describing* what we want to do, and letting the brain work out how to do it in rather mysterious ways; the aim is to achieve the same thing in a computer. In other words, scientists are trying to produce a computer which, together with its software, works in a similar way to the brain, and so could be called *intelligent*.

14.34

What features do you think a machine should have, in order to justify calling it intelligent?   (*D*)

Research is also being done on producing computers to work even faster, not using electricity at all, but light instead. Already communication links using optical fibres are fairly common, but harnessing the same technology to the small scale of a chip is proving difficult, and its commercial use is some years away, if it ever works at all! Light-sensitive devices, in the form of lasers, are making their mark in other fields, though.

Computers which calculate at high speed generate a lot of data, and so naturally other devices are being developed to keep up with them. High speed laser printers are already becoming increasingly common; even they, however, cannot keep up with a high-speed processor unless results are stored temporarily, which means there is a need for high-speed, high-capacity storage devices.

We cannot predict what lies in the future for the technology. In 1981, it seemed that ***bubble memory*** was the solution to the need for large amounts of backing storage with access times as fast as current Immediate Access Storage. In 1986, we now think that this technique will never become cheap enough to be used beyond certain specialist applications.

The latest development in this field is the so-called ***CD-ROM***, which borrows the principle used in compact-disc audio equipment. Information is stored in tiny dots on a highly-polished disk, the position of the dots being sensed by a fine laser beam which reads the data back to the processor. These discs can hold hundreds of megabytes of data; at the time of writing they can only be *read*. The complex technology required to *write* data onto these disks with the necessary accuracy is not cheap, but it is expected that writeable disks will be available in the near future, certainly for business microcomputers.

Fig. 14.24   A CD system.

As you read this, you may know whether CD technology is a common solution to the need for large, fast data stores, or whether it is merely another relic in the Science Museum!

14.35
Give examples of advances in hardware and software which have been designed to make it easier for non-experts to use computers over the years.   (*T*)

14.36
Give an example of some information used by a business which requires the large capacity of a CD-ROM.   (*D*)

With more powerful computers, software can be made more user-friendly. We are always trying to adapt computers to suit humans rather than adapt humans to suit computers! In pursuit of this aim, input devices, too, are receiving their share of development. A number of computers now exist which can recognise voices: obviously it would cut out the time-consuming data preparation stage of computing if we could talk to our computers! At present these *voice recognition* systems can only make use of a few dozen words, but they are being developed rapidly.

We also expect *voice output* from computers and robots to improve considerably in quality and to become very widespread, and for voice recognition to become much more flexible and reliable. We can be certain about one thing, however: in the next few years there will be many new ideas, but only a few of them will have a lasting effect on our lives.

14.37
a   There are a large number of people who cannot use normal computer equipment for various reasons. Write down some of the problems that handicapped people might find, and what developments have helped them to take advantage of information technology.

b   Computers have also helped handicapped people to achieve other things in their lives that they would not otherwise have been able to do. Describe some of the hardware and software that has been developed for this purpose, and what it has achieved. (*R*)

14.38
What other methods of entering data to a computer might there be which would be easy to use?   (*D*)

Shall we all live in the 'electronic cottage'?

During the twentieth century, cities have grown outwards, as people have tended to move away from their work to live in more pleasant suburbs. There are already signs that the growth of computing might reverse this trend. Many people, particularly office workers, spend several hours a day travelling to work and home again. We saw in previous chapters that modern offices rely heavily on computers for their routine paperwork; many workers can integrate their work by the use of local area networks; they can communicate with each other and with other offices by means of electronic mail.

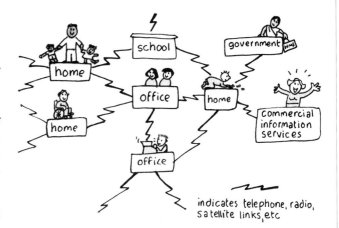

Fig. 14.25   *Communications in the future.*

A few companies have realised that, because electricity travels at nearly the speed of light, their workers can use their word processors and spreadsheets just as effectively at home, sending completed documents, files and reports by telephone links to each other or to the central office. Several people can even attend a meeting by means of tele-conferencing — if they all sit in front of video cameras, linked by closed circuit, with microphones and monitors, they can talk to each other as readily as if they were all sat round a table. As a result, travelling time is saved, and workers suffer less from stress, so they can achieve much more in a typical day.

If this trend continues, there may be some very far-reaching results. The cities themselves may start to shrink instead of expand; people may prefer to live in small communities, as we did before the Industrial Revolution, and as millions of people in the Third World still do. Because of the loss of travelling time, and the labour saved by electronic technology, people will probably have much more leisure time. (A century ago the average working week in the UK was about 60 hours; today it is between 35 and 40 for most people.)

But there is another possible effect which has not happened yet: electronic communications mean that not only can workers do their paperwork *where* they like, but also *when* they want to. Therefore there will be many more opportunities for men and women to integrate their home and work lives, interspersing paid employment with looking after families. As the skills required to work with information technology change, the proportion of women in paid employment could rise from the present level. Furthermore, if employers do not expect workers to leave home, men can play as big a part as women in looking after their children.

14.39

a   Which industries do you think will benefit from the trend to working from home?

b   Which industries do you think will decline? Why?   (*D*)

14.40

If most people eventually have more leisure time than at present, what other effects do you think there might be in the country's economy?   (*D*)

14.41

Do you think the growth of leisure as a result of increased use of information technology will have any effect on the educational system?   (*D*)

'Knowledge is power.' Who will have knowledge in the future?

In some ways, the electronic cottage life-style, with its emphasis on small communities centred on the family, resembles the village life led by the vast majority of the human race in the Third World. There are vast differences, however. In the industrial countries, information technology means that almost everyone, potentially, has access to a huge store of knowledge — knowledge which enables us to make decisions crucial to our prosperity.

For example, farmers having detailed long-term weather forecasts can plan their harvest more effectively, and householders can easily find the cheapest source of food and other necessities from the choice of suppliers available. But this technology is not available to millions of people: it is too expensive for the poorer parts of the world. Politically, this could lead to one of two results.

Either we can make the technology, and the information it provides, available to the poorer countries in order to help them overcome their problems and share the world's riches more equally; or the industrialised nations will use their knowledge to make the gap between rich and poor greater still.

14.42

The majority of microcomputers in the UK are assembled in the UK, America or Japan.

a   Which countries are the chips actually made in?

b   Why do you think this the case?   (*R*)

14.43

In what ways could microcomputers help a poor, mainly agricultural, Third World country?.   (*D*)

The possession of knowledge and information has always been closely connected with power. In 1815, Baron Rothschild paid several men to ride quickly across Europe to bring him the result of the Battle of Waterloo. He realised that the battle, one way or the other, would affect the price of British Government stocks. During the few hours when he was the only man in London who knew the result, he was able to make a fortune, which has remained in his family to this day.

Can computers be governed?

Nowadays, governments go to great lengths to gather information about their citizens; but in future there may be further aspects to this. A democratic government is elected by the people every few years. In between elections, the government tries to find out what the electorate thinks of it by means of opinion polls. Information technology could be used in this task; television viewers of song contests have been asked to send their votes (via keypads and telephone lines) to a computer, which computes the winner; there is no technical reason why the same method could not be used to convey the electorate's opinion of government policy to Ministers.

Indeed, it is technically possible to make Parliament redundant; instead of electing representatives who then make decisions based on what they think are the views of the people, we could make decisions on each issue as it arises. In theory, everyone could have a vote, expressed via telecommunications links.

14.44

a   Describe some of the advantages of an 'electronic

Fig. 14.26

democracy' such as that described above.

b Describe the disadvantages you can see in this method of government. (*Advice:* Consider different ways of asking the same question, and how much information is needed to give an answer to a complex question of national importance) (D)

Computers can also be used by governments in more sinister ways. Nowadays much telephone traffic is carried in digital form (see Chapter 13), with computers in telephone exchanges to make connections between lines. It would be very easy for one of these computers to be programmed to intercept all calls from certain phones. Data gathered in this way could be used, in the public interest, to trap terrorists and subversives. But then who decides who is subversive? The same computers could be used to gather information about anyone the government does not like.

14.45

What safeguards could prevent 'spying' of the kind described above? (D)

14.46

a What is a subversive?

b How could a subversive electronics expert cause damage to society? (R)

The **Data Protection Act** was introduced by the Government to fit in with international rules on the storing of personal details and to give people the right to know what was held about them on computer files. Files holding information of a personal nature about identifiable people must be registered with the government, and registered data can only be transferred from one organisation to another under certain conditions. These rights and responsibilities do not, however, extend to certain government databases.

14.47

a Do you agree that anyone should have a right to see a copy of data stored about them by an organisation, provided that they pay a fee? Give reasons for your answer.

b Personal data held on a large number of people by the Police, Military and other Government security organisations is exempt from parts of the Data Protection Act, so you do not have a right to see it. These organisations are also able to obtain information from other databases without the Data Protection Registrar's approval. Give reasons for and against this exemption.

c Personal records which contain only names, addresses and telephone numbers are also exempt. Explain why you think these files do not have to be registered. (D)

What will 'custom-made' mean in the 1990s?

For the past century or more, it has been expensive to build machines. Changing the tools for a re-designed product has been just as expensive. The cost of, for example, building a machine to cut the pieces of cloth needed for a suit, or the metal sheets needed for a car, could only be justified if the manu-facturer could sell many thousands. Compare this with the Model T Ford, of which fifteen million were sold, all of them black! So products such as clothes have been either mass-produced and iden-tical to thousands of others, or expensive. One result was that large factories were needed to make things in economic quantities, and in turn this led to the growth of large cities to house the necessary workers. Computer-controlled machinery may change all this.

A computer-controlled machine tool is very flexible; it can be set up to produce several different parts simply by changing its program, which usually means nothing more elaborate than replacing one floppy disk with another.

'Made-to-measure' can take on a new meaning. A tailor, for example, no longer needs to make a thousand size 38 jackets and wait for a thousand size 38 customers to come along. He could measure a customer, key the measurements into a micro-computer, and let the computer control the cutting-out and sewing processes in far less time (and therefore cost) than a hand-made item would take. The day may even come when you could be

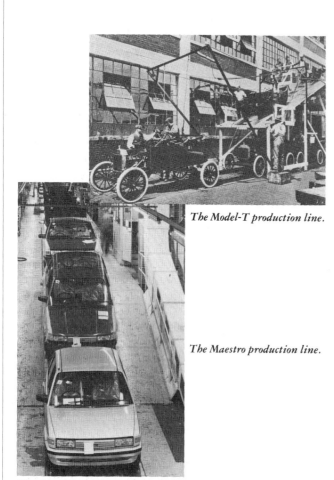

The Model-T production line.

The Maestro production line.

Fig. 14.27

measured directly by a computer, using a television camera, which then makes your suit automatically.

As we saw in Chapter 6, this kind of change is already happening in some industries. Several car factories are now robotised: the components are brought to the production line, picked up, put together and welded — all without human intervention. The assembly line workers' jobs have changed; instead of hard manual labour, they now spend their days monitoring computers, changing programs over, and so on.

14.48
Describe some of the differences between the Model-T production line and the Maestro production line. *(T)*

14.49
Suggest some other household items which could, in theory at least, be customised in the way described above. *(D)*

14.50
At present, instead of everyone gaining leisure time from the effects of automation, there is a trend for some people to work even longer hours, whilst others are unemployed.

a What type of people tend to become unemployed as a result of automation?

b Could information technology be used to help unemployed people contribute more to society and gain the benefits of prosperity? *(R)*

Naturally technology like this has its price. The workers at British Leyland enjoy much better working conditions than their ancestors of a generation ago, and they produce far more cars, but there are many fewer of them. Throughout the industrialised world, one cost of increased computerisation has been unemployment, which has tripled in the UK in a decade of world recession. Part of this unemployment may be permanent, though some researchers expect that the automation of businesses will *increase* employment, because cheaper goods will increase demand sufficiently to counteract the effects of greater productivity.

Some people, however, argue that this is not a bad thing. Machines can make the things we need, so men and women should not exhaust themselves doing this when there are far more enjoyable things to do. But they want to devise a fair economic system so that the goods, and therefore wealth, created by computers and machines are shared equally among everyone, rather than just the few people directly involved. We could all then enjoy far more leisure time, and a far higher standard of living, than our forefathers.

On the other hand, it is possible that society may evolve in a different direction — those who design, program and work with the computers that produce goods and wealth may become a hard-working elite, with everyone else relegated to the status of unemployable second-class citizens. Which way we go in this regard depends on a number of factors, not least of which is the extent to which those who are replaced at work by computers make their voices heard and use their talents to devise alternative occupations.

Are we getting carried away? . . .

We have seen already that a computer system requires a great deal of thought in the design of the hardware, if it is to work properly. We have also seen that the software must be carefully designed. VIP's computer system, however good the machine, will be useless to the firm if Parvesh's programs keep destroying valuable information. We must also bear in mind, though, that a computer system is only as good as the information fed into it (garbage in, garbage out).

In the future, there is likely to be much more emphasis on the *reliability* of computer systems, considered as a whole: hardware, software, liveware (the people involved with a computer system) and data collection. Murphy's Law (if anything can possibly go wrong, then sooner or later it will) applies to computer systems just as to everything else, and designers must take this into account.

In the early 1970s, a technician was doing some routine maintenance on the control panel of a nuclear reactor in the USA, when he dropped a small light bulb into the mass of wires underneath, causing several short circuits. Unfortunately, some of these wires carried the inputs to the computer which controlled the plant, and the resulting short circuits caused it to get false readings from some of its sensors. The reactor was in fact nearly at the highest temperature allowed, but the computer reacted as if it was too cool, and shut off the flow of cooling water to the reactor. The gauges on the control panel, which were actually functioning properly, showed totally different readings from those which the operators expected, given what the computer was doing.

In fact the computer, although its programs were designed to ensure the plant's safety, was causing an extremely dangerous situation, with possibly horrendous consequences, simply because its data was wrong. It was more than hour before the baffled operators regained control of the station.

14.51

Make a list of as many different situations as you can think of, where a faulty computer system could cause danger to the public.   (D)

Safety is likely to become even more important in other ways, too, as computers take over more and more tasks. Already a modern airliner spends much of its time on autopilot, where the pilot instructs an on-board computer where he wants to go, and the computer flies the plane, constantly monitoring height, speed, direction and so on, using its outputs to control flaps, engines, rudder and many other controls. This is even more the case in military planes: a Tornado can fly at a thousand miles an hour, fifty feet above the ground, but no human

pilot could possibly react fast enough to control it in that situation.

British Aerospace is developing a fighter plane, the EAP, which is actually impossible for a human to fly, because it is so unstable (but very manoeuvrable). The only way it can be controlled is by its computer, which, every thousandth of a second, makes all the decisions a pilot needs to make. Other forms of transport, too, use computers extensively, and need to consider safety very extensively in the design of their systems. Complex railway junctions are signalled by electronic systems, to prevent conflicting train movements.

14.52

There are many tools which electronic technicians use which quickly tell them exactly where the fault lies in a machine, and some machines can even do this diagnosis for themselves. Do you think that in future machines will be able actually to *repair* themselves?   (D)

Paradise — or purgatory?

We have seen that the computer, and information technology, can between them greatly improve people's lives. We have also seen that, if we are too careless, computer systems can cause extremely dangerous situations, can lead to totalitarian societies, and can be used in many undesirable ways. It is up to all of us, as computer users, and citizens, to ensure that they are used wisely. In the words of the American historian Alvin Toffler,

'The Third Wave {the computer revolution} brings with it a genuinely new way of life based on methods of production that make most factory assembly lines obsolete; on a novel institution that might be called the "electronic cottage"; and on radically changed schools and corporations of the future... This new civilisation, as it challenges the old, will topple bureaucracies and reduce the role of the nation-state. It requires governments that are simpler, more effective, yet more democratic than any we know today ... For these reasons, among many, it could — with some intelligent help from us — turn out to be the first truly humane civilisation in recorded history.'
   (*Alvin Toffler,* The Third Wave, *1980*)

Or, if we, the human race, are not careful, the new technology could destroy us all.

And which path we follow will depend on all of you. . . .

Index

Acknowledgements

The authors and publisher would like to thank the following for permission to reproduce copyright material:

Amstrad plc p.138;   **Apple Computers plc** p.9 top centre;   **Austin Rover** p.80 (both), 81, 82, 87; **Avery** p.55;   **BBC** p.150, 152, 164 left;   **British Telecom/Datacom** p.156;   **Peter Fox** p.125; **Halifax Building Society** p.123, 126, 129 (both), 130 (all);   **Holt Studios** p.60 (both), 61, 69 (both); **IBM** p.9 top left, 131 left;   **ICL** p.94 btm;   **Inmac** p.82;   **Meteorological Office** (Crown Copyright) p.162 (both), 164 left;   **Miele** p.51;   **Milk Marketing Board** p.70;   **Peter Newark's Western Americana** p.204 top;   **Ocean Software Ltd** p.139; **Oracle** p.153 left;   **Panasonic** p.44 btm;   **Research Machines** p.12, 19, 38, 74, 109, 159 (all);   **Ann Ronan** p.190 top left and top right;   **Science Museum** p.190 btm, 191, 192;   **Science Photo Library** p.141 (both), 143 (both), (Nasa) 164 top right and btm right, 197;   **Singer** p.44 top right;   **Telefocus** p.153 right, 154 both, 157;   **West Air** p.188;   **Zanussi** p.44 top left.

All other photographs have been specially taken by Archie Miles for this book. We would like to thank all those who assisted him, particularly at United Biscuits.

The authors would like to acknowledge their thanks to the following organisations for their help: Caterpillar Tractor Company; MYM Video, Lichfield; *Avery & Co.*, Smethwick; Cadbury Schweppes plc; Austin Rover Group; *Fullwoods Ltd*; *Smith, Knight & Stone*; Birmingham City Council; Nationwide Building Society; and Halifax Building Society.

The authors would also like to thank their wives and families for their support during the production of this book.

Illustrations by: Clive Goodyer, Nick Hawken, Nigel Page and Viv Quillin.